TALES OF THE HASIDIM

★

THE EARLY MASTERS

MARTIN BUBER

TALES OF THE HASIDIM

THE EARLY MASTERS

SCHOCKEN BOOKS / NEW YORK

Eighth Printing, 1975

Translated by Olga Marx

Library of Congress Catalog Card No. 47-2952

Printed in the United States of America

PREFACE

One of the most vital aspects of the hasidic movement is that the hasidim tell one another stories about their leaders, their "zaddikim." Great things had happened, the hasidim had been present, they had seen them, and so they felt called upon to relate and bear witness to them. The words used to describe these experiences were more than mere words; they transmitted what had happened to coming generations, and with such actuality that the words in themselves became events. And since they serve to perpetuate holy events, they bear the consecration of holy deeds. It is told that the "Seer" of Lublin once saw a pillar of light rise out of a klaus; when he entered he saw hasidim telling one another about their zaddikim. According to hasidic belief, the primeval light of God poured into the zaddikim; from them it poured into their works, and from these into the words of the hasidim who relate them. The Baal Shem, the founder of hasidism, is supposed to have said that when a hasid spoke in praise of the zaddikim, this was equivalent to dwelling on the mystery of the divine Chariot which Ezekiel once saw. And a zaddik of the fourth generation, Rabbi Mendel of Rymanov, a friend of the "Seer," added in explanation: "For the zaddikim *are* the chariot of God."* But story is more than a mere reflection. The holy essence it testifies to lives on in it. The miracle that is told, acquires new force; power that once was active, is propagated in the living word and continues to be active—even after generations.

A rabbi, whose grandfather had been a disciple of the Baal Shem, was asked to tell a story. "A story," he said, "must be told in such a way that it constitutes help in itself." And he told: "My grandfather was lame. Once they asked him to tell

* Quoted from Midrash Genesis Rabba LXXXII 7; cf. Rashi on Genesis 17:22.

v

a story about his teacher. And he related how the holy Baal Shem used to hop and dance while he prayed. My grandfather rose as he spoke, and he was so swept away by his story that he himself began to hop and dance to show how the master had done. From that hour on he was cured of his lameness. That's the way to tell a story!"

Side by side with the oral transmission went a written transmission which began far back in the history of the movement, but of the written recollections of the first generations only very few uncorrupted texts have been preserved. In their youth a number of zaddikim wrote down the deeds and utterances of their masters, but apparently for their own use rather than for the public at large. Thus we know from a reliable source that the rabbi of Berditchev, of all rabbis the closest to the people, noted down everything his teacher, Dov Baer of Mezritch, the Great Maggid, said and did, including everyday utterances, and read and re-read the pages, straining his soul to the utmost in the effort to understand the meaning of every word. But his notebook has been lost and very few similar notations have been preserved.

For the most part the legend, this late form of the myth, developed in the literatures of the world in epochs in which the development of the literary narrative either occurs side by side with it or even has already been in the main completed. In the first case, the form of the legend is influenced, in the second it is determined by its sister form. Buddhist legends and tales of India composed as literature, Franciscan legend and the short story of Italy, go hand in hand.

It is quite otherwise with the hasidic legend. The Jews of the Diaspora transmitted legends orally from generation to generation and not until our own era were they couched in literary form. The hasidim could not model the tales they told in praise of their zaddikim on a literary form either extant or in the making, nor could they wholly adapt them to the style of tales current among the people. The inner tempo of the hasidim is frequently too impassioned, too violent for the calm form of such tales, a form which could not contain the abundance of what they had to say. And so the hasidim never shaped their legend into a precious vessel; with few exceptions it never became either the work of an individual artist or a work of folk-art; it remained unformed. But due to the holy element with which it is informed, the life of the zaddikim and the hasidim's rapturous joy therein, it is precious metal, though all too often not pure, but weighted with dross.

Taking the Baal Shem legend as an instance, we can trace the shaping of legendary transmission in hasidism. Even during his lifetime, his family and his disciples circulated tales which were brief indications of his greatness. After his death, these grew into stories which, a quarter of a century later, were set down in book form: the family stories developed into the tales which Rabbi Moshe Hayyim Efraim, the Baal Shem's grandson whom he himself had trained, scattered through his work, "The Camp Flag of Efraim," while the legends perpetuated by his disciples were published at about the same time in the first collection of utterances of the Baal Shem, "The Crown of the Good Name." But twenty-five more years had to pass before the first great legendary biography of the Baal Shem, "In Praise of the Baal Shem Tov," appeared. Every story in this traces back to someone in the immediate circle of the Baal Shem's friends and disciples. Side by side with this are other traditions, such as the oral tradition in the Great Maggid's family, and in the family of Rabbi Meir Margaliot or the written tradition in the school of Koretz. And all of these differ from the published collections and maintain a characteristic life of their own. The second half of the nineteenth century marks the corruption of transmitted motifs. They appear as thin and wordy narratives patched with later inventions and worked into a cheap form of popular literature. But only our own era (since about 1900) heralded the beginnings of critical selection and compiling. These and similar processes are characteristic of the development in hasidic transmission.

After excluding the spurious products in which we frequently cannot find a shred of the original motifs, we still have an enormous mass of largely unformed material: either—and at best!—brief notes with no attempt to shape the event referred to, or—far oftener, unfortunately—crude and confused attempts to give it the form of a tale. In this second category of notes either too much is said or too little, and there is hardly ever a clear thread of narrative to follow. For the most part they constitute neither true art nor true folk-tale but a kind of setting down, the rapturous setting down of stupendous occurrences.

One like myself, whose purpose it is to picture the zaddikim and their lives from extant written (and some oral) material, must above all, to do justice simultaneously to legend and to truth, supply the missing links in the narrative. In the course of this long piece of work I found it most expedient to begin by giving up the available form (or rather formlessness) of the notes with their meagerness or excessive detail, their obscurities and digressions, to reconstruct the events in question with the utmost accuracy (wherever possible, with the aid of variants and other relevant material), and to relate them as coherently as I could in a form suited to the subject matter. Then, however, I went back to the notes and incorporated in my final version whatever felicitous turn or phrase they contained. On the other hand, I considered it neither permissible nor desirable to expand the tales or to render them more colorful and diverse, a method the brothers Grimm for instance employed when they wrote down the stories they had by word of mouth from the people.* Only in those few cases where the notes at hand were quite fragmentary did I compose a connected whole by fusing what I had with other fragments, and filling the gaps with related material.

There are two genera of legend which can be designated in analogy to the two genera of the narrative on which they are modelled: the legendary short story and the legendary anecdote. To exemplify: compare *The Golden Legend* with *The Little*

* See (particularly) Leffz, *Maerchen der Brueder Grimm,* published in their original form from the posthumous papers of Clemens Brentano.

Flower of Saint Francis, or the classical Buddha legend with the tales of the monks of the East-Asiatic Zen sect. Even the formless hasidic material can be grouped in these two categories. For the most part the tales are potential legendary anecdotes. True short stories are rare, but there is a sort of hybrid between story and anecdote. The preponderance of the anecdote is primarily due to the general tendency of the Jewish Diaspora spirit to express the events of history and of the present in a pointed manner: Events are not merely seen and reported so as to signify something, but they are so cleanly hulled from the mass of the irrelevant and so arranged that the report culminates in a significant dictum. In hasidism, life itself favors this mode of interpretation. The zaddik expresses his teachings, deliberately or indeliberately, in actions that are symbolic and frequently go over into utterance which either supplements or helps to interpret them.

By the term short story I mean the recital of a destiny which is represented in a single incident; by anecdote the recital of a single incident which illumines an entire destiny. The legendary anecdote goes one stop beyond: the single incident in question conveys the meaning of life. In the literature of the world, I know of no other group of legendary anecdotes which illustrates this to such a degree, so homogeneously and yet with such variety as the hasidic anecdotes.

The anecdote, as well as the short story, is a species of condensed narrative, that is, of narrative concentrated in one clearly outlined form. Psychology and adornment must be eschewed. The more "naked" it is, the more adequately it fulfills its function.

These considerations determined my attitude toward the material at my disposal.

The zaddik, however, should not be presented merely in actions that tend to go over into dicta, but also in the very act of teaching by word of mouth, for with him speech is an essential part of action. And so this book includes still another species. It includes some pieces which I should like to designate as "Teaching in Answers." The teacher, the zaddik, is asked to interpret a verse in the Scriptures or to expound the meaning of a rite. He replies, and in replying, gives more than the questioner had set out to learn. In the texts I worked on, this species frequently does not employ the form of a conversation; the answer embodies the question. In most instances I have reconstructed the questions and thus restored the dialogue form. And — since a sharp distinction is impossible — this led me to include a number of passages where the speaker puts questions to himself. In addition to these, there are several teachings and sermons which are given because of their profound significance. But not a single passage hails from the extensive theoretical writings of hasidism; all are taken from the popular literature, where they supplement what is told of the lives of the zaddikim. All this has an entirely oral character, not a literary one.

In those selections directly concerned with the teachings, I tried to keep to the actual words of my texts, at least as far as this was compatible with the demands of clarity. But in many cases the texts were so obscure, so fused with alien elements, that it was often necessary to scrape away an entire layer of obvious additions, in order to get down to the true sayings of the master.

This book contains less than a tenth of the material I collected. The first criterion for the inclusion of a tale was, of course, significance *per se*, as well as special significance for the understanding of hasidic life. But many passages which were suitable from this point of view had to be set aside because they did not serve to characterize one of the zaddikim about which this book centers. And this was the deciding factor.

Thus, from the numerous legends transmitted about almost every zaddik, I had to choose those which gave the best account of the character and the way of a certain zaddik, and then to arrange them to give the pattern of his life. Sometimes my material was such that I had only to select among tales and utterances those that furnished together an almost perfect picture of a life; at others there were gaps which I had to fill with my own conjectures, given in my introductions to these two volumes. In a few instances, my data were so meager that I had to resign myself to offering the "static" portrait of a man, instead of the "dynamic" picture of a human life.

Within the individual chapters, I have arranged the tales in biographical, but not in chronological order, since this would have obscured rather than clarified the total effect I had in mind. From the material at hand, it was easier to compose the picture of a man and his way, by projecting the various elements of his character and of his work individually and—if possible—each in the light of its own particular development, until they all fused into a sort of inner biography. Thus, for instance, in the chapter on the Baal Shem, the following sequence was observed: 1) the soul of the Baal Shem; 2) preparation and revelation; 3) ecstasy and fervor; 4) his community; 5) with his disciples; 6) with a variety of people; 7) the strength of vision; 8) holiness and miracles; 9) the Holy Land and redemption; 10) before and after his death. Each passage comes at its appointed place, though occasionally this breaks the chronological order, and the teachings supplement the tales wherever this seems desirable.

At a first quick reading, there will seem to be a number of repetitions in the book, but they are not really repetitions, and wherever a motif recurs, the meaning is altered, or it appears in a different connotation. There is, for example, repeated mention of the "Satan's hasidim," viz., of the false hasidim who join the true and threaten to disrupt the community. But the careful reader will note a different situation and a different form of expression in every single case.

My work of re-telling hasidic legends began more than forty years ago. Its first fruits were the books entitled: "Tales of Rabbi Naham (1906), and "The Legend of the Baal Shem" (1907). Subsequently, however, I rejected my method of dealing with the transmitted material, on the grounds that it was too free. I applied my new concept of the task and the means to accomplish it, in the books "The Great Maggid and His Succession" (1921) and "The Hidden Light" (1924). The content of these two books has been reproduced almost entirely in this

book, but by far the greater part of it was written since my
arrival in Palestine in 1938. Along with much else, I owe the
urge to this new and more comprehensive composition to the
air of this land. Our sages say that it makes one wise; to me
it has granted a different gift: the strength to make a new
beginning. I had regarded my work on the hasidic legends as
completed. This book is the outcome of a beginning.

Jerusalem, Summer 1946

MARTIN BUBER

TABLE OF CONTENTS

INTRODUCTION

INTRODUCTION

1.

The purpose of this book is to introduce the reader to a world of legendary reality. I must call it legendary, for the accounts which have been handed down to us, and which I have here tried to put into fitting form, are not authentic in the sense that a chronicle is authentic. They go back to fervent human beings who set down their recollections of what they saw or thought they had seen, in their fervor, and this means that they included many things which took place, but were apparent only to the gaze of fervor, and others which cannot have happened and could not happen in the way they are told, but which the elated soul perceived as reality and, therefore, related as such. That is why I must call it reality: the reality of the experience of fervent souls, a reality born in all innocence, unalloyed by invention and whimsy. These souls did not give an account of themselves but of what stirred them, and so, whatever we learn from this account is not only a fact in the psychological sense, but a fact of life as well. Something happened to rouse the soul, and it had such and such an effect; by communicating the effect, tradition also reveals its cause; the contact between those who quicken and those who are quickened, the association between the two. That is true legend and that is its reality.

The men who are the subject of these tales, the men who quicken, are the zaddikim, a term which is usually translated by "the righteous," but which actually means "those who stood the test" or "the proven." They are the leaders of the hasidic communities. And the men who do the telling,* whose tales constitute the body of transmitted legends, the men who were

* I have prefaced the so-called "miracle tales," i.e., those in which the unreal aspects of reality are especially evident, with the phrase: "It is told."

1

quickened, are the hasidim, "the devout," or, more accurately, those who keep faith with the covenant. They are the members of such communities. This book, then, purports to express and document the association between zaddikim and hasidim, and should be accepted as the expression and documentation of the life of the zaddikim with their hasidim.

2.

The core of hasidic teachings is the concept of a life of fervor, of exalted joy. But this teaching is not a theory which can persist regardless of whether it is translated into reality. It is rather the theoretic supplement to a life which was actually lived by the zaddikim and hasidim, especially in the first six generations of the movement, of which this book treats — three in each volume.

The underlying purpose of all great religions and religious movement is to beget a life of elation, of fervor which cannot be stifled by any experience, which, therefore, must spring from a relationship to the eternal, above and beyond all individual experiences. But since the contacts a man makes with the world and with himself are frequently not calculated to rouse him to fervor, religious concepts refer him to another form of being, to a world of perfection in which his soul may also grow perfect. Compared to this state of perfect being, life on earth seems either only an antechamber, or mere illusion, and the prospect of a higher life has the task of creating fervor in the face of disappointing outer and inner experiences, of creating the fervent conviction that there is such a higher life, and that it is, or can gradually become accessible to the human soul, under certain conditions beyond the bounds of earthly existence. Although faith in a life hereafter is integral to Judaism, there has always been a strong tendency to provide an earthly residence for perfection. The great Messianic concept of coming perfection on earth which everyone can actively help prepare for, could not, in spite of the power it exerted over souls, endow daily life with that constant, undaunted and exalted joy in the Now and Here, which can spring only from fulfilment in the present, not from hope in a future fulfilment.

This was not altered when the Kabbalistic teaching of the trans-migration of souls made it possible for everyone to identify his soul with that of a person of the Messianic generation, and thus have the feeling of participating in it. Only in the Messianic movements themselves, which always were based on the belief that perfection was just on the verge of being realized, did the fervor break through and permeate all of life. When the last of these movements, the Sabbatian movement, and its after-effects ended in renegacy and despair, the test for the living strength of religion had come, for here no mere soften-ing of sorrow, but only a life of fervent joy could aid the Jew to survive. The development of hasidism indicates that the test was passed.

The hasidic movement did not weaken the hope in a Messiah, but it kindled both its simple and intellectual followers to joy in the world as it is, in life as it is, in every hour of life in this world, as that hour is. Without dulling the prick of con-science or deadening the sense of chasm between the ideal pattern of the individual limned by his Creator, and what he actually is, hasidism shows men the way to God who dwells with them "in the midst of their uncleannesses," a way which issues forth from every temptation, even from every sin. With-out lessening the strong obligation imposed by the Torah, the movement suffused all the traditional commandments with joy-bringing significance, and even set aside the walls separating the sacred and the profane, by teaching that every profane act can be rendered sacred by the manner in which it is performed. It had nothing to do with pantheism which destroys or stunts the greatest of all values: the reciprocal relationship between the human and the divine, the reality of the I and the You which does not cease at the rim of eternity. Hasidism did, however, make manifest the reflection of the divine, the sparks of God that glimmer in all beings and all things, and taught how to approach them, how to deal with them, how to "lift" and redeem them, and re-connect them with their original root. The doctrine of the Shekhinah, contained in the Talmud and expanded in the Kabbalah, of the Shekhinah as the Divine Presence which resides in this world, receives a new and in-

3

timate significance and applicability. If you direct the un-
diminished power of your fervor to God's world-destiny, if you
do what you must do at this moment—no matter what it may
be!—with your whole strength and with kavvanah, with holy
intent, you will bring about the union between God and
Shekhinah, eternity and time. You need not be a scholar or a
sage to accomplish this. All that is necessary is to have a soul
united within itself and indivisibly directed to its divine goal.
The world in which you live, just as it is and not otherwise,
affords you that association with God, which will redeem you
and whatever divine aspect of the world you have been entrusted with. And your own character, the very qualities which
make you what you are, constitutes your special approach to
God, your special potential use for Him. Do not be vexed at
your delight in creatures and things! But do not let it shackle
itself to creatures and things; through these, press on to God.
Do not rebel against your desires, but seize them and bind them
to God. You shall not stifle your surging powers, but let them
work at holy work, and rest a holy rest in God. All the contradictions with which the world distresses you are only that
you may discover their intrinsic significance, and all the contrary trends tormenting you within yourself, only wait to be
exorcised by your word. All innate sorrow wants only to flow
into the fervor of your joy.
But this joy must not be the goal toward which you strive.
It will be vouchsafed you if you strive to "give joy to God."
Your personal joy will rise up when you want nothing but the
joy of God—nothing but joy in itself.

3.

But how was man, in particular the "simple man," with whom
the hasidic movement is primarily concerned, to arrive at living
his life in fervent joy? How, in the fires of temptation, was he
to recast the Evil Urge into an urge for what is good? How,
in the wonted fulfilling of the commandments was he to develop
the rapturous bond with the upper worlds? How, in his meeting with creatures and things, grow aware of the divine sparks
hidden within them? How, through holy kavvanah illumine

4

everyday life? We do, indeed, know that all that is necessary is to have a soul united within itself and indivisibly directed to its divine goal. But how, in the chaos of life on our earth, are we to keep the holy goal in sight? How retain unity in the midst of peril and pressure, in the midst of thousands of disappointments and delusions? And once unity is lost, how recover it? Man needs counsel and aid, he must be lifted and redeemed. And he does not need all this only in regard to his soul, for in some way or other, the domains of the soul are intertwined with the big and little cares, the griefs and despairs of life itself, and if these are not dealt with, how shall those loftier concerns be approached? A helper is needed, a helper for both body and soul, for both earthly and heavenly matters. This helper is called the zaddik. He can heal both the ailing body and the ailing soul, for he knows how one is bound up with the other, and this knowledge gives him the power to influence both. It is he who can teach you to conduct your affairs so that your soul remains free, and he can teach you to strengthen your soul, to keep you steadfast beneath the blows of destiny. And over and over he takes you by the hand and guides you until you are able to venture on alone. He does not relieve you of doing what you have grown strong enough to do for yourself. He does not lighten your soul of the struggle it must wage in order to accomplish its particular task in this world. And all this also holds for the communication of the soul with God. The zaddik must make communication with God easier for his hasidim, but he cannot take their place. This is the teaching of the Baal Shem and all the great hasidim followed it; everything else is distortion and the signs of it appear relatively early. The zaddik strengthens his hasid in the hours of doubting, but he does not infiltrate him with truth, he only helps him conquer and reconquer it for himself. He develops the hasid's own power for right prayer, he teaches him how to give the words of prayer the right direction, and he joins his own prayer to that of his disciple and therewith lends him courage, an increase of power—wings. In hours of need, he prays for his disciple and gives all of himself, but he never permits the soul of the hasid to rely so wholly on his own that

5

it relinquishes independent concentration and tension, in other words, that striving-to-God of the soul without which life on this earth is bound to be unfulfilled. Not only in the realm of human passions does the zaddik point over and over to the limits of counsel and help. He does this also in the realm of association with God; again and again he emphasizes the limits of mediation. One man can take the place of another only as far as the threshold of the inner sanctum.

Both in the hasidic teachings and in the tales, we often hear of zaddikim who take upon themselves the sorrow of others, and even atone for others by sacrificing their own lives. But on the very rare occasions (as in the case of Rabbi Nahman of Bratzlav) when we read that the true zaddik can accomplish the act of turning to God for those nearest and dearest to him, the author immediately adds that this act done in place of the other, facilitates the hasid's own turning to God. The zaddik helps everyone, but he does not relieve anyone of what he must do for himself. His helping is a delivery. He even helps the hasid through his death; those near him in the hour of his death receive "a great illumining."

Within these limits the zaddik has the greatest possible influence not only on the faith and mind of the hasid, but on his active everyday life, and even on his sleep, which he renders deep and pure. Through the zaddik, all the senses of the hasid are perfected, not through conscious directing, but through bodily nearness. The fact that the hasid looks at the zaddik perfects his sense of sight, his listening to him, his sense of hearing. Not the teachings of the zaddik but his existence constitute his effectiveness; and not so much the circumstance that he is present on extraordinary occasions as that he is there in the ordinary course of days, unemphatic, undeliberate, unconscious; not that he is there as an intellectual leader but as the complete human being with his whole worldly life in which the completeness of the human being is tested. As a zaddik once said: "I learned the Torah from all the limbs of my teacher." This was the zaddik's influence on his true disciples. But his mere physical presence did not, of course, suffice to exert influence on the many, on the people at large, that influence which made hasidism a popular movement. To achieve this, he had to work with the people until they were ready to receive what he had to give them, to present his teachings in a form the people could accept as their own, he must "participate in the multitude." He had to mix with the people and, in order to raise them to the rung of what perfection they were capable of, he had to descend from his own rung. "If a man falls into the mire," says the Baal Shem, "and his friend wants to fetch him out, he must not hesitate to get himself a little dirty."

One of the great principles of hasidism is that the zaddik and the people are dependent on one another. Again and again, their relationship is compared to that between substance and form in the life of the individual, between body and soul. The soul must not boast that it is more holy than the body, for only in that it has climbed down into the body and works through its limbs can the soul attain to its own perfection. The body, on the other hand, may not brag of supporting the soul, for when the soul leaves, the flesh falls into decay. Thus the zaddikim need the multitude, and the multitude need the zaddikim. The realities of hasidic teaching depend on this inter-relationship. And so the "descending from the rung" is not a true descent. Quite the contrary: "If the zaddik serves God," says Rabbi Nahman of Bratzlav, "but does not take the trouble to teach the multitude, he will descend from his rung."

Rabbi Nahman himself, one of the most spiritual of all the zaddikim, felt a deep and secret sense of union between himself and "simple men." This union is the point of departure for his strange utterances about two months before he died. At first he was in a state of such spiritual exhaustion that he declared he was nothing but a "simple man." But when this state suddenly went over into the loftiest elation of spirit, he said that in such periods of descending, the zaddik was infused with vital strength which poured out from him into all the "simple men" in the world, not only those of Israel, but of all people. And the vital strength which flowed into him, hailed from "the treasure trove of gratuitous gifts" stored up in the land of Canaan from time immemorial, time before Israel, and this treasure trove, he added, consists of that secret substance

7

which is also accorded to the souls of simple men and makes them capable of simple faith.

Here we come to the very foundation of hasidism, on which the life between those who quicken, and those who are quickened, is built up. The quintessence of this life is the relationship between the zaddik and his disciples, which unfolds the interaction between the quickener and the quickened in complete clarity. The teacher helps his disciples find themselves, and in hours of desolation the disciples help their teacher find himself again. The teacher kindles the souls of his disciples and they surround him and light his life with the flame he has kindled. The disciple asks, and by his manner of asking unconsciously evokes a reply, which his teacher's spirit would not have produced without the stimulus of the question.

Two "miracle tales" will serve to demonstrate the lofty function of discipleship.

Once, at the close of the Day of Atonement, the Baal Shem is greatly troubled because the moon cannot pierce the clouds and so he cannot say the Blessing of the New Moon, which in this very hour, an hour when Israel is threatened with grave danger, was to have a particularly salutary effect. In vain he strains his soul to alter the state of the sky. Then his hasidim, who know nothing of all this, begin to dance just as every year at this time, in joyful elation at the service performed by their master, a service like that of the high priest in the Temple of Jerusalem. First they dance in the outer room of the Baal Shem's house, but in their elation they enter his room and dance around him. At last, at the peak of ecstasy, they beg him to join the dance and draw him into the circle. And then the moon breaks through the heavy clouds and shines out, a marvel of flawless light. The joy of the hasidim has brought about what the soul of the zaddik, straining to the utmost of its power, was not able to effect.

Among the disciples of Rabbi Dov Baer the Great Maggid, the greatest disciple of the Baal Shem, Rabbi Elimelekh was the man who kept alive the core of the tradition and preserved the school as such. Once, when his soul rose up to heaven, he learned that with his holiness he was rebuilding the ravaged altar in the sanctuary of heavenly Jerusalem, which corresponds to the sanctuary of Jerusalem on this earth. At the same time, he learned that his disciples were helping him in this task of restoration. In a certain year, two of these were absent from the Festival of Rejoicing in the Law, Rabbi Jacob Yitzhak, later the rabbi of Lublin (the "Seer"), and Rabbi Abraham Joshua Heshel, later the rabbi of Apt. Heaven had told Elimelekh that Jacob Yitzhak would bring the Ark into the sanctuary, and that Abraham Joshua Heshel would bring the tables of the law. Yet now they were both missing! Then the zaddik said to his son: "Eighteen times over I can cry: 'Rise up, O Lord!' (as Israel, in the day of old, called toward the Ark, which was to precede them into battle)—and it will be of no use."

In this second story, the disciples participate in the work of the zaddik as individuals, in the first they take part in it as a "holy community." This form of collective effect is undoubtedly the more significant, though we have many and varied tales concerning the participation of individuals. The community of hasidim who belong to a zaddik, especially the close-knit circle of those who are constantly with him, or—at least—visit him regularly, is felt as a powerful dynamic unit. The zaddik unites with this circle both in prayer and in teaching. They are his point of departure in praying, for he does not pray merely as one speaking for them, but as their focus of strength in which the blaze of the community-soul is gathered, and from which this blaze is borne aloft fused with the flame of his own soul. On the sabbath when, at the third meal, he expounds the Scriptures and reveals what is hidden, his teaching is directed toward them: they are the field of force in which his words make manifest the spirit in expanding circles, like rings widening on the waters. And this meal itself! We can approach an understanding of its tension and bliss only when we realize that all—each giving himself utterly—are united into an elated whole, such as can only form around an elated center, which through its very being, points to the divine center of all being. This is a living connection which sometimes expresses itself strangely and even grotesquely, but the grotesque in itself is so

9

genuine that it bears witness to the genuineness of the impulses. For hasidism must not be interpreted as an esoteric movement but one charged with primitive vitality which—as all primitive vitality—sometimes vents itself rather crudely. It is this very vitality which lends peculiar intensity to the relationship of one hasid toward another. Their common attachment to the zaddik and to the holy life he embodies binds them to one another, not only in the festive hours of common prayer, and of the common meal, but in all the hours of everyday living. In moments of elation, they drink to one another, they sing and dance together, and tell one another abstruse and comforting miracle tales. But they help one another too. They are prepared to risk their lives for a comrade, and this readiness comes from the same deep source as their elation. Everything the true hasid does or does not do mirrors his belief that, in spite of the intolerable suffering men must endure, the heartbeat of life is holy joy, and that always and everywhere, one can force a way through to that joy—provided one devotes one's self entirely to his deed.

There are many distorted aspects of hasidism which are by no means inherent only in the later stages of the movement. Side by side with the fervent love for the zaddik we find a coarsened form of reverence on the part of those who regard him as a great magician, as one who is an intimate of heaven and can right all that is wrong, who relieves his hasidim of straining their own souls and secures them a desirable place in the hereafter. Though the hasidim of a zaddik were often united by a feeling of true brotherliness, they frequently held aloof from and sometimes were even hostile to the followers of other zaddikim. A like contrast obtained between the free life in religion of a hasidic community and their thick-skinned opportunism in regard to the powers of the state. Sometimes, dull superstition settled down side by side with the innocent fantasy of the elated spirit and made shallows of its depths, and sometimes crass fraud made its appearance and abused it. Most of these phenomena are familiar to us through the history of other religious movements that sprang from the vitality of the people, others become understandable when we consider the pathological premises of life in exile. My aim was not to go into all this, but to show what it was that made hasidism one of the most significant phenomena of living and fruitful faith that we know, and—up to this time—the last great flowering of the Jewish will to serve God in this world and to consecrate everyday life to him.

In the very beginnings of the movement, hasidism disintegrated into separate communities whose inner life had small connection, and early in its history individual zaddikim display problematic traits. But every hasidic community still contains a germ of the kingdom of God, a germ—no more than that, but no less, and often this germ lives and grows even in substance which has fallen prey to decay. And even the zaddik who has squandered the spiritual inheritance of his forbears has hours in which his forehead gives forth a glow as though the primordial light had touched it with radiance.

4.

In a crisis of faith, when faith is renewed, the man who initiates and leads the renewal is frequently not a spiritual character in the ordinary sense of the world, but one who draws his strength from an extraordinary union between the spiritual and tellurian powers, between heavenly and earthly fire, but it is the sublime which determines the earth-sustained frame. The life of such a man is a constant receiving of fire and transforming it into light. And this, which is and occurs within himself, is the cause of his twofold effect on the world: he restores to the element of earth those whom preoccupation with thought has removed from it, and those who are burdened with the weight of earth he raises to the heights of heaven.

Israel ben Eliezer of Mezbizh (Miedzyboz), called the Baal Shem Tov (1700-1760), the founder of hasidism, was such a man. He first appears merely as one in a series of Baale Shem, of "Masters of the Name," who knew a Name of God that had magic force, were able to invoke it, and with this art of theirs helped and healed the men who came to them—manifestations of a form of magic which was absorbed by religion. The actual basis for their work was their ability to perceive intrinsic connections between things, connections which lay beyond the bounds of time and space (apparent only to what we usually call intuition) and their peculiar strengthening and (consolidating influence on the soul-center of their fellowmen,\which enabled this center to regenerate the body and the whole of life— an influence of which the so-called "suggestive powers" are nothing but a distortion. Certain aspects of Israel ben Eliezer's work constitute a continuation of the work of the Baale Shem, but with one marked difference which even expresses itself in the change of the epithet "Baal Shem" to "Baal Shem Tov." This difference and what it signifies is unambiguously stressed in the legendary tradition.

In various versions we are told how either Rabbi Gershon, the Baal Shem's brother-in-law, who first despised him as an ignorant man but later became his faithful disciple, or one of the descendants of the Baal Shem, went to a great rabbi who lived far away—in Palestine or in Germany—and he told him about Rabbi Israel Baal Shem. "Baal Shem?" said the rabbi questioningly. "I don't know any such person." And in the case of the Baal Shem's brother-in-law, the rejection is more pronounced, for when Rabbi Gershon speaks of the Baal Shem as his teacher, he receives the reply: "Baal Shem? No, there is no teacher by that name." But when Rabbi Gershon quickly rights his first words by giving the full name "Baal Shem Tov," the rabbi he is visiting assumes an entirely different attitude. "Oh!" he exclaims. "The Baal Shem Tov! He, to be sure, is a very great teacher. Every morning I see him in the temple of paradise." The sage refuses to have anything to do with common miracle men, but the Baal Shem Tov—that is quite another matter, that is something new. The addition of one word altered the meaning and the character of the epithet. "Shem Tov" is the "Good Name." The Baal Shem Tov, the possessor of the Good Name, is a man who, because he is as he is, gains the confidence of his fellowmen. "Baal Shem Tov" as a general designation, refers to a man in whom the people have confidence, the confident of the people. With this, the term ceases to designate a rather doubtful vocation and comes to apply to a reliable person and, at the same time, transforms what was, after all, a category of

12

magic, into one religious in the truest sense of the word. For the term "Baal Shem Tov" signifies a man who lives with and for his fellowmen on the foundation of his relation to the divine.

There is a story that Rabbi Yitzhak of Drohobycz, one of the ascetic "hasidim" who first rebelled against the Baal Shem, was full of hostility for the innovator because he had heard that he gave people amulets containing slips of paper inscribed with secret names of God. On the occasion of a meeting, he asked the Baal Shem about it. He opened one of the amulets and showed the questioner that on the slip there was nothing but his own name and that of his mother, "Israel ben Sarah." Here the amulet has completely lost its magical attributes. It is nothing but a sign and pledge of the personal bond between the helper and the one who is given help, a bond based on trust. The Baal Shem Tov helps those who trust him. He is able to help them because they trust him. The amulet is the permanent symbol of his direct influence at the given moment. It contains his name and thus represents him. And through this pledge of personal connection, the soul of the recipient is "lifted." The power at work here is the union of the tellurian and spiritual within the Baal Shem and, proceeding from this union, the relationship between him and his hasidim which involves both domains.

This sheds light on his attitude toward the "Men of Spirit" he wishes to win for the hasidic movement, and on the fact that most of them are willing to subject themselves to him. According to one legendary version, for instance, the greatest of his disciples, the actual founder of the hasidic school of teaching: Rabbi Dov Baer, the Maggid (wandering preacher) of Mezritch (Miedzyrzecze), comes to him to be cured of his illness. His physical suffering is only eased, but he is healed of "teaching without soul." This instance clearly demonstrates that Nature, at work in the person of the helper, guides the spirit, which has strayed too far from her, back into her domain, the only milieu in which the soul can thrive through ceaseless contact with her. And the "Great Maggid," whose powers as thinker are far superior to those of the Baal Shem, bows to the infinitely rare and decisive phenomenon: the union of fire and light in a human being. The same holds for another important exponent of

13

hasidic teachings in the second generation, for Rabbi Jacob Joseph of Polnoye (Polonnoje). He was not an independent thinker, such as the Maggid, but well versed in the teachings, and thus enabled to receive and expound the teachings of the Baal Shem who drew him from his ascetic remoteness into a simple life with his fellowmen. There are various versions of how the Baal Shem won him over, but they all have two traits in common: he does not reveal himself directly, but manifests himself through his particular manner of concealment, and he tells him stories (he always likes to tell stories) which stir the hearer just because of their primitive character and apparent lack of intellectual quality, and finally make him see and accept them as a reference to his own secret needs. Here again, in the telling of simple stories and parables which, however, evoke a strong personal application, the connection between spirit and nature becomes manifest, a union which makes it possible for images to serve as symbols, that is as spirit which assumes form in Nature herself. What both of these disciples have to say about the teachings of the Baal Shem, and about their association with him, is characteristic in the same sense: he taught the Maggid (among other things) how to understand the language of birds and trees, and—so the rabbi of Polnoye tells his son-in-law—it was his "holy custom" to converse with animals. The Gaon of Vilna, the great opponent of hasidism, who was responsible for the ban pronounced upon it, the man who wished to proceed against the hasidim "as Elijah proceeded against the prophets of Baal," accused the Baal Shem of "having led astray" the Maggid of Mezritch "through his magic arts." What seemed magic was the union within a person of heavenly light and earthly fire, of spirit and nature. Whenever this union appears incarnate in human form, this person testifies—with the testimony of life—for the divine unity of spirit and nature, reveals this unity anew to the world of man which again and again becomes estranged from it, and evokes ecstatic joy. For true ecstasy hails neither from spirit nor from nature, but from the union of these two.

14

5.

Not many of the immediate disciples of the Baal Shem stand in the limelight of legendary tradition. It is as though, for the time being, the power of ecstatic vision, which was his to so great a degree, narrowed and concentrated on a few persons beloved by their people, while of the others there are only isolated, though frequently very characteristic tales. Not until the third generation* does the House of Study of the Great Maggid become the focus for a long series of zaddikim, each entirely different from the other, whose memory legend preserved and embroidered with veneration. But aside from this, we are struck by a complete change in tone the moment we turn from the stories which concern the Baal Shem, to those which deal with his disciples and are not immediately connected with his own life. The three men around whom legend has primarily crystallized: the Maggid of Mezritch, Pinhas of Koretz, and Yehiel Mikhal of Zlotchov were, above all, teachers, the first as the head of the hasidic mother-school, the second in a small closed circle which developed hasidic wisdom along its own, independent lines, the third through the powerful influence he exerted in temporary contacts, wide in scope, but not followed up by continuous educational activities. Thus in the case of these three men legend is concerned chiefly with their teachings, while in the stories about the Baal Shem, his teachings only figure as one function, as one part of his life. In the third generation there is a noticeable change: the tales grow more varied, more vivid. They become more like the legends of the Baal Shem. Once more life is expressed in all its abundance — only that the secret of beginnings, the secret of primal magnitude is lacking.

Rabbi Dov Baer, the Maggid of Mezritch (died 1772), was a teaching thinker, or rather, the Baal Shem, who liberated him

* In keeping with the contents of this book, this introduction deals only with the first three generations of zaddikim. The introduction to the second volume will treat of the others. This division into generations does not, to be sure, quite correspond to the chronological order: some zaddikim of the third generation chronologically belong to the second volume, some of the fourth to the first.

from his solitude, made a teaching thinker of him. From that time on, the task of teaching determined the deepest core of his thinking. It is significant that his favorite simile is that of the father adjusting himself to his little son who is eager to learn. He regards the world as God's self-adjustment to his little son: Man, whom he rears with tender care to enable him to grow up to his Father. Here then, under the influence of basic pedagogic experience, the Kabbalistic concept of the "contraction" of God to make room for the creation of the world, ceases to be cosmogonic and enters the realm of the anthropological. It is this idea which spurs the Maggid to try to understand the world from the viewpoint of God's educational methods. But the fundamental prerequisite for all education is the strength and tenderness of the relationship between the educator and his pupil. Only one who experienced this like Rabbi Baer could do what he did, could—as Rabbi Shneur Zalman, the most all-inclusive among his disciples, tells us—unite the mercy of God with man's love of God, and the sternness of God with man's fear of God, in other words: set up the reciprocity of this relationship as the fundamental principle.

One must understand the tremendous seriousness the Maggid's own experience in receiving teaching had for his soul, to appreciate not only the intensity with which he handles each of his disciples according to his particular character and his inner destiny, but also what is said of his manner of teaching. We are told that his disciples had very divergent interpretations of what he had said, but that the Maggid refused to decide for one or the other of these, because—no matter which of the seventy faces of the Torah one regards with a true spirit—one sees the truth. This sheds light on another aspect of the Maggid's method: When he spoke, he did not supply systematic connections, but threw out a single suggestion, or a single parable without spinning it out and tying together the threads. His disciples had the task—and it was a task which absorbed them completely—of working over what had been said and supplying the missing links. Each did this for himself or they worked together. One of them wrote in a letter: "We were always content with one saying over a long period of time and

kept it alive within us, pure and whole, until we heard another."
The Maggid was concerned with waking the truth inherent in
the spirit of his disciples, with "lighting the candles."

But we cannot grasp all this in its full significance until we
remember that obviously the Maggid had always been a man
given to ecstasy, only that, under the influence of the Baal
Shem, this ecstasy was diverted from ascetic solitude to the
active life of teaching disciples. From that moment on, his
ecstasy assumed the shape of teaching. Many of his disciples
have testified to the ecstatic character of his words. They say
that he had only to open his lips and they all had the impression that he was no longer in this world, that the Divine
Presence was speaking from his throat. And this phenomenon
too cannot be understood until we probe down to the deepest
depths accessible to us: It is apparent that with all the passion
his soul was capable of, the Maggid put himself into the service of the will of God to lift his "little son" up to him. And
to accomplish this service he regarded himself, his thinking
as well as his teaching, only as a vessel for divine truth. To
use his own words, he "changed the something back into the
nothing." From this angle, we can understand that effect on
his disciples which the youngest of them, later the "Seer of
Lublin," described after his very first visit to the Maggid:
"When I came before the master, before the Maggid, I saw
him on his bed: something was lying there, which was nothing
but simple will, the will of the Most High." That was why his
disciples learned even more and greater things from his sheer
being than from his words.

The founder of hasidism, the Baal Shem, had not been a
teacher in the specific sense of the word. Compared to him,
the Maggid represents the quintessence of what makes up the
teacher, and that is the reason for his special influence. The
Baal Shem had lived, wrought, helped, healed, prayed, preached,
and taught. All this was one and the same thing, all was
an organic part of unified, spontaneous life, and so teaching
was only one among other natural manifestations of effective
living. It was different with the Maggid. He was, of course,
not a professional teacher, not a man with one specialized

function. Only in eras when the world of the spirit is on the decline is teaching, even on its highest level, regarded as a profession. In epochs of flowering, disciples live with their master just as apprentices in a trade lived with theirs, and "learn" by being in his presence, learn many things for their work and their life both because he wills it, or without any willing on his part. That is how it was with the disciples of the Maggid. Over and over they say that he himself as a human being was the carrier of teaching, that, in his effect on them, he was a Torah personified. As far as he himself was concerned, however, the will to teach was the mainspring of his existence. He poured into his disciples all the strength of his life, recreated by contact with the Baal Shem. And all the work of his intellect, he put into the service of teaching. He did not write a book; neither had the Baal Shem. But if—unlike the Baal Shem—he permitted others to take down his words, he did this to transmit his teachings to future genera-tions of disciples, as an indestructible prop.

The Great Maggid did not found an institute of learning. His spirit created only disciples, generations of disciples and dis-ciples of disciples. No other religious movement of the modern era has produced so many and so varied independent person-alities in so short a space of time.

Concerning the son of the Great Maggid, Rabbi Abraham, "the Angel," who died only a few years after him (1776), Rabbi Pinhas of Koretz said that had he lived longer, all the zaddikim of his generation would have subjected themselves to him. And in the autobiography of one of his contemporaries who, on the ninth day of Av, the commemorative day of the destruction of the Temple, saw him lamenting for a night and a day, we read: "Then I realized that it was not for nothing that all called him an angel, for his was not the strength of one born of woman." But in one most significant respect, he cannot be considered a disciple of Rabbi Baer's, in this one respect he even leaves the teachings of the Baal Shem: he sets out to accomplish the "change of something into nothing" by returning to the way of ascetic solitude. Accordingly, he neither associates with the people at large, like the Baal Shem, nor with disciples, like the

Baal Shem and the Great Maggid. He gave instruction in the Kabbalah to only one person, to Shneur Zalman, a man of his own age. In the preface to his posthumous book, he refers to the fact that the true teachings of the Baal Shem and the Great Maggid "grew dark and material before our eyes," in contrast to the steadfastness of a superior zaddik "who cannot descend to the lowest rung to uplift his generation." Here, as in other instances, the bodily descendants of a leading zaddik cease to transmit the teachings. As early as the second generation the problematic character of hasidic development becomes evident, in its most sublime aspect.

Rabbi Pinhas of Koretz (Korzec, died 1791) was the second among those who belonged to the Baal Shem's circle to become the focus of a tradition. He was not one of his disciples in the strict sense of the word, since he is said to have visited the Baal Shem only twice, the second time during the last days of his life. Apparently his contacts with Rabbi Israel ben Eliezer did not bring about any fundamental change in his views, but only confirmed and strengthened them. Yet he must certainly be included here. Although in his mention of the Baal Shem he does not designate him as his teacher, he and his school give important data about the Baal Shem and cite important utterances of his, for which we have no other source, and which therefore probably go back to oral transmission. One such utterance is the basis of one of the Rabbi Pinhas' major teachings: that we should "love" the evil-doer and hater "more" in order to compensate for the lack of the power of love he himself has caused in his place in the world. And other basic teachings of Rabbi Pinhas also derive from words of the Baal Shem. To gain a better understanding of the relationship, we must remember that the Baal Shem—as we glean from a number of indications—found kindred trends to which his influence afforded increased vitality and, frequently, a deeper rooting. Among these kindred trends, those of Rabbi Pinhas (who was about thirty-two when the Baal Shem died) approximated his own most nearly, and he accepted him more as a companion than as a disciple.

Rabbi Leib, son of Sarah, the zaddik who wandered over the earth for secret purposes of his own, is said to have called Rabbi Pinhas the brain of the world. He was, at any rate, a true and original sage. In the period between the Baal Shem and his great-grandson Nahman of Bratzlav, he has no equal in fresh and direct thinking, in daring and vivid expression. What he says often springs from a profound knowledge of the human soul, and it is always spontaneous and great-hearted. In contrast to the Baal Shem and the Great Maggid, no ecstasies are reported of Rabbi Pinhas. Ecstasy wanes into the background and the mystic teachings are reduced to the precept of constant renewal through immersion in nothingness, a doctrine of dying and arising which, however, sponsors also sturdy living in tune with all the things of this earth, and a give-and-take community with one's fellowmen. Rabbi Pinhas' circle had no great influence on the outside world, but such as it is, it represents a unique and invaluable phenomenon, for its members were distinguished by the simple honesty of their personal faith, the unrhetorical telling of the teaching, a telling even tinged with humor, and by their loyal readiness to satisfy the demands put upon them, at the cost of their very lives.

One cannot consider Rabbi Pinhas apart from his most distinguished disciple, Rafael of Bershad. In the whole history of hasidism, rich in fruitful relationships between master and disciple, there is no other instance of so pure a harmony, of so adequate a continuation of the work. In reading the records, we sometimes hardly know what to ascribe to Pinhas and what to Rafael, and yet we have a number of utterances of the latter which bear the stamp of independent thinking. But more important than his independence is the matter of course devotion with which the disciple embodied his master's teachings in his life and—according to tradition—even in his death, which quietly and solemnly sealed the proclamation of the commandment of truth, for which the master had striven so many years.

Rabbi Yehiel Mikhal, the maggid of Zlotchov (died about 1786)* who first learned from the Baal Shem and, after his

* The dates given for his death vary between 1781 and 1792.

death, from the Great Maggid, was also a unique phenomenon, as yet insufficiently understood and difficult to understand. He came from a family of those ascetic mystic hasidim whom the new movement found ready to hand and tried to win for its own, because the earnestness of their faith which colored their whole attitude toward life rendered them particularly valuable for the task of renewal. Mikhal's father was that Rabbi Yitzhak of Drohobycz who had criticized the amulets of the Baal Shem. All manner of uncanny rumors were circulated about him, that he once did a favor to the "prince of the forest," for instance, or that he sent those of his new-born children who displeased him back to the upper world. (It was said that Mikhal remained alive only because his mother refused to let his father see his face, before he had promised to let him live.) Rabbi Yitzhak's mother, who was called "Yente, the prophetess," used to repeat the threefold "holy" of the choir of angels whose song she heard. To understand Mikhal, it is necessary to know his milieu. In spite of the fact that his father was close to the movement, he himself became a follower of the Baal Shem only after some hesitation. From what we are told it is quite evident that his father's suspicion lived on in him and was only gradually overcome. But he never wholly overcame his basic asceticism.

While he was still young, Mikhal became a great preacher, like his father before him, and went preaching from town to town. He fascinated and intimidated his audiences although he emphasized that the reproof in his sermons was directed toward himself as well as them. The Baal Shem chided him for imposing too heavy penances on sinners and apparently induced him to adopt a milder attitude. But even after his death they tell of souls who come to a younger zaddik to complain of Rabbi Mikhal who, as the chief justice of a court in heaven, censures unintentional earthly faults with the utmost severity because he, who remained pure, does not understand the temptations of men. Though he wholly accepted and absorbed the hasidic teachings and followed the trend of the Baal Shem in his doctrine of the Evil Urge as a helper and of the uplifting of sexuality, he never quite rid himself of asceticism whose extreme forms, however, he emphatically rejected. According to a report, which all but crosses the border between the sublime and the ridiculous, he never warmed himself at the stove, for this would have been a concession to sloth, never bent down to his food, for this would have been yielding to greed, and never scratched himself, since this would have verged on voluptuousness. But Rabbi Mikhal's special endowment made for true hasidism in a very significant fashion. The most notable instance of this is that he carried on the tradition of those "first hasidim" of whom the Talmud says that they waited with praying until they had prepared the kavvanah within themselves. But he expanded this motif into something that embraced the whole community: in order to make his prayer representative for the community, he strove to unite with both the mightier and the humbler to form a single, continuous and powerful chain of prayer, and—taking as his point of departure the tradition of his father and a saying of the Baal Shem's—he also wanted to raise up the limp prayers which had not the strength to rise from the ground. This attitude, for which he incurred violent hostility, exerted an effective influence on later generations who accorded him deep veneration. But even a contemporary zaddik said of him that he was "a soul of the soul," and, in his own generation, played the same role as Rabbi Simeon ben Yohai, the founder of the secret teachings, in his.

Like Rabbi Mikhal himself, two of his five sons figure in tales of strange journeys of the soul to heaven. But a third, Rabbi Zev Wolf of Zbarazh (died about 1802),* who was reputed to have been a very wild child, was made of quite other stuff. Like his contemporary Rabbi Moshe Leib of Sasov (who belonged to the fourth generation), he became one of the great friends of man and the earth. In contrast to his father—though we must not forget that Rabbi Mikhal bade his sons pray for their enemies—he obstinately refused to treat the wicked differently from the good. Wolf lavished his love on all human beings who came his way and even on animals. He held that man

* The dates of his death given, vary between 1800 and 1820.

should love all that lives, and that this love must not be determined by the way the object of his love behaves toward him.
Among the disciples of Rabbi Mikhal was Rabbi Mordecai of Neskhizh (Niesuchojce, died 1800), whom his teacher took with him to visit the Great Maggid. He figures in a great number of miracle tales, and it is told that even demons recognized his power. The source of such a statement is actual power over the souls of men, and in the case of Rabbi Mordecai such power definitely sprang from the unity in his own soul. This unity, however, did not find adequate expression in power itself, but rather in the unity of his own life. This is what the "Seer" of Lublin must have meant when he said that all his activities were, in reality, one.

6.

According to hasidic tradition, the Great Maggid had three hundred disciples. About forty of these have come down to us as individuals with their personal characteristics, the most of them also through their writings. Ten are represented in this volume, but—as in the case of the Baal Shem's disciples—these ten do not include all of those who were most significant as human beings, because the legends about them, current among the people, do not suffice to give a connected account of their lives. These ten are: Menahem Mendel of Vitebsk (died 1788), whom the Maggid brought to the Baal Shem when he was a boy; Aaron of Karlin (died 1772); Shmelke of Nikolsburg (died 1778); Meshullam Zusya (yiddish Zishe) of Hanipol (Annopol, died 1800); his younger brother, Elimelekh of Lizhensk (Lezajsk, died 1809); Levi Yitzhak of Berditchev (died 1809); Shneur Zalman of Ladi (died 1813); Shelomo of Karlin (died 1792); Israel of Koznitz (Kozienice, died 1814); Jacob Yitzhak of Lublin (died 1815).
What makes Rabbi Menahem Mendel of particular importance in the history of hasidism is that he transplanted the movement to Palestine where, to be sure, other zaddikim had settled before him. From the days of the Baal Shem who, according to legend, had to turn back at the border, the focus of hasidic, as of the pre-hasidic, yearning for redemption, was "the Land." After

having taken a leading part in the struggle against those who pronounced the ban, he translated this yearning into action by going to Palestine (1777) with three hundred of his hasidim. There he first settled near Safed, the ancient city of Kabbalists, and later in Tiberias. Thus he gave the movement a site which was not central in location but in spirit, and linked it organically with the past. And he brought the Land an element of new life. Concerning this, a grandson of his friend Shneur Zalman (who had not been able to accompany Mendel to Palestine) said that once, when the Land of Israel was on its highest rung, it had the power to uplift man, but that now that it had sunk so low, and strangely enough kept on sinking, it could no longer uplift man, that now man must uplift the Land, and only a man on so high a rung as Rabbi Mendel had been able to do this. In a letter from Palestine, Rabbi Mendel wrote that he regarded himself as an envoy to the palace of the king, dispatched by the governors of the provinces, that he must not for a moment lose sight of both the physical and spiritual welfare of the provinces. He remained in especially close and constant contact with the hasidim he had left behind in exile, so close that— as one of those who accompanied him writes—everything connected with them, everything taking place in their hearts, was manifest to him when he prayed before falling asleep.

From among all of his disciples, the Maggid chose Aaron of Karlin as his envoy, because he knew how to win souls as none other, even though his courting of them was linked with stern demands upon their whole attitude toward life. He died young, and in his funeral sermon his successor, Rabbi Shelomo of Karlin, said that the Lord had taken him before his time, because his power of converting men to God was so great, that he deprived them of the freedom of choice which is of prime importance. When the Maggid heard of his death, he said: "He was our weapon in war. What shall we do now?" Rabbi Aaron did not wish to go contrary to the folk-character of the movement which not only persisted in the Karlin school but experienced a curious development there. Nevertheless, what he obviously wanted was to create an elite body dedicated to a life of faith. One main device by which he sought to accomplish this was the regulation of one day a week devoted to solitary meditation accompanied by fasting and the ritual bath. But this was to have nothing of the ascetic, for Rabbi Aaron regarded asceticism as a bait thrown out by Satan himself. His demands sprang from his own intrinsic experience. His "testament" expresses his deepest purpose for his own person: to prepare the proper kavvanah for the hour in which the soul departs from the body. His friend Shneur Zalman says of him that he was a veritable fountain of the love of God and that whoever heard him pray was seized by the love for God. But the picture becomes complete only through the words the same zaddik said about Rabbi Aaron's great fear of God after his death.* His love was only the flowering of his fear, for only through great fear—this was Rabbi Aaron's basic feeling—can one attain to great love. He who has not this fear does not love the great and terrible God himself, but only a small convenient idol. One of the sayings of his great-grandson who followed this trend is: "Fear without love is something imperfect; love without fear is nothing at all." And this world in which we live is the site where through fear one can attain to love, and where fear and love can fuse. That is why in another of his sayings we read: "This world is the lowest, and yet the loftiest of all."

Among the disciples of the Great Maggid, Rabbi Shmelke of Nikolsburg was the preacher par excellence; not a preacher who exhorted, as Rabbi Mikhal did in his youth, but a preacher per se. The sermon was his true element because he fervently believed that words inspired by God had the power to transform, and he never gave up this belief, even in the face of disappointments. He regarded the sermon as an action which lifts the prayer of the congregation to the highest level of purity. And so, in his sermons, he repeatedly demanded two things from those who prayed: first, that with the rivers of their love they wash away all separating walls and unite to one true congregation to furnish the site for the union with God; secondly, that they detach their prayers from individual wishes,

* See the story of "The Little Fear and the Great Fear."

25

and concentrate the full force of their being on the desire that God unite with his Shekhinah. This was the spirit in which he himself prayed and this holy intent of his lifted him to ecstasy, so that in the very midst of prayer, he abandoned the charted track of memory and custom and sang new melodies, never heard before. He left his Polish congregation for Nikolsburg in Moravia, which was utterly remote from the world of hasidism, and where a man such as he was bound to provoke constant annoyance. He exerted a profound influence on many a spirit that was still open and responsive, but the majority of those he stirred up from their usual ways did all they could to make his life in their community intolerable. We have various versions of the tale of how Rabbi Elimelekh, his younger friend in the Maggid's House of Study, visited him and in a coarse and pithy sermon told the burghers that they were not fit patients for so noble a doctor, that first he, Elimelekh, the barber, would have to subject them to drastic treatment. And the next instant, fixing now one, now the other with his gaze, he hurled at them the full description of all their secret vices and faults. Rabbi Shmelke never could have done that, if only because the weaknesses of individuals were not of sufficient importance in his eyes. His basic attitude to all men, including his foes, was love, the vast tide of love which he preached. His House of Study in Nikolsburg became one of the main centers of the movement. He exerted a great influence on his disciples and friends and through them on countless others.

In sharp contrast to Shmelke, Rabbi Meshullam Zusya, known as the Rabbi Reb Zishe, was a true man of the people. Here, in the narrow confines of an eastern ghetto, in a much later century, the "Fool of God" reappears, the singular character, known to us from the legends of Chinese Buddhists, from Sufis, and from the disciples of St. Francis of Assisi. Yet he may also be interpreted as the East European Jewish type of badhan, the jester who figures chiefly at weddings, but now sublimated into something holy. He is a human being who, because of his undamaged direct relationship with God, has quitted the rules and regulations of the social order, though he continues to participate in the life of his fellowmen. He does not sequester himself; he is only detached. His loneliness in the face of the eternal "Thou" is not the loneliness of the recluse, but of one who is composed and true to the world, a loneliness which includes intrinsic oneness with all living creatures. He leads his life among his fellows, detached and yet attached, regarding their faults as his own and rejoicing in them and in all creatures in the freedom of God. But since men are so made that they cannot endure an attitude such as this, which blocks their evasion of the eternal, they are content to jeer at the "fool." They make him suffer. They do not impose sharp and brief martyrdom, but life-long sorrows, and he delights in them. Yet men are also so made that such a destiny kindles them to the most sublime love, and it was with sublime love that Rabbi Zusya was loved by the people.

Rabbi Elimelekh, called the Rabbi Reb Melekh, was Zusya's brother and shared the wanderings of his youth. Year after year, they went on and on without a goal, making their lives an imitation of the journeying of the exiled Presence of God, watching for souls wakened or ready to be wakened. But then they parted ways. Zusya did, to be sure, settle down, but again and again he felt the urge to wander and into his old age he continued to be a boy who whistles a song for God. Elimelekh had the vocation to be a leader of men. He too knew the timeless world of ecstasy, but his clear and unerring reason taught him to protect himself against its dangers and enabled him to combine the life of the spirit with the activities of an organizer. Here again was a man who simultaneously headed the hasidic school and the hasidic congregation, and so Rabbi Elimelekh must be considered the true successor of the Great Maggid. While he did not approach him in originality of teaching, he was almost his equal in his power to build up, and even outstripped him in his intuitive knowledge of the many different types of people, their flaws and their needs, and the means to minister to these. In the legend-shaping memory of the people, he stands out as a doctor of souls, as a man who could exorcise demons, as a wonder-working counselor and guide.

Levi Yitzhak, the rav of Berditchev, the most original of the Maggid's disciples, and the one who came closest to the people,

was very different from Elimelekh. He was akin to Zusya, but
more of the stuff of this earth, and part and parcel of his nation. His ecstasy penetrated his strong and solid life. The transports of Rabbi Shmelke, whose devoted follower he was, passed
over into him, only translated into something more substantial,
as it were. In lieu of the strange new songs which broke from
Rabbi Shmelke, Rabbi Yitzhak's whole body shook with un-
controllable tremors when he prayed. He liked to converse with
crude and ignorant people, but even the worldliest of his words
was holy and had for its purpose Yihudim, the uniting of the
upper worlds. He was harsh enough when something displeased
him about a man, but he was always willing to learn from
others and had the greatest reverence for simplicity. Even his
communings with God were colored by unvarnished intimacy.
He confronted him not only as the passionate intercessor for
Israel, he took him to account, made demands on him, and even
ventured to hurl threats, a bitter and sublime jest which would
have been blasphemy in another, but was irreproachable coming from the lips of this unique character. In his own fashion,
however, he also praised God and often interrupted the flow of
prescribed prayer by interpolating endearment for him.

Rabbi Shneur Zalman, the rav of Northern White Russia, who
was called simply "the rav," or "the Tanya" after the title of
his main work, intended to voyage to the Holy Land together
with Rabbi Mendel of Vitebsk. But Mendel asked him to turn
back—legend makes of it a command received in a dream
vision—and the rav later founded the special Lithuanian school
of hasidism, the Habad, a term made up of the initial letters
of the three upper of the ten Sefirot which, according to the
teachings of the Kabbalah, emanated from God: Hokhmah,
wisdom; Binah, intelligence; Daat, knowledge. This very
name, which detaches the specifically intellectual Sefirot out
of the closely linked structure, points to the principle underlying this school: reason and intellect are to be reinstated as a
way to find God. The Habad School represents an attempt to
reconcile rabbinism with hasidism by incorporating both in a
system of thought, a method which of necessity weakened certain fundamental concepts of hasidism. The very separating

28

off of the spheres threatened to deprive hasidism of its strongest base: the teaching that sparks of God are inherent in all things and creatures, in all concepts and urges, sparks which desire us to redeem them and, linked with this teaching, the affirmation of the soul-body entity of man, provided he is able to turn all his stirrings toward God. The average man is no longer asked to transform "alien thoughts"; he is requested to turn away from them and this spells his renunciation of attaining all-embracing unity. The only ones who are not forbidden contact with the powers of temptation are the superior men. (Here, to be sure, the Habad teachings connect up with certain warnings of Rabbi Efraim of Sadylkov, the Baal Shem's grandson.) But in order to give the reason of the individual its due, the zaddik is deprived of the essential office which is his, according to the teachings of the Baal Shem and especially of the Great Maggid, the great office of cosmic helper and mediator. The things misused are discarded together with misuse itself. Yet in spite of everything, the special position of the Habad must not be interpreted as leading to schism. For the rav was exposed to the hostilities of the mitnagdim, the opponents of hasidism, no less, but even more, than the other zaddikim of his time. The anti-hasidic rabbis plotted against him and had him arrested again and again. He was confined in the fortress of Petersburg and subjected to lengthy cross-examination. What he was charged with were distorted teachings of the Baal Shem whose true intent he avowed. A certain zaddik said of the Habad—and he was not altogether wide of the mark— that it resembled a loaded gun in the hand of a man who can aim and who knows the target—only that the fuse was lacking. But even this branch movement with its rationalized mysticism (aided and abetted by the rational tendencies of the Lithuanian Jew) still manifests the old flight of the soul. The life of the zaddik with his hasidim is warmer and stronger than the chilly doctrine, and besides this the rav counted among his disciples distinguished men who again brought the teachings closer to the original tenets of hasidism. Surely the hasidic "flame" burned in the rav himself. We are told of certain traits in his life which give evidence of impassioned personal religiosity, and his clinging to God is documented by his melodies, particularly those known simply as "the rabbi's melodies." Sometimes these are linked with a Kabbalistic song, at others they revolve around "Tatenyu" (little father), a name by which God is addressed. Again and again, at a feast or in solitude, the Habad-hasidim sing them, expressing their fervor and renewing it by its expression.

Rabbi Shelomo of Karlin was instructed by his fellow-pupil Aaron of Karlin and later became his successor. He was a man of prayer in even a stricter sense than Levi Yitzhak, who prayed primarily in behalf of the people while Shelomo prayed only to pray. Rabbi Shelomo as none other accepted as his own the Baal Shem's doctrine that before praying man should prepare to die, because the intention of prayer demands the staking of his entire self. For him prayer was a stupendous venture to which one must give one's self up so completely that thought beyond that point is wholly impossible, that it is impossible to imagine what could take place afterwards. From his youth on, this capacity for self-surrender made his prayer indescribably forceful. Before presenting him to the Great Maggid, Rabbi Aaron told him about this youth who, on the eve of the Day of Atonement, spoke the words of the psalm: "How glorious is Thy name in all the earth," in such a way that not a single one of the fallen sparks remained unlifted. There is a significant story of how some of the hasidim of the "Tanya" came to see him and went into a long ecstasy over the way he recited a psalm before saying grace. The "Tanya" did, indeed, commend him with the words that he was "a hand's-breadth above the world," but it is also told that after Rabbi Mendel of Vitebsk's departure for Palestine, when a number of hasidim thought of joining Rabbi Shelomo, "the Tanya" deterred them with the very same words, saying: "How can you go to him? You know he is a hand's-breath above the world!"—a statement which implied that while Shelomo's ecstasies were commendable, they were not beneficial. This furnishes a clue to what later happened between those two. During a crisis in the hasidic school of Karlin, brought about mostly by the Tanya's growing power of attraction, Rabbi Shelomo conceived the idea of settling in the region of Vitebsk, which had been Rabbi Mendel's main rallying point and which was now included in the Tanya's sphere of influence, and went to him, requesting his consent to this. The rav made three conditions which serve to characterize both men: Rabbi Shelomo was not to look down upon the scholars; he was not to look down upon "natural piety" (that is, piety which lacks ecstasy); and he must no longer declare that the zaddik has to carry the sheep (a phrase by which he designated the zaddik's function to mediate). Shelomo accepted the two first conditions but he rejected the third, and thus relinquished his plan. Later he visited the rav and the two had a lengthy discussion which—so the Habad-hasidim say—"could not be noted down" because of its "shocking" character. In the period of Poland's desperate battles of 1792, in the course of which Shelomo died, he prayed for Poland, while the Tanya (just as twenty years later during Napoleon's campaigns) prayed for Russia. According to tradition, which represents Shelomo of Karlin as a reincarnation of the first, suffering Messiah who re-appears "from generation to generation," he was killed in the midst of prayer by a bullet a Cossack fired, but continued his work of prayer even after his death.

The Great Maggid's youngest disciple, Rabbi Israel, maggid of Koznitz, manifested a gentler, more composed form of Rabbi Shelomo's power of praying. Legend relates that the Baal Shem promised a bookbinder and his wife the birth of a son in their old age, because they had gladdened his heart by their joyful celebration of the sabbath. The son, Rabbi Israel, was sickly all through life and often on the verge of death, but his prayers were so potent that the rows of devotees gazed at that frail form of his as though at a victorious general. When the Great Maggid died, Rabbi Israel attached himself to Rabbi Shmelke, after his death to Rabbi Elimelekh, and after his, to Rabbi Levi Yitzhak. At the very zenith of his life and his work, he still wished to be a disciple. Whenever he cited the words of the talmudic and later masters, he said their names with fear and trembling. On the eve of the Day of Atonement, the entire congregation, men, women, and children, used to come to his threshold and implore atonement with sobs and tears. And he himself came out to them weeping, prostrated himself in the dust, and cried: "I am more sinful than all of you!" Then they wept together and together they went to the House of Prayer to say the Kol Nidre prayer. The power of living prayer—of which he once said that its function was to waken and lift the dead prayers—radiated continually from his sick-bed. People came to him from all over: Jews, peasants, and nobles, to receive his blessing, to implore his mediation, or just to look on his face. No zaddik since the day of the Baal Shem had so many cures of the possessed placed to his credit. And legend even has him play an important role in the history of his time. He is said to have predicted Napoleon's triumph and later his defeat—the outcome of the Russian expedition is traced back to the force of Rabbi Israel's prayers.

Rabbi Jacob Yitzhak of Lublin, a friend of Rabbi Israel and his fellow-pupil in the school of the Great Maggid and later in those of Rabbi Shmelke and Rabbi Elimelekh, also took part in the cosmic struggle. He was called "the Seer" because his intuition was even greater than that of his teacher, Rabbi Elimelekh. One of his disciples said: "If I may take the liberty of saying so, even the Rabbi Reb Melekh did not have the eyes of the Seer of Lublin." He is the only zaddik to whom the people accorded this by-name which is, however, used in quite another sense than in the case of the biblical prophets. The prophet is the mouthpiece of the *will* of God. He does not see or predict a future reality. In fact, the future concerns him only in so far as it cannot yet be grasped and beheld as reality, in so far as it is still latent in the will of God and also in the free relationship of man to this divine will, and hence is, in a certain way, dependent on the inner decision of man. The seer in the hasidic meaning of the word, on the other hand, sees and sees only whatever reality is present in time and space, but his seeing reaches beyond the perception of the senses, beyond the grasp of intelligence on to what is in the process of becoming and back into the past which he recognizes in that and through that which is. Thus the rabbi of Lublin could read not only character and deeds, but the origin of souls (which according to the genealogy of souls, have their own law of propagation) and the migrations of the souls of his visitors. And he read this from their foreheads or even from the notes of request they handed him. Countless men came to him to have their souls illumined and suffused by the light of his eyes. And his disciples felt so secure in the shelter of his radiance that, while they dwelt in its pale, they forgot the exile and thought themselves in the Temple of Jerusalem. But he did not forget the exile. He was filled with ceaseless waiting for the hour of redemption and finally initiated and played the chief part in the secret rites which he and certain other zaddikim—among them Israel of Koznitz, who strove against Napoleon, and Mendel of Rymanov who sided with Napoleon—performed with the purpose of converting the Napoleonic wars into the pre-Messianic final battle of Gog and Magog. The three leaders in this mystic procedure all died in the course of the following year.* They had "forced the end": they died at its coming. The magic, which the Baal Shem had held in check, broke loose and did its work of destruction.

Barukh of Mezbizh (died 1811) grew up under the Great Maggid's care but lived his life remote from the master's other disciples. He was the younger of the two sons of Odel, the Baal Shem's daughter. His elder brother Efraim, whom his grandfather had still been able to educate himself, was a quiet sickly man. We know him almost only through the book in which he cites and interprets the teachings of the Baal Shem and tells the legendary anecdotes about him which—together with similar notes taken down by Rabbi Jacob Joseph of Polnoye—form the nucleus of a legendary biography. Beyond this, the book contains a description of his dreams in which the Baal Shem frequently appeared to him.

Barukh offers us quite another picture, one that is full of contradictions and yet an integrated whole. There has been much and legitimate mention of his interest in wealth and power, his pride and love of splendor, and what we know of these qualities of his would suffice to account for his quarrels with the most

* I have related these happenings in my book *Gog and Magog* (English title: *For the Sake of Heaven*).

prominent zaddikim of his time, even if he had not almost always been the one to start them. And yet it would be a mistake to place him in the category of a later degenerate type of zaddik. Many things we have from his own lips, and others told about him, prove that he led the life of a true and impassioned mystic. But his form of mystic life did not make for harmony with the world of man. It caused him to regard this world as an alien region in which he was an exile, and to consider it his duty to challenge and oppose it. His preference for the Song of Songs, which he recited with such fervor and abandon, helps us to gain insight into his soul, and no less important is the fact that he once designated God and himself as two strangers in an unknown land, two castaways who make friends with each other. But the picture of his soul which takes shape through these characteristics is complicated by the circumstance that Barukh liked to interpret the actions and incidents (even such as seem trivial to us) of his own life as the symbolizing of heavenly events, and wanted others to do likewise. A little deeper probing, however, makes it clear that, in the final analysis, he was concerned with something utterly different from the desire for recognition. Apparently he really meant what he once said: that he would rather be stricken dumb than "coin fine phrases," that is to say, to talk in a manner that would please his hearer rather than unbolt the gates of truth. By and large we must agree with what Rabbi Israel of Rizhyn, the Great Maggid's great-grandson, once said about him: "When a wise man went to the Rabbi Reb Barukh, he could spoon up the fear of God with a ladle, but the fool who visited him, became much more of a fool." And this, of course, does not hold for this one zaddik alone.

THE EARLY MASTERS

ISRAEL BEN ELIEZER
THE BAAL SHEM TOV

The Tree of Knowledge

They say that once, when all souls were gathered in Adam's soul, at the hour he stood beside the Tree of Knowledge, the soul of the Baal Shem Tov went away, and did not eat of the fruit of the tree.

The Sixty Heroes

It is said that the soul of Rabbi Israel ben Eliezer refused to descend to this world below, for it dreaded the fiery serpents which flicker through every generation, and feared they would weaken its courage and destroy it. So he was given an escort of sixty heroes, like the sixty who stood around King Solomon's bed to guard him against the terrors of night—sixty souls of zaddikim to guard his soul. And these were the disciples of the Baal Shem.

The Test

It is told:

Rabbi Eliezer, the Baal Shem's father, lived in a village. He was so hospitable that he placed guards at the outskirts of the village and had them stop poor wayfarers and bring them to his house for food and shelter. Those in Heaven rejoiced at his doing, and once they decided to try him. Satan offered to do this, but the prophet Elijah begged to be sent in his stead. In the shape of a poor wayfarer, with knapsack and staff, he came to Rabbi Eliezer's house on a sabbath afternoon, and said the greeting. Rabbi Eliezer ignored the desecration of the sabbath, for he did not want to mortify the man. He invited him to the meal and kept him in his house. Nor did he utter a word of reproof the next morning, when his guest took leave of him. Then the prophet revealed himself and promised him a son who would make the eyes of the people of Israel see the light.

His Father's Words

Israel's father died while he was still a child.
When he felt death drawing near, he took the boy in his arms and said: "I see that you will make my light shine out, and it is not given me to rear you to manhood. But, dear son, remember all your days that God is with you, and that because of this, you need fear nothing in all the world."
Israel treasured these words in his heart.

Vain Attempts

After the death of Israel's father, the people looked out for the boy for the sake of Rabbi Eliezer, whose memory was dear to them, and sent his son to a melammed.
Now, Israel studied diligently enough, but always only for a few days running. Then he played truant and they found him somewhere in the woods and alone. They ascribed this behavior to the fact that he was an orphan without proper care and supervision, and returned him to the melammed over and over, and over and over the boy escaped to the woods until the people despaired of ever making an honest and upright man of him.

The First Fight

When the boy grew up, he hired himself out as teacher's assistant. Early in the morning, he called for the children in their homes and brought them to school and the House of Prayer. In a clear and moving voice, he recited to them those words of prayer which are said in chorus, such as "Amen, let His great name be blessed forever and in all eternity." While he walked with them, he sang to them and taught them to sing with him. And when he took them home, he went by way of fields and woods.
The hasidim say that those in heaven rejoiced in these songs every morning, just as they had once rejoiced in the song of the Levites in the Temple of Jerusalem. The hours when the

hosts of Heaven gathered to listen to the voices of mortals, were hours of grace. But Satan was there too. He knew very well that what was in the making down there would threaten his power on earth. So he entered into the body of a sorcerer who could change himself into a werewolf.

Once when Israel was walking through the woods and singing with the little ones in his care, the monster fell on them, and the children screamed and scattered in all directions. Some of them fell ill from the shock and the parents decided to put a stop to the doings of the young school assistant. But he remembered what his father had said as he lay dying, went from house to house, promised the people to protect their children, and succeeded in persuading them to entrust them to him once more. The next time he shepherded them through the wood, he took a sound stick with him and when the werewolf attacked again, he struck him between the eyes, so that he was killed on the instant. The following day they found the sorcerer dead in his bed.

Conjuring

After this, Israel was employed as a servant in the House of Study. Since he had to be there day and night, but felt that Heaven wished him to keep secret his fervor and intentness, he made a habit of sleeping while those in the House of Study were awake, and to pray and study while they slept. But what they thought was that he slept all night and on into the day. The hasidim tell of wonderful happenings that occurred in those days.

Before the time of the Baal Shem Tov—so they say—a wonder-working man by the name of Adam lived, no one knows just where, but it was probably in the imperial city of Vienna. Like the succession of wonder-working men before him, Adam was called Baal Shem, that is the Master of the Name, because he knew the secret, full name of God, and could say it in such a way that—with its help—he was able to effect strange things and especially to heal men in body and soul. When this man knew he was about to die, he did not know to whom to leave the age-old writings from which he had learned his secrets, the writings which had been handed down from Abraham, the patriarch. While his only son was a man both learned and devout, he was not worthy of a heritage such as this. And so Adam, in his dream, asked Heaven what he should do and was told to have the writings given to Rabbi Israel ben Eliezer in the city of Okup, who would then be fourteen years old. On his death-bed, Adam entrusted his son with the errand.

When his son reached Okup, he first found it difficult to believe that the servant in the House of Study, who was generally regarded as a crude and ignorant boy, could be the person he was looking for. He let the boy wait on him in the House of Study, observed him closely and secretly and soon realized that Israel was hiding his true character and preoccupations from the world. Now he told him who he was, gave him the writings and only asked that he might participate in studying them under the boy's direction. Israel consented on condition that their agreement remain secret and that he continue to serve the stranger. Adam's son rented a small house outside the city and apart from others, and the people were only too glad to give him Israel for his servant. They thought, indeed, that this devout and learned man was willing to put up with the boy only because his father had been a person of such merit.

Once Rabbi Adam's son asked the boy to conjure up the Prince of the Torah with the aid of the directions given in the writings, so that they might ask him to solve certain difficulties in the teachings. For a long time, Israel refused to undertake so great a venture, but in the end he let himself be persuaded. They fasted from sabbath to sabbath, immersed themselves in the bath of purification, and—at the close of the sabbath—fulfilled the rites prescribed. But, probably because Adam's son did not fix his soul utterly on the teachings themselves, an error crept in. Instead of the Prince of the Torah, the Prince of Fire appeared and wanted to burn up the entire town. It was only by a great effort that it was saved.

After a long time, Adam's son urged the boy to make another attempt. Israel steadfastly refused to do again what was obviously displeasing to Heaven. But when his companion called on him in the name of his father, who had bequeathed the

38

miraculous writings to the boy, he consented. Again they fasted from one sabbath to the next. Again they immersed themselves in the bath of purification and, at the close of the sabbath, fulfilled the rites prescribed. Suddenly the boy cried out that they were condemned and would die unless they watched through the night with unflagging spiritual intentness. All night they remained standing. But when day was just dawning, Rabbi Adam's son could not fight his drowsiness any longer and fell asleep on his feet. In vain Israel tried to wake him. They buried him with great honors.

His Marriage

In his youth, Israel ben Eliezer was an assistant teacher in a small community not far from the city of Brody. No one knew anything much about him, but the children he taught were so eager and happy to learn, that their fathers also came to like him. Presently it was bruited about that he was wise, and people came to ask his advice. When a quarrel broke out, the young teacher was asked to mediate and this he did so well that a man against whom he decided was no less pleased than his opponent in whose favor he had spoken, and both went their ways serene and happy.

At that time, a great scholar, Rabbi Gershon of Kitov, lived in Brody. His father, Rabbi Efraim, was carrying on a law-suit with a member of the small community whose children the Baal Shem taught. He looked up his opponent and suggested that they both go to Brody to submit their disagreement to the rabbinical court. But the other man kept telling him about the wisdom and sense of justice of the young teacher until Rabbi Efraim agreed to put the matter up to him. When he entered his room and looked at him, he was startled, for shining from Israel's forehead, he saw a curved sign exactly like that he had seen for an instant—and never forgotten!—on the little forehead of his own daughter, when the midwife had shown him the new-born child. He lowered his gaze, his tongue was numb and he could hardly utter his request. When he raised his eyes again, the sign had vanished. Israel listened, put questions, listened again, and then pronounced judgment. Soon after, the hearts of both men were at peace, and it seemed to them that shining justice itself had blazed forth from the mists of their differences.

Later Rabbi Efraim went to the Baal Shem and asked him to take his daughter to wife. Israel consented but insisted on two conditions: that their agreement should remain secret for the time being, and that in the contract about to be drawn up, his scholarship should not even be mentioned; that he should be designated merely by name: Israel ben Eliezer, for—he added —"You want me and not my knowledge, as a husband for your daughter." Everything was done according to his wish.

When Rabbi Efraim returned from his trip, he fell suddenly ill and died after a few hours. His son, Rabbi Gershon Kitover, came to bury him. Among his father's papers he found the marriage contract and read that his sister had been promised to a man who had no learned title and who was not of a famous family. Not even the native town of the stranger was mentioned. He immediately informed his sister of this unheard-of arrangement, but she only replied that since this had been her father's wish, only this and nothing else could be right for her.

Israel waited until he had completed his year of teaching. The fathers of his pupils did not want him to go, but he did not let them hold him back. He put aside his robe and clothed himself in a short sheepskin with a broad leather belt, such as peasants wear, and he adopted their speech and gestures. Thus he came to Brody and to Rabbi Gershon's house. There he stood in the door, on the inner threshold. The scholar, who was just comparing various interpretations of a difficult passage in the Talmud, had them give a coin to the stranger who looked needy to him, but the man said he had something to tell him. They went into the adjoining room together and Israel informed the rabbi that he had come to fetch his wife. In great consternation, Gershon called his sister to see the man her father had chosen for her. All she said was: "If he has commanded this, then it is God's command," and bade them prepare for the wedding. Before they went to the marriage canopy, the Baal Shem talked to his wife and revealed his secret to her. But she had to promise never to breathe a word of it, no matter what might happen. He also told her that great misery and many troubles were in store for them. She only said that all this was as it should be.

After the wedding, Rabbi Gershon spent day after day trying to teach his ignorant brother-in-law the Torah, but it was impossible to get him to remember a single word of the teachings. Finally he said to his sister: "I am ashamed of your husband. It would be a good thing for you to divorce him. If you do not want to do this, I shall buy you horses and a carriage and you can go with him wherever you like." She was well satisfied with the second alternative.

They drove until they came to a little town in the Carpathian Mountains, where the woman found a place to live. Israel went to the nearby hills, built himself a hut, and quarried clay. Two or three times a week, she went to him, helped him load the clay in the wagon, took it into the town and sold it for a small sum. When Israel was hungry, he put water and flour into a little pit, kneaded the dough, and baked it in the sun.

The Helpful Mountain

It is told:
The summits of the mountains on whose gentle slopes Israel ben Eliezer lived are straight and steep. In hours of meditation he liked to climb these peaks and stay at the very top for a time. Once he was so deep in ecstsay, he failed to notice that he was at the edge of an abyss, and calmly lifted his foot to walk on. Instantly a neighboring mountain leaped to the spot, pressed itself close to the other, and the Baal Shem pursued his way.

With Robbers

It is told:
A small band of robbers who lived in the eastern section of the Carpathian Mountains and had witnessed the miraculous happenings which occurred wherever the Baal Shem showed himself, came to him and offered to take him to the Land of Israel by a special route, through caves and holes under the earth, for they had heard—we do not know how—that that was where he

41

wanted to go. The Baal Shem was willing and ready to go with them. The way took them through a gorge filled with mud and slime. Only at the very edge, there was a narrow foothold and there they walked, step by step, holding to blocks of stone which they had rammed into the earth. The robbers went first. But when the Baal Shem wanted to follow them, he saw the flame of the sword wielded in a circle forbidding him to advance, and he turned back.

Obstacles to Blessing

The Baal Shem once asked his disciple Rabbi Meir Margaliot: "Meirly, do you still remember that sabbath, when you were just beginning to study the Pentateuch? The big room in your father's house was full of guests. They had lifted you up on the table and you were reciting what you had learned?"
Rabbi Meir replied: "Certainly I remember. Suddenly my mother rushed up to me and snatched me down from the table in the middle of what I was saying. My father was annoyed, but she pointed to a man standing at the door. He was dressed in a short sheepskin, such as peasants wear, and he was looking straight at me. Then all understood that she feared the Evil Eye. She was still pointing at the door when the man disappeared."
"It was I," said the Baal Shem. "In such hours a glance can flood the soul with great light. But the fear of men builds walls to keep the light away."

The First

When Rabbi Israel ben Eliezer was employed as ritual slaughterer for the village of Koshilovitz, he did not reveal himself and no one could tell the difference between him and an ordinary butcher. Rabbi Zevi Hirsh Margaliot, the rav of the neighboring town of Yaslovitz, had two sons, Yitzhak Dov Baer and Meir. Yitzhak was seventeen at the time, his brother eleven. Suddenly each of the boys was overcome with the burning desire to visit the slaughterer in Koshilovitz. They could see neither rhyme nor reason in it, and even when they had told each other about their longing, they still did not understand it, and both felt that they could not talk about it either to their father nor to anyone else.

One day they stole out of the house and went to the Baal Shem. What was said at this visit, neither he nor they ever told. They stayed with the Baal Shem. At home they were missed. People looked for them all over the town and in the entire region. In Koshilovitz too, they went from house to house until the boys were found and taken home. For the first few days, their father was so happy to have them back that he did not question them. Finally he asked them quietly what was so remarkable about the slaughterer in Koshilovitz. "It is impossible to describe," they replied. "But you can believe us that he is wiser than all the world and more devout than all the world."

Later, when the Baal Shem became known, they attached themselves to him and went to see him every year.

Shaul and Ivan

It is told:

Once when Rabbi Meir Margaliot, the author of the book "Illuminator of the Paths," was visiting the Baal Shem with his seven-year-old son, his host asked him to leave the boy for a time. Little Shaul remained in the house of the Baal Shem Tov. Soon after, the Baal Shem took him and his disciples on a journey. He had the carriage stop in front of a village inn and entered with his companions and the boy. Inside they were playing the fiddle and peasant men and women were dancing. "Your fiddler is no good," the Baal Shem said to the peasants. "Let my boy here sing you a dance song, and then you will be able to dance much better."

The peasants were willing. The boy was stood on the table and in his silvery voice sang a hasidic dance song without words, that went straight to the feet of the villagers. In a reel of wild happiness they danced around the table. Then one of them, a young fellow, stepped forward from among them and asked the boy: "What is your name?" "Shaul," he said. "Go on

43

singing," the peasant cried. The boy started another song and the peasant faced him and danced in time to the tune. But in the midst of his wild leaps and bounds, he repeated over and over in charmed tones: "You Shaul and I Ivan, you Shaul and I Ivan!" After the dance, the peasants treated the Baal Shem and his disciples to vodka, and they drank together.

About thirty years later, Rabbi Shaul, who had become both a wealthy merchant and a Talmud scholar of sorts, was traveling through the country on business. Suddenly robbers attacked him, took his money and wanted to kill him. When he begged them to have pity on him, they took him to their chieftain. He gave Rabbi Shaul a long penetrating look. Finally he asked: "What is your name?" "Shaul," said the other. "You Shaul and I Ivan," said the robber chief. He told his men to return Shaul's money and take him back to his carriage.

The Peasant at the Stream

It is told:

When Rabbi Israel ben Eliezer lived in the village of Koshilo-vitz, he frequently bathed in the stream. When it was covered with ice, he hacked an opening and dipped down into the water-hole. A peasant whose hut was near the stream once saw him wrenching at his foot which had gotten stuck in the ice, until the skin came off and blood spurted out. After that the peasant watched the weather and put down straw for the Baal Shem to step on. Once he asked the peasant: "What would you like best: to get rich, to die old, or to be mayor?" "Rabbi," said the peasant, "that all sounds pretty good." The Baal Shem had him build a bath-house beside the stream. Soon it became known that the peasant's sick wife had bathed in the water of the stream and recovered from her ailment. The fame of the healing waters spread more and more until the doctors heard of it and made such a to-do about it in government quarters that the bath-house was closed. But in the meantime the peasant who lived near the stream had become rich and the people had chosen him for their mayor. He bathed in the stream every day and grew very old.

Fasting

When Rabbi Elimelekh of Lizhensk once said that fasting was no longer service, they asked him: "Did not the Baal Shem Tov fast very often?"

"When the Baal Shem Tov was young," he replied, "he used to take six loaves of bread and a pitcher of water at the close of the sabbath, when he went into seclusion for the entire week. On a Friday, when he was ready to go home, and about to lift his sack from the ground, he noticed that it was heavy, opened it, and found all the loaves still in it. He was very much surprised. Fasting such as this, is allowed!"

The Tap at the Window

It happened in the days of the Baal Shem's youth, that one Friday he had nothing at all in the house to prepare for the sabbath, not a crumb, not a penny. So early in the morning, he tapped at the window of a well-to-do man, said: "There is some one who has nothing for the sabbath," and walked on. The man, who did not know the Baal Shem, ran after him and asked: "If you need help, why do you run away?" The Baal Shem laughed and replied: "We know from the Gemara that every man is born with his livelihood. Now, of course, the heavier the load of one's sins, the greater effort one must make to get the appointed livelihood to come. But this morning I felt scarcely any weight on my shoulders. Still there was enough to make me do a little something—and that is what I just did."

The Call

When Heaven revealed to the Baal Shem that he was to be the leader of Israel, he went to his wife and said to her: "You must know that I have been appointed to be the leader of Israel." She answered: "What shall we do?" He said: "We must fast." So they fasted for three nights and three days without a break, and one day and one night they lay on the earth with outstretched hands and feet. On the third day, toward evening, the Baal Shem heard a call from above: "My son, rise

and lead the people!" He rose and said: "If it is the will of
God that I be their leader, I must take this burden upon myself."

The Baal Shem Reveals Himself

It is told:

Israel ben Eliezer had held successively the posts of school
assistant, servant in the House of Study, teacher of children,
and ritual slaughterer and for a time he acted as driver for his
brother-in-law. Finally this man rented a piece of land for him
in a village on the Prut River. On the land was an inn which
also had rooms for guests. A short distance away, across the
ford, a cave had been hewn into the side of a mountain. There
the Baal Shem spent the week sunk in meditation. Whenever a
guest came to the inn, Israel's wife went to the door and called
over to him, and he always responded, and immediately came
to wait on the guest. On the sabbath he stayed at home and
wore the white sabbath robe.

One day—it was on a Tuesday—a disciple of Rabbi Gershon's,
the Baal Shem's brother-in-law, was on the way to his teacher
who lived in the town of Brody. He passed through the village
on the Prut, stopped, and went into the inn. Then the woman
called to her husband and the Baal Shem came and served the
guest his meal. When he had finished eating, he said: "Israel,
harness the horses; I have to go on."

The Baal Shem harnessed the horses, reported that the carriage
was ready, and added: "But how about staying here over the
sabbath?" The guest smiled at this foolish suggestion. But
hardly had he driven half a mile, when a wheel broke.

He found that it would be some time before it could be fixed,
and so he had to go back and spend the night at the inn. The
next day, and the next after that, and even on Friday morning,
one obstacle after another presented itself, and finally he had
no choice but to stay for the sabbath. On Friday morning he
went about troubled and sad. To his astonishment he saw that
the innkeeper's wife was baking twelve sabbath loaves. He
asked her what she needed them for. "Well," she said, "my
husband is, to be sure, an ignorant man, but he does the right

46

thing, and I do in my husband's house what I saw done in my brother's."

"Perhaps you also have a bath for the purification?" he asked.

"Certainly," she said. "We have such a bath."

"But what do you need the bath for?" he continued.

"Well," she said, "my husband is, to be sure, an ignorant man, but he does the right thing, and so he immerses himself in the bath every day."

In the afternoon, when the time for prayer was come, he asked the woman where her husband was. "Out in the field with the sheep and cows," she said. So the guest had to say the Afternoon and Evening prayer, and the words to receive the sabbath, alone, and still the innkeeper did not come. For he was praying in his cave. When he finally returned to the house, he again assumed the speech and gestures of a peasant, and greeted his guest in this manner.

"So you see!" he said. "You are spending the sabbath here after all." He stood up against the wall as if to pray, and then —in order not to give himself away by the fervor he knew he could not conceal—he asked his guest to pronounce the benediction over the wine. They sat down and ate together. When they had finished their meal, the Baal Shem asked the guest to say words of teaching. In order not to tax the mental powers of his host too greatly, Rabbi Gershon's disciple merely gave a brief and dry account of the chapter for the week, of the enslavement in Egypt of the children of Israel.

That very night, the last before the day the Baal Shem would complete the thirty-sixth year of his life, Heaven sent him a message that the time for concealment was over.

In the middle of the night, the guest woke up, and from his bed in the main room of the inn, saw a great fire burning in the hearth. He ran there because he thought the logs had caught fire. But then he saw that what he had taken for fire, was a great light. A great white light shone out from the hearth and filled the house. The man started backward and fainted. When the Baal Shem had restored him to consciousness, he said: "A man should not look upon what is not granted to him."

47

In the morning the Baal Shem went into his cave in his white sabbath robe, came home, head held high, went about in the house, his face shining, and sang: "I shall prepare the meal on the sabbath morning." Then he spoke the "great Kiddush" in his usual manner, with miraculous power of clinging to God. At table, he again asked his guest to say words of the teaching, but he was so confused that all he could utter was a few words interpreting a passage in the Scriptures. "I heard another expounding of that," said the Baal Shem.

Together they said the Afternoon Prayer, and then the Baal Shem spoke words of teaching and revealed secrets of the teachings which no one had ever heard before. Then they said the Evening Prayer together and pronounced the benediction which marks the separation between the sabbath and the workaday week.

When Rabbi Gershon's disciple reached Brody, he went to the community of the "great hasidim" in that town even before visiting his teacher, told what had happened to him and added: "A great light dwells close to you. It would be no more than right that you go and bring it into the city." They went and met the Baal Shem at the edge of the woods which skirts the village. They wove a seat of green withes for him, set him upon it, took it on their shoulders, and he spoke words of teaching to them.

Themselves

The Baal Shem said:

"We say: 'God of Abraham, God of Isaac, and God of Jacob,' and not: 'God of Abraham, Isaac, and Jacob,' for Isaac and Jacob did not base their work on the searching and service of Abraham; they themselves searched for the unity of the Maker and his service."

The Torah Is Perfect

Concerning the verse of the psalm: "The law of the Lord is perfect," the Baal Shem said:

"It is still quite perfect. No one has touched it as yet, not a whit and not a jot of it. Up to this hour, it is still quite perfect."

The hasidim tell:
Rabbi Dov Baer, the maggid of Mezritch, once begged Heaven
to show him a man whose every limb and every fibre was holy.
Then they showed him the form of the Baal Shem Tov, and it
was all of fire. There was no shred of substance in it. It was
nothing but flame.

Trembling

1.

On a certain day of the new moon, the Baal Shem joined in
the Morning Prayer standing in his own place, for it was his
custom to go to the reader's pulpit only when the reading of the
psalms began. Suddenly he trembled and the trembling grew
greater and greater. They had seen this happen before while
he prayed, but it had never been more than a slight quiver
running through his body. Now he was violently shaken. When
the reader had ended, and the Baal Shem was to go to the desk
in his stead, they saw him stand in his place and tremble violently. One of his disciples went up to him and looked him in
the face: it was burning like a torch and his eyes were wide
open and staring like those of a dying man. Another disciple
joined the first, they took him by the hands, and led him to
the desk. He stood in front of it and trembled. Trembling he
recited the psalms and after he had said the Kaddish, he remained standing and trembled for a good while, and they had
to wait with reading the Scriptures until his trembling had
left him.

2.

The maggid of Mezritch told:
"Once—it was on a holiday—the Baal Shem was praying in
front of the desk with great fervor and in a very loud voice.
Because I was ill, it was too much for me, and I had to go
into the small room and pray there alone. Before the festival
service, the Baal Shem came into the small room to put on his
robe. When I looked at him, I saw that he was not in this
world. Now, as he was putting on his robe, it wrinkled at the

49

shoulders and I put my hand on it to smooth out the folds. But hardly had I touched it, when I began to tremble. I held fast to the table, but the table began to tremble too. The Baal Shem had already gone into the big hall, but I stood there and begged God to take the trembling from me."

3.

Rabbi Jacob Joseph of Polnoye told:
"Once a large water-trough stood in the room in which the Baal Shem was praying. I saw the water in the trough tremble and sway until he had finished."
Another disciple told:
"Once, on a journey, the Baal Shem was praying at the east wall of a house at whose west wall stood open barrels filled with grain. Then I saw that the grain in the barrels was trembling."

When the Sabbath Drew Near

The disciples of a zaddik who had been a disciple of the Baal Shem Tov, were sitting together at noon, before the sabbath, and telling one another about the miraculous deeds of the Baal Shem. The zaddik, who was seated in his room which adjoined theirs, heard them. He opened the door and said: "What is the sense of telling miracle tales! Tell one another of his fear of God! Every week, on the day before the sabbath, around the hour of noon, his heart began to beat so loudly that all of us who were with him could hear it."

The Fringes

A zaddik told:
The fringes of the prayer robe of the holy Baal Shem Tov had their own life and their own soul. They could move even when his body did not move, for through the holiness of his doing, the holy Baal Shem Tov had drawn into them life and soul.

To His Body

The Baal Shem said to his body: "I am surprised, body, that you have not crumbled to bits for fear of your Maker!"

In the midst of praying, the Baal Shem once said the words in the Song of Songs: " 'New and old, which I have laid up for thee, O my beloved.' " And he added: "Whatever is in me, everything, new and old, for you alone."

They asked him about this, saying: "But the rabbi tells words of teaching to *us* too!" He answered: "As when the barrel overflows."

What the Mouth Will

The Baal Shem said: "When I weld my spirit to God, I let my mouth say what it will, for then all my words are bound to their root in Heaven."

How Ahijah Taught Him

The rav of Polnoye told:

"At first the Baal Shem Tov did not know how to talk to people, so wholly did he cling and cleave to God, and he talked softly to himself. Then his God-sent teacher Ahijah, the prophet, came and taught him which verses of the psalms to say every day, to gain the ability of talking to people without disrupting his clinging to God."

The Money That Stayed in the House

Never did the Baal Shem keep money in his house overnight. When he returned from a journey, he paid all the debts which had accumulated in his absence and distributed whatever he had left, among the needy.

Once he brought a large amount of money back from a journey, paid his debts, and gave the rest away. But in the meantime, his wife had taken a little of the money so that she might not have to buy on credit for a few days. In the evening, the Baal Shem felt something impeding his prayer. He went home and said: "Who took of the money?" His wife confessed it was she who had done so. He took the money from her and had it distributed among the poor that very evening.

51

Knowledge

The Baal Shem said:

"When I reach a high rung of knowledge, I know that not a single letter of the teachings is within me, and that I have not taken a single step in the service of God."

The Bath of Immersion

The Baal Shem said: "I owe everything to the bath. To immerse oneself is better than to mortify the flesh. Mortifying the flesh weakens the strength you need for devotions and teaching, the bath of immersion heightens this strength."

Against Mortification of the Flesh

Rabbi Barukh, the Baal Shem's grandson, told:

They once asked my grandfather, the Baal Shem Tov: "What is the essence of service? We know that in former times 'men of deeds' lived who fasted from one sabbath to the next. But you have done away with this, for you said that whoever mortifies his flesh will have to render account as a sinner, because he has tormented his soul. So do tell us: what is the essence of service?"

The Baal Shem Tov replied: "I have come into this world to point another way, namely that man should try to attain to three loves: the love of God, the love of Israel, and the love of the Torah—it is not necessary to mortify the flesh."

Without the Coming World

Once the spirit of the Baal Shem was so oppressed that it seemed to him he would have no part in the coming world. Then he said to himself: "If I love God, what need have I of a coming world!"

The Dance of the Hasidim

At the festival of Simhat Torah, the day of rejoicing in the law, the Baal Shem's disciples made merry in his house. They danced and drank and had more and more wine brought up from the cellar. After some hours, the Baal Shem's wife went to his room and said: "If they don't stop drinking, we soon won't have any wine left for the rites of the sabbath, for Kiddush and Havdalah."

He laughed and replied: "You are right. So go and tell them to stop."

When she opened the door to the big room, this is what she saw: The disciples were dancing around in a circle, and around the dancing circle twined a blazing ring of blue fire. Then she herself took a jug in her right hand and a jug in her left and— motioning the servant away—went into the cellar. Soon after she returned with the vessels full to the brim.

The Master Dances Too

One Simhat Torah evening, the Baal Shem himself danced together with his congregation. He took the scroll of the Torah in his hand and danced with it. Then he laid the scroll aside and danced without it. At this moment, one of his disciples who was intimately acquainted with his gestures, said to his companions: "Now our master has laid aside the visible, dimensional teachings, and has taken the spiritual teachings unto himself."

The Deaf Man

Rabbi Moshe Hayyim Efraim, the Baal Shem's grandson told: "I heard this from my grandfather: Once a fiddler played so sweetly that all who heard him began to dance, and whoever came near enough to hear, joined in the dance. Then a deaf man who knew nothing of music, happened along, and to him all he saw seemed the action of madmen—senseless and in bad taste."

The Strength of Community

It is told:

Once, on the evening after the Day of Atonement, the moon was hidden behind the clouds and the Baal Shem could not go out to say the Blessing of the New Moon. This weighed heavily on his spirit, for now, as often before, he felt that destiny too great to be gauged depended on the work of his lips. In vain he concentrated his intrinsic power on the light of the wandering star, to help it throw off the heavy sheath: whenever he sent some one out, he was told that the clouds had grown even more lowering. Finally he gave up hope.

In the meantime, the hasidim who knew nothing of the Baal Shem's grief, had gathered in the front room of the house and begun to dance, for on this evening that was their way of celebrating with festal joy the atonement for the year, brought about by the zaddik's priestly service. When their holy delight mounted higher and higher, they invaded the Baal Shem's chamber, still dancing. Overwhelmed by their own frenzy of happiness they took him by the hands, as he sat there sunk in gloom, and drew him into the round. At this moment, someone called outside. The night had suddenly grown light; in greater radiance than ever before, the moon curved on a flawless sky.

The Bird Nest

Once the Baal Shem stood in the House of Prayer and prayed for a very long time. All his disciples had finished praying, but he continued without paying any attention to them. They waited for him a good while, and then they went home. After several hours when they had attended to their various duties, they returned to the House of Prayer and found him still deep in prayer. Later he said to them: "By going away and leaving me alone, you dealt me a painful separation. I shall tell you a parable.

You know that there are birds of passage who fly to warm countries in the autumn. Well, the people in one of those lands once saw a glorious many-colored bird in the midst of a flock which was journeying through the sky. The eyes of man had never seen a bird so beautiful. He alighted in the top of the tallest tree and nested in the leaves. When the king of the country heard of it, he bade them fetch down the bird with his nest. He ordered a number of men to make a ladder up the tree. One was to stand on the other's shoulders until it was possible to reach up high enough to take the nest. It took a long time to build this living ladder. Those who stood nearest the ground lost patience, shook themselves free, and everything collapsed."

The Address

Every evening after prayer, the Baal Shem went to his room. Two candles were set in front of him and the mysterious Book of Creation put on the table among other books. Then all those who needed his counsel were admitted in a body, and he spoke with them until the eleventh hour.

One evening, when the people left, one of them said to the man beside him how much good the words the Baal Shem had directed to him, had done him. But the other told him not to talk such nonsense, that they had entered the room together and from that moment on the master had spoken to no one except himself. A third, who heard this, joined in the conversation with a smile, saying how curious that both were mistaken, for the rabbi had carried on an intimate conversation with him the entire evening. Then a fourth and a fifth made the same claim, and finally all began to talk at once and tell what they had experienced. But the next instant they all fell silent.

Faith

Rabbi David Leikes, a disciple of the Baal Shem Tov, once asked some hasidim of his son-in-law Rabbi Motel of Tchernobil, who had come to meet him on his way to the town of Tchernobil: "Who are you?"

They said: "We are hasidim of Rabbi Motel of Tchernobil." But he went on questioning them. "Have you perfect faith in your teacher?" They did not answer, for who would dare to say he had perfect faith! "Then I shall tell you," he said, "what faith is. One sabbath, the third meal—as so often happens— went on into the night. Then we said grace and remained standing and said the Evening Prayer and made Havdalah and at once sat down to the 'escort of the sabbath.' Now we were all poor, and had not a penny of our own, especially on the sabbath. And yet, when the meal was over and the holy Baal Shem Tov said to me: 'David, give something for mead,' I put my hand in my pocket, although I knew I had nothing in it, but I drew out a gulden, and gave it for mead."

The Story Teller

There are many versions of how the Baal Shem gained for his disciple Rabbi Jacob Joseph, later the rav of Polnoye, who subsequently set down the teachings of his master in many a book. These versions include tales of miracles—even the awakening of the dead. I shall here give an account taken from other stories which supplement one another.

When Rabbi Jacob Joseph was still a rav in Szarygrod and bitterly averse to the hasidic way, a man whom no one knew came to his town one summer morning, at the hour when the cattle were taken to pasture, and stopped in the market-place with his wagon. He called to the first man who came along leading his cow, and began to tell him a story, which pleased his listener so well that he could not break away. A second man caught a few words in passing; he wanted to go on and could not, so he stayed and listened. Soon a whole group of people were gathered about the story teller and still their number grew. Right among them stood the servant of the House of Prayer who had been on his way to open the doors, for in summer the rav always prayed there at eight o'clock and the doors had to be opened well ahead of that time, around seven. Now, at eight the rav came to the House of Prayer and found it locked. It is well-known that he was very particular and quick to fly into a temper; now too he angrily set out to look for the servant. But there he was, right in front of him, for the Baal Shem—it was he who was telling the stories—had signed to him to go, and he had run to open the House of Prayer. The rav shouted at him and asked why he had failed in his duty and why the men, who were usually there by that time, had not come. The servant replied that, like himself, all those who had been on the way to the House of Prayer, had been irresistibly captivated by the great story. The angry rav had to say the Morning Prayer alone. But then he told the servant to go to the market-place and fetch the stranger. "I'll have him beaten up!" he cried.

In the meantime, the Baal Shem had finished his story and gone to the inn. There the servant of the House of Prayer found him and delivered his message. The Baal Shem immediately followed him out, smoking his pipe, and in this manner came before the rav. "What do you think you are doing!" shouted the rav. "Keeping people from prayer!"

"Rabbi," said the Baal Shem calmly, "it does not become you to fly into a rage. Rather let me tell you a story."

"What do you think you are doing!" was what the rav wanted to repeat, and then he looked at the man closely for the first time. It is true that he immediately turned his eyes away, nevertheless the words he had been about to say stuck in his throat. The Baal Shem had begun his story, and the rav had to listen like all the others.

"Once I drove cross-country with three horses," said the Baal Shem, "a bay, a piebald, and a white horse. And not one of the three could neigh. Then I met a peasant coming toward me and he called: 'Slacken the reins!' So I slackened the reins, and then all three horses began to neigh." The rav could say nothing for emotion. "Three," the Baal Shem repeated. "Bay, piebald and white did not neigh. The peasant knew what to do; slacken reins—and they neighed." The rav bowed his head in silence. "The peasant gave good advice," said the Baal Shem. "Do you understand?"

"I understand, rabbi," answered the rav and burst into tears. He wept and wept and knew that up to this time he had not known what it was to weep.

"You must be uplifted," said the Baal Shem. The rav looked up to him and saw that he was no longer there.

Every month Rabbi Jacob Joseph fasted one week, from sabbath to sabbath. Since he always took his meals in his room, no one knew this except his niece who brought him his food. In the month which followed his meeting with the Baal Shem, he fasted as always, because it never occurred to him that the uplifting predicted for him could be attained without mortifying the flesh. The Baal Shem was on another one of his journeys, when he suddenly felt: if the rav of Szarygrod continues as he is doing, he will lose his mind. He had the horses urged on so vehemently that one fell and broke a leg. When he entered the rav's room, he said: "My white horse fell because I was in such a hurry to get here. Things cannot go on in this way. Have some food brought for yourself." The rav had food brought and ate. "Your work," said the Baal Shem, "is one of sorrow and gloom. The Divine Presence does not hover over gloom but over joy in the commandments."

The month after this, the rav was sitting over a book in Mezbizh in the "Klaus" of the Baal Shem, when a man entered and immediately began to converse with him. "Where are you from?" he asked. "From Szarygrod," answered the rav. "And what do you do for a living?" the man continued. "I am rav in the city," said Rabbi Jacob Joseph. "And how do you make out?" the other went on to ask. "Do you make a good living or are you strapped for money?" The rav could no longer endure this empty talk. "You are keeping me from my studies," he said impatiently. "If you fly into a temper," said the other, "you curtail God in making his living." "I do not understand what you mean," said the rav. "Well," said the man, "everyone makes his living in the place God has appointed for him. But what is the livelihood of God? It is written: 'And thou, holy one, art enthroned upon the praises of Israel'; that is God's living! If two Jews come together and one asks the other how he makes his living, he answers: 'Praise be to God, I make my living thus and so,' and his praise is the living of God. But you, who do not talk to anyone, you who only want to study, are curtailing God's living." The rav was taken aback. He wanted to reply, but the man had vanished. The rav went back to his book, but he could not study. He shut the book and went into the Baal Shem's room. "Well, rav of Szarygrod," he said smilingly, "Elijah got the best of you, after all, didn't he?"

When the rav had returned to his home, he invited the congregation to the third sabbath meal, as was the custom among the hasidim. Some came, but most of them were annoyed that he had joined that juggler of a hasid! They grew more and more hostile to him until they finally succeeded in driving him out of town. At the last, they would not suffer him to remain in his house for even a day longer and, since it was a Friday, he had to spend the sabbath in a village near by. The Baal Shem was on a journey with some of his intimate friends and on that very Friday he was close to that village. "Let us keep the sabbath together with the rav of Szarygrod and gladden his heart," he said. And that was what they did.

Soon afterward, Rabbi Jacob Joseph became rav in the city of Rashkov. He issued a proclamation far and wide that he would return all fines he had ever received, and there had been many. He did not rest until he had distributed all the money he had. From that time on, he used to say: "Worry and gloom are the roots of all the powers of evil."

The Seventy Languages

Rabbi Leib, son of Sarah, the hidden zaddik, told:

"Once I was with the Baal Shem Tov over the sabbath. Toward evening, his great disciples gathered around the table before the third meal and waited for his coming. And while waiting, they discussed a passage in the Talmud about which they wanted to ask him. It was this: "Gabriel came and taught Joseph seventy languages.' They could not understand this, for does not every language consist of countless words? Then, how could the mind of one man grasp them all in a single night, as the passage implied? The disciples decided that Rabbi Gershon of Kitov, the Baal Shem's brother-in-law, should be the one to ask him.

"When he came and seated himself at the head of the table, Rabbi Gershon put the question. The Baal Shem began to say words of teaching, but what he said seemed to have nothing to do with the subject of the question, and his disciples could not glean an answer from his words. But suddenly something unheard-of and incredible happened. In the middle of the Baal Shem's address, Rabbi Jacob Joseph rapped on the table and called out: 'Turkish!' and after a while: 'Tartar!' and after another interval: 'Greek!' and so on, one language after another. Gradually his companions understood: from the master's speech, which was apparently concerned with quite different things, he had come to know the source and the character of

59

every single language—and he who teaches you the source and character of a language, has taught you the language itself."

The Battle Against Amalek

Once Rabbi Pinhas of Koretz felt confused about his faith in God, and could think of no way to help himself except to travel to the Baal Shem. Then he heard that the master had just arrived in Koretz. Full of happiness he ran to the inn. There he found a number of hasidim gathered about the Baal Shem Tov, and he was expounding to them the verse in the Scriptures in which the hands Moses held up in the hour of the struggle against Amalek, are spoken of as being emunah, that is, trusting and believing. "It sometimes happens," said the Baal Shem, "that a man grows confused about his faith. The remedy for this is to implore God to strengthen his faith. For the real harm Amalek inflicted on Israel was to chill their belief in God through successful attack. That was why Moses taught them to implore God to strengthen their faith, by stretching to Heaven his hands which were, in themselves, like trust and faith, and this is the only thing that matters in the hour of struggle against the power of evil." Rabbi Pinhas heard, and his hearing of it was in itself a prayer, and in the very act of this prayer he felt his faith grow strong.

The Passage of Reproof

When Rabbi Nahum of Tchernobil was young, he once happened to be with the Baal Shem the sabbath on which the great passage of reproof is read from the Scriptures, and which goes by the name of the "Sabbath of Blessings" in order to avoid using the ominous words. On this occasion he was called to the reading of the Torah in the House of Prayer, and it was this very passage of reproof he was to assist with. He was annoyed that just this chapter had fallen to his share. The Baal Shem himself read aloud. Now Rabbi Nahum was sickly and plagued with all manner of aches and pains. But when the Baal Shem began to read, Rabbi Nahum felt pain leave one of his limbs after another with each successive part of the passage of reproof, and when the reading was over, he was rid of all his complaints: sound and well.

Losing the Way

Rabbi Yehiel Mikhal, later the maggid of Zlotchov, did, indeed, seek out the Baal Shem while he was quite young, but was not sure whether or not he should become his disciple. Then the zaddik took him with him on a journey to a certain place. When they had been driving for a while, it became evident that they were not on the right road. "Why, rabbi!" said Mikhal. "Don't you know the way?"

"It will make itself known to me in due time," answered the Baal Shem, and they took another road; but this too did not take them to their destination. "Why, rabbi!" said Mikhal. "Have you lost your way?"

"It is written," the Baal Shem said calmly, "that God 'will fulfill the desire of them that fear him.' And so he has fulfilled your desire to have a chance to laugh at me."

These words pierced young Mikhal to the heart and without further arguing or analyzing, he joined the master with his whole soul.

The Cantor of the Baal Shem Tov

One of the Baal Shem's disciples once asked him: "How shall I make my living in the world?"

"You shall be a cantor," said the master.

"But I can't even sing!" the other objected.

"I shall bind you to the world of music," said the zaddik.

This man became a singer without peer, and far and wide they called him the cantor of the Baal Shem Tov.

After many years he arrived in Lizhensk in the company of his bass singer, who always went with him, and visited Rabbi Elimelekh, the disciple of the disciple of the Baal Shem Tov. For a long time, the rabbi and his son Eleazar could not make up their minds to let these two sing with the chorus in the House of Prayer on the sabbath, for Rabbi Elimelekh feared that the artistry of their singing might disturb his devotions. But Rabbi

Eleazar argued that because of the holiness of the Baal Shem Tov, it would not be right to withhold the honor from the man, and so it was agreed that he should sing at the inauguration of the sabbath. But when he began, Rabbi Elimelekh noticed that the great fervor of his singing flowed into his own, and threatened to drive him out of his mind, and so he had to retract his invitation. But he kept the cantor with him over the sabbath, and paid him many honors.

After the conclusion of the sabbath, the rabbi invited him to his house again and asked him to tell him about the holy Baal Shem Tov, the light of Israel. Then the eyes of the man kindled with new life, and it was clear that there was new life in his throat and in his heart as well. He began to speak and it became manifest that now, since he had not been allowed to sing, all the fervor in his heart, which he usually poured into his song, flowed into his spoken word. He told how, in the great sequence of the songs of praise, the master never recited a verse until he had seen the angel of this verse and heard his special strain. He told of the hours in which the soul of the master rose to Heaven, while his body remained behind as if dead, and that there his soul spoke with whomever it would, with Moses the faithful shepherd, and with the Messiah, and asked and was answered. He told that the master could speak to each creature on earth in its own language, and to every heavenly being in its own language. He told that, the moment the master saw an implement, he at once knew the character of the man who had made it, and what he had thought about, while making it. And then the cantor rose and testified that once he and his companions had received the Torah through the mouth of the master as Israel had once received it at Mount Sinai through the sound of thunder and trumpets, and that the voice of God was not yet silenced on earth, but endured and could still be heard.

Some time after his visit in Lizhensk, the cantor lay down and died. Thirty days after that, and again on a Friday, the bass singer came from the bath of purification and said to his wife: "Summon the Holy Brotherhood quickly to see to my burial, for in paradise they have commissioned my cantor to sing for the inauguration of the sabbath, and he does not want to do that without me." He lay down and died.

The Wrong Answer

It is told:

When Rabbi Wolf Kitzes took leave of his teacher, before setting out for the Holy Land, the Baal Shem stretched out his second finger, touched him on the mouth, and said: "Heed your words, and see to it that you give the right reply!" He refused to say anything more.

The ship on which the Baal Shem's disciple had taken passage was driven from its course by a tempest, and forced to land on an unknown, and apparently desert island. Presently the storm died down, but the vessel had suffered damage and could not put out to sea again immediately. Some of the passengers, Rabbi Wolf among them, went ashore to have a look at the unfamiliar foreign landscape. The others turned back after a while, but he was so deep in meditation that he went on and on and finally came to a big house built in an old-fashioned style, which looked as if no one had ever lived in it. Only then did he remember that the ship would not wait for him, but before he could decide one way or another, a man in a linen garment appeared on the threshold. His features were age-old, his hair was white, but he bore himself erect. "Do not be afraid, Rabbi Wolf," he said. "Spend the sabbath with us. The morning after, you will be able to resume your journey." As in a dream, Rabbi Wolf followed the old man to the bath, prayed in the company of ten tall majestic old men, and ate with them. The sabbath passed as in a dream. The next morning, the age-old man accompanied him down to the shore where his ship was lying at anchor, and blessed him in parting. But just as Rabbi Wolf was hurrying to set foot on the gangplank, his host asked him: "Tell me, Rabbi Wolf: How do the Jews fare in your country?"

"The Lord of the world does not abandon them," Rabbi Wolf replied quickly and walked on. Not until he was on the high seas, did his mind clear. Then he recalled the words of his teacher and was seized with such bitter remorse that he resolved not to continue his voyage to the Holy Land, but to go home at once. He spoke to one of the crew and gathered from his reply that he was already homeward bound.

When Rabbi Wolf came to the Baal Shem, his master looked at him sorrowfully but not angrily and said: "That was the wrong answer you gave our father Abraham! Day after day he asks God: 'How are my children?' And God replies: 'I do not abandon them.' If only you had told him of the sufferings of exile!"

The Axe

Once the Baal Shem had his disciple Rabbi Wolf Kitzes learn the kavvanot of blowing the ram's horn, so that, on New Year's Day, he might announce before him the order of the sounds. Rabbi Wolf learned the kavvanot but, for greater security, noted everything down on a slip of paper which he hid in his bosom. This paper, however, dropped out soon after and he never noticed it. They say that this was the work of the Baal Shem. Now when it was time to blow, Rabbi Wolf looked for his slip in vain. Then he tried to remember the kavvanot, but he had forgotten everything. Tears rose to his eyes, and weeping, he announced the order of sounds quite simply without referring to the kavvanot at all. Later the Baal Shem said to him: "There are many halls in the king's palace, and intricate keys open the doors, but the axe is stronger than all of these, and no bolt can withstand it. What are all kavvanot compared to one really heartfelt grief!"

The Word of the Disciple

On a Friday, at the hour the zaddik examines his soul, the whole world once grew dark for the Baal Shem, and the spark of life almost died within him. That was how one of his great disciples found him. "My master and teacher!" he said. His voice trembled and he could not utter another word. But even so he had caused new strength to flow into the Baal Shem's heart, and the flame of life grew strong within him.

A disciple asked the Baal Shem: "Why is it that one who clings to God and knows he is close to him, sometimes experiences a sense of interruption and remoteness?"

The Baal Shem explained: "When a father sets out to teach his little son to walk, he stands in front of him and holds his two hands on either side of the child, so that he cannot fall, and the boy goes toward his father between his father's hands. But the moment he is close to his father, he moves away a little, and holds his hands farther apart, and he does this over and over, so that the child may learn to walk."

Praying in the Field

A hasid who was traveling to Mezbizh in order to spend the Day of Atonement near the Baal Shem, was forced to interrupt his journey for something or other. When the stars rose, he was still a good way from the town and, to his great grief, had to pray alone in the open field. When he arrived in Mezbizh after the holiday, the Baal Shem received him with particular happiness and cordiality. "Your praying," he said, "lifted up all the prayers which were lying stored in that field."

The Scholars

Moshe Hayyim Efraim, a grandson of the Baal Shem's, dedicated himself to study in his youth and became so great a scholar that this made him deviate somewhat from the hasidic way of life. His grandfather, the Baal Shem, made a point of often going walking with him beyond the town, and Efraim went with him, though with a hint of reluctance, for he begrudged the time he might have spent in studying.

Once they met a man coming from another city. The Baal Shem asked him about one of his fellow-citizens. "He is a great scholar," said the man.

"I envy him his scholarship," said the Baal Shem. "But what am I to do? I have no time to study because I have to serve my Maker." From this hour on, Efraim returned to the hasidic way again with all his strength.

The disciples of the Baal Shem heard that a certain man had a great reputation for learning. Some of them wanted to go to him and find out what he had to teach. The master gave them permission to go, but first they asked him: "And how shall we be able to tell whether he is a true zaddik?"

The Baal Shem replied. "Ask him to advise you what to do to keep unholy thoughts from disturbing you in your prayers and studies. If he gives you advice, then you will know that he belongs to those who are of no account. For this is the service of men in the world to the very hour of their death; to struggle time after time with the extraneous, and time after time to uplift and fit it into the nature of the Divine Name."

Writing Down

A disciple secretly wrote down all the teachings he had heard from the Baal Shem. One day the Baal Shem saw a demon going through the house. In his hand was a book. The Baal Shem asked him: "What book is that you have in your hand?"

"That is the book," the demon replied, "of which you are the author."

Then the Baal Shem knew that some one was secretly setting down in writing what he said. He gathered all his people around him and asked: "Who of you is writing down what I teach you?" The disciple who had been taking notes said it was he, and brought the master what he had written. The Baal Shem studied it for a long time, page for page. Then he said: "In all this, there is not a single word I said. You were not listening for the sake of Heaven, and so the power of evil used you for its sheath, and your ears heard what I did not say."

Beside the Tree of Life

The Baal Shem told:

"Once I went to paradise and many people went with me. The closer I came to the garden, the more of them disappeared, and when I walked through paradise, there were only a very few left. But when I stood beside the Tree of Life and looked around, I seemed to be alone."

The Sermon

Once they asked the Baal Shem to preach after the prayer of the congregation. He began his sermon, but in the middle of it he was shaken with a fit of trembling, such as sometimes seized him while he was praying. He broke off and said: "O, Lord of the world, you know that I am not speaking to increase my own reputation . . ." Here he stopped again, and then the words rushed from his lips. "Much have I learned, and much have I been able to do, and there is no one to whom I could reveal it." And he said nothing further.

Like Locusts

Rabbi Mikhal of Zlotchov told:
"Once when we were on a journey with our teacher, Rabbi Israel Baal Shem Tov, the Light of the Seven Days, he went into the woods to say the Afternoon Prayer. Suddenly we saw him strike his head against a tree and cry aloud. Later we asked him about it. He said: 'While I plunged into the holy spirit I saw that in the generations which precede the coming of the Messiah, the rabbis of the hasidim will multiply like locusts, and it will be they who delay redemption, for they will bring about the separation of hearts and groundless hatred.' "

Happy Is the People

Concerning the verse in the psalm: "Happy is the people that know the joyful shout; they walk, O Lord, in the light of Thy countenance," the Baal Shem said: "When the people do not depend upon heroes but are themselves versed in the joyful shout of battle, then they will walk in the light of your countenance."

Simplicity

Once the Baal Shem said to his disciples: "Now that I have climbed so many rungs in the service of God, I let go of all of them and hold to the simple faith of making myself a vessel for God. It is, indeed, written: 'The simple believeth every word,' but it is also written: 'The Lord preserveth the simple.' "

The Hose-Maker

Once, in the course of a journey, the Baal Shem stopped in a little town whose name has not come down to us. One morning, before prayer, he smoked his pipe as usual and looked out of the window. He saw a man go by. He carried his prayer shawl and phylacteries in his hand and set his feet as intently and solemnly as though he were going straight to the doors of Heaven. The Baal Shem asked the disciple in whose house he was staying, who the man was. He was told that he was a hose-maker who went to the House of Prayer day after day, both summer and winter, and said his prayer even when the pre-scribed quorum of ten worshippers was not complete. The Baal Shem wanted to have the man brought to him, but his host said: "That fool would not stop on his way—not if the emperor called him in person."

After prayer, the Baal Shem sent someone to the man with the message that he should bring him four pairs of hose. Soon after, the man stood before him and displayed his wares. They were of good sheep's wool and well-made. "What do you want for a pair?" asked Rabbi Israel.

"One and a half gulden."

"I suppose you will be satisfied with one gulden."

"Then I should have said one gulden," the man replied.

The Baal Shem instantly paid him what he had asked. Then he went on questioning him. "How do you spend your days?"

"I ply my trade," said the man.

"And how do you ply it?"

"I work until I have forty or fifty pairs of hose. Then I put them into a mould with hot water and press them until they are as they should be."

"And how do you sell them?"

"I don't leave my house. The merchants come to me to buy. They also bring me good wool they have bought for me, and I pay them for their pains. This time I left my house only to honor the rabbi."

"And when you get up in the morning, what do you do before you go to pray?"

"I make hose then too."

"And what psalms do you recite?"

"I say those psalms which I know by heart, while I work," said the man.

When the hose-maker had gone home, the Baal Shem said to the disciples who stood around him: "Today you have seen the cornerstone which will uphold the Temple until the Messiah comes."

The Busy Man's Prayer

The Baal Shem said:

"Imagine a man whose business hounds him through many streets and across the market-place the livelong day. He almost forgets that there is a Maker of the world. Only when the time for the Afternoon Prayer comes, does he remember: 'I must pray.' And then, from the bottom of his heart, he heaves a sigh of regret that he has spent his day on vain and idle matters, and he runs into a by-street and stands there, and prays: God holds him dear, very dear and his prayer pierces the firmament."

The Little Whistle

A villager, who year after year prayed in the Baal Shem's House of Prayer in the Days of Awe, had a son who was so dull-witted that he could not even grasp the shapes of the letters, let alone the meaning of the holy words. On the Days of Awe his father did not take him to town with him, because he did not understand anything. But when he was thirteen and of age according to the laws of God, his father took him along on the Day of Atonement, for fear the boy might eat on the fast-day simply because he did not know any better.

Now the boy had a small whistle which he always blew when he sat out in the fields to herd the sheep and the calves. He had taken this with him in the pocket of his smock and his father had not noticed it. Hour after hour, the boy sat in the House of Prayer and had nothing to say. But when the Additional Service commenced, he said: "Father, I have my little whistle with me. I want to sing on it." The father was greatly perturbed and told him to do no such thing, and the boy restrained himself. But when the Afternoon Service was begun, he said again: "Father, do let me blow my little whistle." The father became angry and said: "Where did you put it?" And when the boy told him, he laid his hand on his pocket so that the boy could not take it out. But now the Closing Prayer began. The boy snatched his pocket away from his father's hand, took out the whistle and blew a loud note. All were frightened and confused. But the Baal Shem went on with the prayer, only more quickly and easily than usual. Later he said: "The boy made things easy for me."

The Court Sweeper

Once, just before New Year's, the Baal Shem came to a certain town and asked the people who read the prayers there in the Days of Awe. They replied that this was done by the rav of the town. "And what is his manner of praying?" asked the Baal Shem.

"On the Day of Atonement," they said, "he recites all the confessions of sin in the most cheerful tones."

The Baal Shem sent for the rav and asked him the cause of this strange procedure. The rav answered: "The least among the servants of the king, he, whose task it is to sweep the forecourt free of dirt, sings a merry song as he works, for he does what he is doing to gladden the king."

Said the Baal Shem: "May my lot be with yours."

In the Hour of Doubt

It is told:

In the city of Satanov there was a learned man, whose thinking and brooding took him deeper and deeper into the question why what is, is, and why anything is at all. One Friday he stayed in the House of Study after prayer to go on thinking, for he was snared in his thoughts and tried to untangle them and could not. The holy Baal Shem Tov felt this from afar, got into his carriage and, by dint of his miraculous power which made the road leap to meet him, he reached the House of Study in Satanov in only an instant. There sat the learned man in his predicament. The Baal Shem said to him: "You are brooding on whether God is; I am a fool and believe." The fact that there was a human being who knew of his secret, stirred the doubter's heart and it opened to the Great Secret.

The Famous Miracle

A naturalist came from a great distance to see the Baal Shem and said: "My investigations show that in the course of nature the Red Sea had to divide at the very hour the children of Israel passed through it. Now what about that famous miracle!" The Baal Shem answered: "Don't you know that God created nature? And he created it so, that at the hour the children of Israel passed through the Red Sea, it had to divide. That is the great and famous miracle!"

Truth

The Baal Shem said: "What does it mean, when people say that Truth goes over all the world? It means that Truth is driven out of one place after another, and must wander on and on."

To One Who Admonished

The Baal Shem said this to a zaddik who used to preach admonishing sermons: "What do you know about admonishing! You yourself have remained unacquainted with sin all the days of your life, and you have had nothing to do with the people around you—how should you know what sinning is!"

With the Sinners

The Baal Shem said:
"I let sinners come close to me, if they are not proud. I keep the scholars and the sinless away from me if they are

71

proud. For the sinner who knows that he is a sinner, and therefore considers himself base—God is with him, for He 'dwell-
eth with them in the midst of their uncleannesses.' But concerning him who prides himself on the fact that he is unburdened
by sin, God says, as we know from the Gemara: 'There is not
enough room in the world for myself and him.' "

Love

The Baal Shem said to one of his disciples:
"The lowest of the low you can think of, is dearer to me than
your only son is to you."

False Hospitality

It is told:
In the days of the Baal Shem, a rich and hospitable man
lived in a nearby city. To every poor wayfarer, he gave food
and drink and money to boot. But he felt the urgent need to
hear words of praise from everyone he received into his house,
and if such words did not come spontaneously, he threw out a
deft phrase as bait, and then a big or little praise-fish was
always sure to bite.
Once the Baal Shem sent one of his disciples, Rabbi Wolf
Kitzes, cross-country, and told him to visit that rich man in
the course of his journey. He was lavishly entertained and
presented with a generous gift, but gave only sparse words of
thanks. Finally his host said: "Don't you think that this is the
proper way to practice hospitality?"
"We shall see," answered Rabbi Wolf. And not another word
could the rich man get out of him. At nightfall, the host
lay down among his guests according to his custom, for before
falling asleep he liked to chat with them and hear something
pleasing to his person. Just as he was dozing off, Rabbi Wolf
touched him on the shoulder with his little finger. In his dream
the man thought he was called to the king and had tea with
him. But suddenly the king fell and was dead and they accused
him of poisoning him and put him in jail. A fire broke out in
the jail and he escaped and fled until he was far away. Then he
became a water-carrier, but that was hard work and got him a

72

meagre living, so he moved to another region where water was scarce. But there they had a law that you were not paid unless the pail was full to the brim, and to walk with a full pail and never spill a drop was a difficult matter. Once when he was walking carefully, slow step by step, he fell and broke both legs, and there he lay and thought of his former life, and was amazed and wept. Then Rabbi Wolf touched him on the shoulder again with his little finger, and the man woke up and said: "Take me with you to your master."

The Baal Shem received the rich man with a smile. "Would you like to know where all that hospitality of yours has gone to?" he asked. "It has all gone into a dog's mouth."

The man's heart awoke and turned to God, and the Baal Shem instructed him how to lift up his soul.

The Crowded House of Prayer

Once the Baal Shem stopped on the threshold of a House of Prayer and refused to go in. "I cannot go in," he said. "It is crowded with teachings and prayers from wall to wall and from floor to ceiling. How could there be room for me?" And when he saw that those around him were staring at him and did not know what he meant, he added: "The words from the lips of those whose teaching and praying does not come from the hearts lifted to heaven, cannot rise, but fill the house from wall to wall and from floor to ceiling."

The Jug

Once the Baal Shem said to his disciples: "Just as the strength of the root is in the leaf, so the strength of man is in every utensil he makes, and his character and behavior can be gauged from what he has made." Just then his glance fell on a fine beer jug standing in front of him. He pointed to it and continued: "Can't you see from this jug that the man who made it had no feet?"

When the Baal Shem had finished speaking, one of his disciples happened to pick up the jug to set it on the bench. But the moment it stood there it crumbled to bits.

In the days of the Baal Shem, there lived a man who cruelly mortified his flesh in order to attain a holy spirit. The Baal Shem once said this about him: "In the world of changes, they laugh at him. They bestow on him higher and higher rungs and do it only to make fun of him. If he did not have me to help him, he would be lost."

One Small Hand

Rabbi Nahman of Bratzlav has handed down to us these words of his great-grandfather, the Baal Shem Tov:
"Alas! the world is full of enormous lights and mysteries, and man shuts them from himself with one small hand!"

Across the Dniester

A zaddik told:
When the master was no more than a little boy, the prophet Ahijah, the Shilonite, came to him and taught him the wisdom of the holy names. And because he was still so young, he wanted to find out what he could accomplish. So one day he cast his belt into the Dniester River when the current was very strong, pronounced a name and crossed the river walking on his belt. All his days he did penance for this to erase the flaw from his soul, and he succeeded. For once he had to cross the river at a time the current again ran strong, because a number of Jew-haters were after him with the intent to kill. So again he cast his belt into the waters and crossed on it but without pronouncing a holy name and with the aid of nothing but his great faith in the God of Israel.

The Icicle

A zaddik told:
"On a winter's day, I went to the bath with the master. It was so cold that icicles hung from the roofs. We entered and as soon as he did the Unification, the bath grew warm. He stood in the water for a very long time, until the candle began to drip and gutter. 'Rabbi,' I said, 'the candle is guttering and going out.'

'Fool,' he answered, 'take an icicle from the roof and light it! He who spoke to the oil and it leaped into flame, will speak to this too, and it will kindle.' The icicle burned brightly for a good while, until I went home, and when I got home there was a little water in my hand."

The Creatures
It is told:
Once the Baal Shem was forced to inaugurate the sabbath in an open field. A flock of sheep was at pasture nearby. When he pronounced the hymn to greet the coming Sabbath Bride, the sheep rose on their hind legs and remained in this position, turned toward the master, until he had finished the prayer. For while listening to the Baal Shem's devotions, every creature assumed the original position it had held when it stood at the throne of God.

The Visit

The Baal Shem's disciples could always tell from his face if the Seven Shepherds, or one of them, were with him. Once, at the meal of the New Moon they looked at him and knew that one of the shepherds was present. Later they asked him which of the seven it had been. He said: "When I pronounced the benediction over the bread, I had in mind the secret of eating and plunged into it. Then Moses, our teacher, peace be with him, came to me and said: 'Hail to you, that you have in mind the very secret into which I plunged when I waited at table at the meal of Jethro, my father-in-law.' "

The Debate
It is told:
Once the Baal Shem Tov was seated at his table with his disciples around him. Among them was Rabbi Nahman of Horodenka, whose son married a granddaughter of the Baal Shem and with her begot the other Nahman: Rabbi Nahman of Bratzlav.
The Baal Shem said: "The time has come to reveal to you something of the deeper significance of the bath of immersion."

75

He paused for a little, and then, with mighty words, built up before them the foundation and structure of meanings. When he had done, he threw back his head, and his face began to shine with that radiance which announced to his disciples that his soul was rising to the worlds above. He was utterly motionless. His disciples rose with trembling hearts and looked at him, for this was one of the times when it was vouchsafed them to see their master as he really was. Rabbi Nahman wanted to rise with the rest, but he could not. Sleep overwhelmed him. He tried to ward it off, but failed.

In his dream he came to a city where tall men were striding through the streets, on toward a great house. He went as far as the gate with them. He could go no further, for the throng of men filled the house. Now, from within, he could catch the voice of a teacher whom he could not see, though he could hear what was said quite clearly. He was speaking about the bath of immersion and revealing all its secret significance. Toward the end of his speech, it became clearer and clearer that he was presenting a teaching different from the traditional doctrine of Ari, the holy "lion" Rabbi Yitzhak Luria, and in conclusion, this was openly stated. And now the throngs moved apart. From the door came Ari himself, pacing toward the pulpit and almost brushing Rabbi Nahman as he went. The movement of the throngs closing behind him swept Rabbi Nahman along. Suddenly he found himself standing in front of the pulpit. He looked up, and recognized the face of his master whose voice he had not recognized. And now the debate took place close before him. The "lion" and the Baal Shem Tov opposed each other by quoting different passages from the holy Book of Splendor and giving different interpretations. Contradictions between one passage and another gaped and closed again, and in the end both flames leaped up in a single blaze which soared to the heart of Heaven. There was no vista through which eyes could see and find a solution. Then those two resolved to ask Heaven to decide. Together they performed the rite that leads to uplifting. What came to pass, happened beyond the confines of time, and instantly Ari said: "The decision has been made in favor of the words of the Baal Shem

Tov." At that Nahman awoke. Before his eyes, the master bowed
forward his head which he had flung back, and said to him:
"And it was you I chose to accompany me as my witness."

In His Image

Once the Baal Shem summoned Sammael, lord of demons, because of some important matter. The Lord of demons roared at
him: "How dare you summon me! Up to now this has happened to me only three times; in the hour at the Tree of Knowledge, the hour of the golden calf, and the hour of the destruction of Jerusalem."
The Baal Shem bade his disciples bare their foreheads, and on
every forehead, Sammael saw the sign of the image in which
God creates man. He did what was asked of him. But before
leaving, he said: "Sons of the living God, permit me to stay
here a little longer and look at your foreheads."

The Miraculous Bath

It is told:
Once the Baal Shem bade Rabbi Zevi, the scribe, write the
verses for phylacteries and instructed him in the special attitude
of the soul which befits this action. Then he said to him: "Now
I shall show you the phylacteries of the Lord of the world."
He took him to a lonely wood. But another one of his disciples,
Rabbi Wolf Kitzes, had discovered where they were going and
hid in that same wood. He heard the Baal Shem cry out: "The
bath of Israel is the Lord!" And suddenly he saw a bath in a
place where there had been none. At the same instant, the Baal
Shem said to Rabbi Zevi: "Some man is hiding here." In a
moment he discovered Rabbi Wolf and told him to go away.
No one has ever found out what happened in the wood after
that.

The Effect of the Mixed Multitude

The Baal Shem said:
"The Erev Rav, the mixed multitude, prevented Moses from
reaching the rung of an angel."

It is told:

Sabbatai Zevi, the "false Messiah" long dead, came to the Baal Shem and begged him to redeem him. Now it is well known that the work of redemption is accomplished by binding the stuff of life to the stuff of life, by binding mind to mind, and soul to soul. In this way, then, the Baal Shem began to bind himself to that other, but slowly and cautiously, for he feared he might try to harm him. Once, when the Baal Shem lay asleep, Sabbatai Zevi came and tried to tempt him to become as he himself was. Then the Baal Shem hurled him away with such vigor that he fell to the very bottom of the nether world. When the Baal Shem spoke of him, he always said: "A holy spark was within him, but Satan caught him in the snare of pride."

A Halt Is Called

1.

It is told:

In the company of his daughter Odel and Rabbi Zevi, the scribe, the Baal Shem was on his way to the Land of Israel to prepare for the hour of deliverance. But Heaven called a halt to his journey. On the way from Stambul to the Land of Israel, the ship stopped at an unknown island. They went ashore, and when they tried to return to the ship, they lost their way and fell into the hands of robbers. Rabbi Zevi said to the Baal Shem: "Why are you silent? Just do as you usually do and then we shall be free."

But the Baal Shem replied: "I know nothing at all any more. Everything has been taken from me. It is up to you to recall something of all you have learned from me, and stir up my memory."

Rabbi Zevi said: "I too know nothing at all any more! The only thing I still remember is the alphabet."

"Why are you delaying?" cried the Baal Shem. "Recite it to me!" Then the scribe recited the letters of the alphabet, and he said them with the great fervor he always put into his prayers. A bell chimed, an old captain came with a troop of soldiers

and freed them without saying a word. He took them aboard
his ship and brought them back to Stambul, and neither he nor
any of his people said a single word. When they went ashore—
it was the seventh day of Passover—the ship and the crew vanished. Then the Baal Shem knew that it was Elijah who had
saved them, but he also realized that he was not to travel on,
so he set out on his journey home.

2.

But it is also told:
During the festival of Passover, when the Baal Shem and his
companions boarded a ship in Stambul, Heaven let him know
that he was to go ashore again and start for home. But in his
soul he refused to obey, and the ship sailed off with him. Then
all the spiritual rungs he had attained were taken from him,
and his teaching and his prayer was taken from him too. When
he looked into a book, he no longer even understood the symbols. But in his soul he said: "What does it matter! Then I
shall enter the Holy Land as a crude and ignorant fellow."
But a tempest rose and a huge wave rushed upon the ship and
swept Odel, the Baal Shem's daughter, into the sea. At this
moment Satan came to him and said what he said. But he cried
out: "Hear, o Israel!" He turned his back on Satan and said:
"Lord of the world, I am going home." And immediately his
teacher, the prophet Ahijah the Shilonite, came through the
air, snatched Odel out of the sea, and carried them all back
to Stambul through the clouds.

Sound the Great Horn!

A zaddik told:
The holy community had a little house outside the city, and
there they met after every sermon of the Baal Shem Tov, to discuss what he had said. I knew where the house was, but I did
not dare go there either with them or after them, because I was
very young at the time.
The year I was in the house of the Baal Shem Tov, on the first
day of the New Year, right after grace, the holy Baal Shem

preached on the words of prayer: "Sound the great horn for our freedom." Immediately after the sermon he went to his room and locked the door. But his disciples went to the house outside the city. I remained behind alone. Then it occurred to me that the Messiah would come this very day, and every moment I grew more and more convinced that now he was walking along the road, soon he would enter the city, and there would be no one there to receive him. And what I imagined seemed to me so overpoweringly true that I could do nothing but run to the disciples to tell them about it. I ran through the town, and the people wanted to stop me and question me. But I ran on until I reached the house where the others were. There I saw them all sitting around a big table, and no one uttered a word, and you could see that not one of them had the strength to utter a word. But later I learned that—in his thoughts—every one of them saw the Messiah coming this very hour. And I did not know what to do except sit down with them. So we sat around the big table until the stars of the second night stood in the sky. Only then the thought broke off in all of us, and we returned to the town.

The Third Failure

It is told:

When the number of renegades who followed Jacob Frank, the false Messiah, grew greater and greater, Heaven revealed to the Baal Shem that their impure strength was stronger than his holy strength, and that, if he hoped to overcome them, he would have to enlist someone to help him, and that this other was to be Rabbi Moshe Pastuch, which means, Rabbi Moshe, the Shepherd. Without a moment's delay, the Baal Shem set out for the city to which he had been directed. When he asked for Rabbi Moshe Pastuch, it evolved that the man who bore that name was a shepherd who pastured his flock in the hills beyond the city. There he found him. The sheep were scattered over the slopes, but the shepherd, whom the Baal Shem approached unobserved, was standing over a ditch and saying to himself: "Dear Lord, how can I serve you? If you had flocks of sheep, I should pasture them for you without pay. But as it is, what can I do?" Suddenly he began to jump back and forth over the ditch. Full of fervor he jumped and jumped and somersaulted and cried: "I am jumping for the love of God! I jump for the love of God!" Then the Baal Shem realized that the service of this shepherd was greater than his own.

When the shepherd paused in his jumping, the Baal Shem went up to him and said: "I must talk with you."

"I am a hired man," said the other, "and may not waste my time."

"But you were just jumping back and forth over the ditch," the Baal Shem reminded him.

"That is true," said the man. "I am permitted to do that because it is for the love of God."

"What I have in mind for you is also for the love of God," said the zaddik. Then the other let him talk and listened, and his soul was just as much aflame as when he had leaped the ditch. He made the Baal Shem tell him everything, beginning with the destruction of the Temple; how twice before, in hours of disaster, when thousands sanctified the great Name with their death, the great work had been undertaken, but that Satan had come between and prevented it, and that now the third hour had come.

"Yes," cried the shepherd. "Let us free the Divine Presence from exile!"

"Is there a place here where we can immerse ourselves?" asked the Baal Shem.

"There is a living spring at the foot of the mountain," said the shepherd, and was already on his way down the slope. The zaddik followed him as best he could. Down below, they both dipped down into the spring, and the Baal Shem prepared to confide to him the secret of the work in hand.

In the meantime, rumor had spread in Heaven that men on earth were about to hasten the hour of salvation. Heavenly powers rose up against the plan, Satan grew strong and went to work. Fire broke out in the city, and soon the alarm rang over to the hills. The shepherd ran to his sheep. "Where are you running and why?" asked the Baal Shem.

The other replied: "The owners of the flocks have most likely heard that the sheep went astray and now they will come and ask what has become of them."

The Baal Shem was unable to hold him back and he realized who it was that had put in his oar.

Before the Coming of the Messiah

The Baal Shem said:

"Before the coming of the Messiah there will be great abundance in the world. The Jews will get rich. They will become accustomed to running their houses in the grand style and moderation will be cast to the winds. Then the lean years will come; want and a meagre livelihood, and the world will be full of poverty. The Jews will not be able to satisfy their needs, grown beyond rhyme or reason. And then the labor which will bring forth the Messiah, will begin."

After the Death of His Wife

A zaddik tells:

The Baal Shem Tov believed that, like Elijah, he would rise up to Heaven in a storm. When his wife died, he said: "I thought that a storm would sweep me up to Heaven like Elijah. But now that I am only half a body, this is no longer possible."

Omission

It is told:

Rabbi Pinhas of Koretz went to the Baal Shem for Passover, and saw that he was very tired.

On the day before the last day of the festival, Rabbi Pinhas debated with his soul whether or not he should go to the bath of immersion. He did not go.

On the last day of Passover he felt in the midst of praying that the Baal Shem was destined to die soon because he had strained himself to the utmost against the throngs of renegades. He concentrated all his strength in prayer, and gave himself wholly up to it, but noticed that he was not accomplishing anything at all. Then he was filled with deep regret that he had not gone to the bath.

82

After prayer, the Baal Shem asked him: "Did you go to the bath yesterday?" He answered "No." Then the Baal Shem said: "It has already come to pass, and after this there is nothing more."

Of the Baal Shem's Death

After Passover, the Baal Shem fell ill. But he continued to pray before the pulpit in the House of Prayer, as long as his strength permitted.

He did not send word to those of his disciples in other towns who were held to be men whose prayers were effective through their fervor, and sent the disciples who were in Mezbizh, to other places. Rabbi Pinhas of Koretz was the only one who refused to leave.

On the eve of the Feast of Weeks, the congregation met as every year at this time, in order to spend the night in the study of the law. The Baal Shem addressed them on the revelation on Mount Sinai.

When morning came, he sent for his close friends. First he summoned two of them and told them to attend to his corpse and his burial. On his own body he showed them, limb by limb, how the soul wished to depart from it, and instructed them to apply what they had learned in the case of other sick persons, for these two belonged to the Holy Brotherhood who care for the dead and their burial.

Then he bade the quorum of ten worshippers pray with him. He asked for the prayer-book and said: "I want to busy myself with God for a bit more."

After the prayer, Rabbi Nahman of Horodenka went to the House of Study to pray for him. The Baal Shem said: "He is shaking the gates of Heaven in vain! He cannot get in at the door by which he used to enter."

Later, when the servant happened to come into the room, he heard the Baal Shem say: "I give you those two hours," and thought that he was telling the angel of death he need not torment him two hours more, but Rabbi Pinhas knew better what was meant. "He had two hours more to live," he said.

"And he was saying that he would make God a gift of those two hours. This is a true sacrifice of the soul."

Then, just as every year on this day, the people from the city came to him and he spoke words of teaching to them.

Some time later he said to the disciples who stood about him: "I have no worries with regard to myself. For I know quite clearly: I am going out at one door and I shall go in at another." And again he spoke and said: "Now I know for what I was created."

He sat up in bed and spoke brief words of teaching about the "pillar" by means of which the souls, after death, mount from the lower paradise to the upper paradise, to the "Tree of Life," and expounded the verse from the Book of Esther: "And with that the maiden came unto the king." He also said: "I shall surely return, but not as I am now."

After that he had them say the prayer: "And let the graciousness of the Lord our God be upon us," and stretched out in his bed. But several times he sat up again and whispered, as they knew he did when he shaped and directed his soul to fervor. For a while they heard nothing and he lay there quietly. Then he bade them cover him with a sheet. But they still heard him whisper: "My God, Lord of all worlds!" And then the verse of the psalm: "Let not the foot of pride come upon me." Later on, those whom he had bidden attend to his body and his burial, said they had seen the Baal Shem's soul ascend as a blue flame.

The River and the Light

It is told:

A woman who lived in a village not far from Mezbizh often went there and took gifts of fish and poultry, butter and flour, to the house of the Baal Shem. Her way led across a small river. Once the river rose and flooded its banks, and when, notwithstanding, she tried to cross, she was drowned. The Baal Shem grieved for the good woman. In his grief he cursed the river and it dried up. But the prince of the river complained of this in Heaven, and there it was decided that at some time or other for a few hours the bed of the river should fill with water again, that the river should flood its banks, and that one of the descendants of the Baal Shem should try to cross it, and no one should help him but the Baal Shem himself.

Several years after his death, his son lost his way, as he was walking by night, and suddenly found himself close to the river which he did not recognize because of its tiding waters. He tried to cross but was soon seized and swept away by the current. Then, above the shore, he saw a burning light which illumined the banks and the river. He mustered all his strength, fought free of the current, and reached the shore. The burning light was the Baal Shem himself.

The Fiery Mountain

Rabbi Zevi, the Baal Shem's son, told this:
"Some time after my father's death, I saw him in the shape of a fiery mountain, which burst into countless sparks. I asked him: 'Why do you appear in a shape such as this?' He answered: 'In this shape I served God.'"

On the Walls

A zaddik told:
"In a dream I once had the experience of being led to the highest paradise. There I was shown the walls of the Jerusalem of above and they were in ruins. Over these ruins heaped round about, from wall to wall, walked a man incessantly, without stopping. I asked "Who is he?" They replied: "This is Rabbi Israel Baal Shem Tov, who has sworn not to go from here until the Temple has been rebuilt."

"He Will Be"

Rabbi Nahum of Tchernobil, who in his youth was privileged to see the Baal Shem, said: "It is written: 'The sun also ariseth, and the sun goeth down'—'one generation passeth away and another generation cometh.' As for the Baal Shem Tov, whose merit shall be our protection—no one was before him and no one will be after him until the coming of the Messiah, and when the Messiah comes, he will be." And three times he repeated: "He will be."

If

Rabbi Leib, son of Sarah, the hidden zaddik, once said to some persons who were telling about the Baal Shem: "You ask about the holy Baal Shem Tov? I tell you: if he had lived in the age of the prophets, he would have become a prophet, and if he had lived in the age of the patriarchs, he would have become an outstanding man, so that just as one says: 'God of Abraham, Isaac, and Jacob,' one would say 'God of Israel.'"

BARUKH OF MEZBIZH

The Three Men

An old man once asked the Baal Shem Tov: "Concerning the passage in the Scriptures which relates that Abraham saw three men standing before him, the holy Book of Splendor says that these were Abraham, Isaac, and Jacob. But how could Abraham see Abraham standing before him?"

Barukh, the Baal Shem's grandson, who was three years old at the time, was present and heard the question. He said: "Grandfather, what a silly thing for this old man to ask! Abraham, Isaac, and Jacob—those are of course the attributes which, as everyone knows, became the attributes of the fathers: mercy, rigor, and glory."

The Little Sister

After the death of his grandfather, the Baal Shem Tov, the boy Barukh was taken into the house of Rabbi Pinhas of Koretz. He was very secretive and withdrawn, and even when he was no longer a child, he still would not say a word of teaching.

Once, on the day before the sabbath, Rabbi Pinhas went to the bath with him. When they came home they drank mead together. As soon as the rabbi saw that the youth had grown light of heart, he asked him to say some words of teaching. Barukh said: "In the Song of Songs it is written: 'We have a little sister.' This refers to wisdom, as it is written in Proverbs: 'Say to wisdom: You are my sister.' I have a little wisdom! And further on in the Song of Songs, we read: 'And she hath no breasts.' My little sister wisdom has no breasts from which she can suck, she has no longer a teacher from whom she can receive the teachings. And still further on, it is written: 'What shall we do for our sister in the day when she shall be spoken for?' What shall I do with my little wisdom when I have said all there is to say?"

After his marriage, Rabbi Barukh lived in the house of his father-in-law. The other two sons-in-law, who were learned men, complained that Barukh conducted himself differently from them and from all the rest of the world besides, that when they sat over their books, he slept, and when he was awake, he busied himself with all manner of foolish things. Finally the father-in-law decided to take all three of them to the maggid of Mezritch, and put the matter before him. On the way there they made Barukh sit beside the coachman. When they were about to enter the house, only Barukh was admitted. The others had to wait outside until they were asked to come before the maggid. He said to them: "Barukh is conducting himself very well, and what seems idle play to you is directed to sublime matters and effects sublime things." On the way home they gave Barukh the best seat.

Preparation

When Rabbi Barukh had burned the leaven on the eve of Passover and scattered the ashes, he said the words prescribed for this, and expounded them. " 'Any kind of leaven which remains in my possession'—all that seethes; 'which I have or have not seen'—even though I believe I have looked into myself thoroughly, I have probably not looked thoroughly at all; 'which I have burned or not burned'—the Evil Urge within me tries to convince me that I have burned everything, but not until now do I see that I have not burned it, and so I beg of you, God, 'it shall be null and accounted as the dust of earth.' "

To Himself

When Barukh came to those words in the psalm which read: "I will not give sleep to mine eyes, nor slumber to mine eyelids until I find out a place for the Lord," he stopped and said to himself: "Until I find myself and make myself a place to be ready for the descending of the Divine Presence."

Make Us Holy

Once, when Rabbi Barukh was saying grace and came to these words: "Our Holy One, the Holy One of Jacob," he said to

God in the voice of a child who wants to coax his father: " 'Our Holy One'—make us holy, for you are 'the Holy One of Jacob' —when you wanted to, you made Jacob holy."

The Two Strangers

In the hundred and nineteenth psalm, the psalmist says to God: "I am a sojourner on the earth, hide not thy commandments from me."

Concerning this verse Rabbi Barukh said: "He whom Life drives into exile and who comes to a land alien to him, has nothing in common with the people there, and not a soul he can talk to. But if a second stranger appears, even though he may come from quite a different place, the two can confide in each other, and live together henceforth, and cherish each other. And had they not both been strangers, they would never have known such close companionship. That is what the psalmist means: "You, even as I, are a sojourner on earth and have no abiding place for your glory. So do not withraw from me, but reveal your commandments, that I may become your friend."

Blessed Be He Who Spoke

They asked Rabbi Barukh: "Why do we say: 'Blessed he who spoke and the world existed' and not, 'Blessed he who created the world'?"

He replied: "We praise God because he created our world with the word, and not with the thought, like other worlds. God judges the zaddikim for an evil thought they nurse within them. But how could the rank and file of the people persist if he were to judge them in this way, and not—as he does—only for an evil thought they have expressed and made effective through words."

With Yourself

This is how Rabbi Barukh expounded the words in the Sayings of the Fathers, "and be not wicked by facing yourself only" (that is, do not think that you cannot be redeemed):

"Every man has the vocation of making perfect something in this world. The world has need of every single human being. But there are those who always sit in their rooms behind closed doors and study, and never leave the house to talk with others. For this they are called wicked. If they talked to others, they would bring to perfection something they are destined to make perfect. That is what the words mean: 'Be not wicked by facing yourself only.' Since you face yourself only, and do not go among people, do not become wicked through solitude."

Gifts

When, in saying grace, Rabbi Barukh came to the passage: "Let us not require gifts of flesh and blood and not the loan of them, but only your full, open, and holy hand," he repeated these words three times and with great fervor. When he had ended, his daughter asked him: "Father, why did you pray so fervently that you might be able to do without the gifts of man? Your only means of subsistence is that the people who come to you give you things of their own accord, to show their gratitude."

"My daughter," he replied, "you must know that there are three ways of bringing money to the zaddik. Some say to themselves: 'I'll give him something. I am the kind of man who brings gifts to the zaddik.' The words: 'Let us not require gifts . . .' refers to these. Others think: 'If I give something to this devout man, it will profit me hereafter.' These want heaven to pay them interest. That is the 'loan.' But there are some who know: 'God has put this money in my hand for the zaddik, and I am his messenger.' These serve the 'full and open hand.'"

Sweets

On the eve of the Day of Atonement, at the meal which precedes the fast, Rabbi Barukh distributed sweets among his hasidim at his table, and said: "I love you greatly and whatever good I see in the world, I should like to give you. Keep in mind what is said in the psalm: 'O taste and see that the Lord is good.' Just taste—in the right sense of the word—and you will see:

wherever there is something good, there He is." And he broke into the song: "How good is our God, how fair is our lot."

Right Service

Rabbi Barukh's disciples asked him: "When through Moses God commanded Aaron to make the lamps of the candlestick seven and to light the lamps, the Scriptures simply say: 'And Aaron did so.' Rashi thinks that this is said in praise, because he did not deviate from what he was told. How are we to understand this? Is Aaron, appointed by God, to be considered worthy of praise because he did not deviate from God's command?"

Rabbi Barukh replied: "If the righteous man is to serve God in the right way, he must be a man who, no matter what fires he may feel within him, does not allow the flame to burst from the vessel, but performs every tangible action in the manner proper to it. We are told of a holy servant of God who, when he was to fill the lamps in the House of Prayer, was so flooded with fervor that he spilled the oil. That is why it must be regarded as praise when it is said of Aaron that—although he served his Maker with the whole strength of his soul—he saw to the candlestick in the way prescribed, and lit the lamps."

How We Should Learn

The disciples of Rabbi Barukh asked him: "How can a man ever learn the Talmud adequately? For there we find that Abayyi said this, and Raba said that. It is just as if Abayyi were of one world and Raba of quite another. How is it possible to understand and learn both at the same time?"

The zaddik replied: "He who wants to understand Abayyi's words, must link his soul to the soul of Abayyi; then he will learn the true meaning of the words as Abayyi himself utters them. And after that, if he wants to understand Raba's words, he must link his soul to the soul of Raba. That is what is meant in the Talmud when we read: 'When a word is spoken in the name of its speaker, his lips move in the grave.' And the lips of him who utters the word, move like those of the master who is dead."

Without telling his teacher anything of what he was doing, a disciple of Rabbi Barukh's had inquired into the nature of God, and in his thinking had penetrated further and further until he was tangled in doubts, and what had been certain up to this time, became uncertain. When Rabbi Barukh noticed that the young man no longer came to him as usual, he went to the city where he lived, entered his room unexpectedly, and said to him: "I know what is hidden in your heart. You have passed through the fifty gates of reason. You begin with a question and think, and think up an answer—and the first gate opens, and to a new question! And again you plumb it, find the solution, fling open the second gate—and look into a new question. On and on like this, deeper and deeper, until you have forced open the fiftieth gate. There you stare at a question whose answer no man has ever found, for if there were one who knew it, there would no longer be freedom of choice. But if you dare to probe still further, you plunge into the abyss."

"So I should go back all the way, to the very beginning?" cried the disciple.

"If you turn, you will not be going back," said Rabbi Barukh. "You will be standing beyond the last gate: you will stand in faith."

Thanking in Advance

On a certain eve of the sabbath, Rabbi Barukh went back and forth in his house and, as always, first gave the greeting of peace to the angels of peace, and then said the prayer: "Lord of the worlds, Lord of all souls, Lord of peace," until he came to the words: "I offer thanks to you, O Lord my God, and God of my fathers, for all the grace you have done unto me, and which you will do unto me in the future." Here he stopped and was silent for a time. Then he said: "Why should I give thanks for future grace? Whenever grace is done unto me, that is when I shall offer thanks." But instantly he replied to himself: "Perhaps a time will come when you do a grace unto me, and I shall not be able to offer the thanks which are your due. That is why I must do it now." And he burst into tears.

Rabbi Moshe of Savran, his disciple, had stood in a corner of the room unnoticed and heard his master's words. Now, when he saw him weep, he came forward and said: "Why do you weep? Your question was good and your answer was good!" Rabbi Barukh said: "I wept because suddenly I thought: For what offense shall I be punished by not being able to offer thanks?"

The Great Work

Rabbi Barukh said: "Elijah's great work was not that he performed miracles, but that, when fire fell from Heaven, the people did not speak of miracles, but all cried: 'The Lord is God.' "

Everything Is Wonder

They asked Rabbi Barukh: "In the hymn, God is called 'Creator of remedies, awful in praises, lord of wonders.' Why? Why should remedies stand next to wonders and even precede them?" He answered: "God does not want to be praised as the lord of supernatural miracles. And so here, through the mention of remedies, Nature is introduced and put first. But the truth is that everything is a miracle and wonder."

Medicine

Once Rabbi Barukh went to the city and bought medicine for his sick daughter. The servant set it on the window-sill of his room in the inn. Rabbi Barukh went up and down, looked at the little bottles, and said: "If it is God's will that my daughter Raizel recover, she needs no medicine. But if God made his miraculous power manifest to all eyes, then no one would, any longer, have freedom of choice: everyone would know. But God wanted men to have a choice, so he cloaked his doing in the courses of Nature. That is why he created healing herbs." Then he walked up and down the room again, and asked: "But why does one give poisons to the sick?" And answered: "The 'sparks' that fell from the primeval iniquity of the worlds into the 'shells' and penetrated the stuff of stones, plants, and animals—all ascend back to their source through the sanctification of the devout who work at them, use them, and consume them in holiness. But how shall those sparks that fell into bitter poisons and poisonous herbs, be redeemed? That they might not remain in exile, God appointed them for the sick: to each the carriers of the sparks which belong to the root of his soul. Thus the sick are themselves physicians who heal the poisons."

Apparition

When Rabbi Shelomo of Karlin, whose son was the husband of Rabbi Barukh's daughter, once came to visit the rabbi and was on the very threshold of his room, he started back and closed the door. After a while the same thing recurred. On being questioned, Rabbi Shelomo said: "He is standing at the window and looking out. But beside him stands the holy Baal Shem Tov, and is caressing his hair."

The Argument

Rabbi Moshe of Ludmir, the son of Rabbi Shelomo of Karlin, once called on Rabbi Barukh together with his younger son. When they entered the room, they saw and heard the zaddik arguing with his wife. He paid no attention to his guests. The boy was disturbed because his father was not shown the honor due to him. When Rabbi Moshe observed this, he said: "My son, believe me! What you have just heard was an argument between God and his Presence concerning the lot of the world."

Fine Words

One sabbath, a learned man who was a guest at Rabbi Barukh's table, said to him: "Now let us hear the teachings from you, rabbi. You speak so well!" "Rather than speak so well," said the grandson of the Baal Shem, "I should be stricken dumb."

To a Bridegroom

Rabbi Barukh said this to a bridegroom before he stepped under the wedding canopy: "It is written: 'And as the bridegroom rejoiceth over the bride, so shall thy God rejoice over thee.'

In you, bridegroom, God shall rejoice; the god-like part of
you shall rejoice over the bride."

Sabbath Joy

Once Rabbi Barukh was entertaining a distinguished guest
from the Land of Israel. He was one of those who are forever
mourning for Zion and Jerusalem, and cannot forget their
sorrow for a single second. On the eve of the sabbath, the rabbi
sang: "He who sanctifies the seventh day . . ." in his usual
manner. When he came to the words: "Beloved of the Lord,
you who await the rebuilding of Ariel," he looked up and saw
his guest sitting there as gloomy and sad as always. Then he
interrupted himself and, vehemently and joyfully, shouted in
the very face of the startled man: "Beloved of the Lord, you
who await the rebuilding of Ariel, on this holy day of the
sabbath, be joyful and happy!" After this, he sang the song
on to the end.

Forgetting

A learned man from Lithuania who was proud of his knowledge, was in the habit of interrupting the sermons of Rabbi
Levi Yitzhak of Berditchev with all manner of hair-splitting
objections. Time after time the zaddik invited him to visit him
at his home for discussions of this kind, but the Lithuanian did
not come but continued to appear in the House of Prayer, and
interrupted the rabbi again and again. Rabbi Barukh was told
of this. "If he comes to me," he said, "he will not be able to
say anything at all."
These words were reported to the learned man. "What is the
rabbi specially versed in?" he asked. "In the Book of Splendor," was the answer. So he selected a difficult passage in the
Book of Splendor and went to Mezbizh to ask Rabbi Barukh
about it. When he came into the room, he saw the Book of
Splendor lying on the desk and opened to the very passage he
had in mind. "What an odd coincidence," he thought to himself, and immediately began to cast about for another difficult
passage that might serve to embarrass the rabbi. But the zaddik
anticipated him. "Are you well versed in the Talmud?" he

asked. "Certainly I am well versed in it!" the other replied and laughed. "In the Talmud," said Rabbi Barukh, "it is said that when the child is in the mother's womb a light is kindled above his head and he learns the entire Torah, but that—when his appointed time to issue forth into the air of earth has come —an angel strikes him on the mouth and thereupon he forgets everything. How are we to interpret this? Why should he learn everything only to forget it?" The Lithuanian was silent. Rabbi Barukh continued: "I shall answer the question myself. At first glance, it is not clear why God created forgetfulness. But the meaning of it is this: If there were no forgetting, man would incessantly think of his death. He would build no house, he would launch on no enterprise. That is why God planted forgetting within him. And so one angel is ordered to teach the child in such a way that it will not forget anything, and the second angel is ordered to strike him on the mouth and make him forget. But occasionally he fails to do this, and then I replace him. And now it is your turn. Recite the whole passage to me." The man from Lithuania tried to speak, but he stammered and could not utter a single word. He left the rabbi's house and had forgotten everything. He was an ignorant man! After that he became a servant in the House of Prayer in Berditchev.

Blessing of the Moon

In a certain month of winter, one dark and cloudy night followed upon the other; the moon was hidden and Rabbi Barukh could not say the blessing of the moon. On the last night of those set aside for this, he sent someone out to look at the sky, time after time, but again and again he was told that it was dark as pitch and the snow was falling thick and fast. Finally he said: "If things were with me as they should be, the moon would surely do me a favor! So I ought to do penance. But because I am no longer strong enough to do it, I must at least penitently confess my sins." And this penitent confession broke from his lips with such force that all who were there with him, were shaken. A great shudder pulsed through their hearts, and they turned to God. Then someone came and reported: "It isn't snowing any more. You can see a little light!" The rabbi put on his coat and went out. The clouds had scattered. Among the shining stars shone the moon, and he spoke the blessing.

Hide-and-Seek

Rabbi Barukh's grandson Yehiel was once playing hide-and-seek with another boy. He hid himself well and waited for his playmate to find him. When he had waited for a long time, he came out of his hiding-place, but the other was nowhere to be seen. Now Yehiel realized that he had not looked for him from the very beginning. This made him cry, and crying he ran to his grandfather and complained of his faithless friend. Then tears brimmed in Rabbi Barukh's eyes and he said: "God says the same thing: 'I hide, but no one wants to seek me.' "

The Two Wicks

Rabbi Barukh's other grandchild, young Israel, made a habit of crying aloud while he prayed. Once his grandfather said to him: "My son, do you recall the difference between a wick of cotton and a wick of flax? One burns quietly and the other sputters! Believe me, a single true gesture, even if it be only that of the small toe, is enough."

The Twofold World

Rabbi Barukh once said: "What a good and bright world this is if we do not lose our hearts to it, but what a dark world, if we do!"

DOV BAER OF MEZRITCH
THE GREAT MAGGID

The Family Tree

When Rabbi Baer was five years old, a fire broke out in his father's house. Hearing his mother grieve and cry about this, he asked her: "Mother, do we have to be so unhappy because we have lost a house?"

"I am not grieving for the house," she said, "but for our family tree which burned up. It began with Rabbi Yohanan, the sandal-maker, the master in the Talmud."

"And what does that matter!" exclaimed the boy. "I shall get you a new family tree which begins with me!"

The Curse

When Rabbi Baer was young, he and his wife lived in great poverty. They inhabited a ramshackle house beyond the city limits, because they did not have to pay rent for it, and here the woman brought her son into the world. Up to this time she had not complained. But when the midwife asked for money to buy camomile tea for the child, and she hadn't a penny to give her, she moaned: "This is how his service provides for us!"

The maggid heard these words and said to her: "Now I shall go outside and curse Israel because they leave us to our misery." He went out, stood in front of the door, raised his eyes to Heaven, and cried: "O children of Israel, may abundant blessings come upon you!" Then he went back into the room. When he heard his wife moan a second time, he said to her: "Now I shall really curse them!" Once more he went out, lifted his head, and cried: "Let all happiness come to the children of Israel—but they shall give their money to thorn-bushes and stones!"

Silently his wife held the hungry child. It was too weak to cry. Then—for the first time—the maggid sighed. Instantly the answer came. A voice said to him: "You have lost your share in the coming world."

"Well, then," he said, "the reward has been done away with. Now I can begin to serve in good earnest."

Punishment

When the maggid realized that he had become known to the world, he begged God to tell him what sin of his had brought this guilt upon him.

His Reception

Rabbi Baer was a keen scholar, equally versed in the intricacies of the Gemara and the depths of the Kabbalah. Time and again he had heard about the Baal Shem and finally decided to go to him, in order to see for himself if his wisdom really justified his great reputation.

When he reached the master's house and stood before him, he greeted him and then—without even looking at him properly —waited for teachings to issue from his lips, that he might examine and weigh them. But the Baal Shem only told him that once he had driven through the wilderness for days and lacked bread to feed his coachman. Then a peasant happened along and sold him bread. After this, he dismissed his guest.

The following evening, the maggid again went to the Baal Shem and thought that now surely he would hear something of his teachings. But all Rabbi Israel told him was that once, while he was on the road, he had had no hay for his horses and a farmer had come and fed the animals. The maggid did not know what to make of these stories. He was quite certain that it was useless for him to wait for this man to utter words of wisdom.

When he returned to his inn, he ordered his servant to prepare for the homeward journey; they would start as soon as the moon had scattered the clouds. Around midnight it grew light. Then a man came from the Baal Shem with the message that

Rabbi Baer was to come to him that very hour. He went at once. The Baal Shem received him in his room. "Are you versed in the Kabbalah?" he asked. The maggid said he was. "Take this book, the *Tree of Life*. Open it and read." The maggid read. "Now think!" He thought. "Expound!" He expounded the passage which dealt with the nature of angels. "You have no true knowledge," said the Baal Shem. "Get up!" The maggid rose. The Baal Shem stood in front of him and recited the passage. Then, before the eyes of Rabbi Baer, the room went up in flame, and through the blaze he heard the surging of angels until his senses forsook him. When he awoke, the room was as it had been when he entered it. The Baal Shem stood opposite him and said: "You expounded correctly, but you have no true knowledge, because there is no soul in what you know."

Rabbi Baer went back to the inn, told his servant to go home, and stayed in Mezbizh, the town of the Baal Shem.

The Sign

Once, at parting, the Baal Shem blessed his disciple. Then he bowed his own head to receive the blessing from him. Rabbi Baer drew back, but the Baal Shem took his hand and laid it on his head.

The Succession

Before the Baal Shem died, his disciples asked him who was to be their master in his stead. He said: "Whoever can teach you how pride can be broken, shall be my successor."

After the Baal Shem's death, they first put the question to Rabbi Baer. "How can pride be broken?"

He replied: "Pride belongs to God—as it is written: 'The Lord reigneth; He is clothed in pride.' That is why no counsel can be given on how to break pride. We must struggle with it all the days of our life." Then the disciples knew that it was he who was the Baal Shem's successor.

The Visit

Rabbi Jacob Joseph of Polnoye was the other of the two most distinguished disciples of the Baal Shem who fell heir to his work. It was he who wrote down his master's teachings. After the Baal Shem's death, he lived in Mezritch for a time, and during this period the maggid asked him to be his guest over the sabbath. The rabbi of Polnoye said: "On the sabbath I act like any house-father. I lie down after dining. I do not extend the dinner-hour as you who have many disciples and say Torah at table."

"On the sabbath," answered the maggid, "my disciples and I shall stay in two rooms which lie across the courtyard and leave the house to you, so that you can do just as you would in your own home." So the rabbi of Polnoye and his disciple Rabbi Moshe, who had accompanied him on his trip, remained in the house. On the eve of the sabbath they ate together and then Rabbi Jacob Joseph went to sleep. His disciple wanted very much to sit at the maggid's table, for he knew him for the leader of his generation, but he feared his teacher might wake up and notice his absence.

After the meal on the evening of the sabbath, the holy "third meal," the rabbi of Polnoye said to his disciple: "Let us go to the maggid's table and listen in a little." While they crossed the court, they heard the maggid's voice intoning the teachings, but when they reached his door it ceased. Rabbi Jacob Joseph went back into the court and again he heard the maggid speak. Once more he turned to the door. Once more he stood on the threshold. Once more all was silent within. When this happened a third time, the rabbi of Polnoye walked back and forth in the court, his hands pressed to his heart, and said: "What can we do? On the day our master died, the Divine Presence packed her knapsack and journeyed to Mezritch!" He did not try to go to the maggid's table again. When the sabbath was over, he made his farewells in cordial words and went home with his disciple.

Palm and Cedar

"The righteous [zaddik] shall flourish like the palm-tree; he shall grow like a cedar in Lebanon." Concerning this verse in the psalm, the maggid of Mezritch said: "There are two kinds of zaddikim. Some spend their time on mankind. They teach them and take trouble about them. Others concern themselves only with the teachings themselves. The first bear nourishing fruit, like the date-palm; the second are like the cedar: lofty and unfruitful."

Nearness

A disciple told:

Whenever we rode to our teacher—the moment we were within the limits of the town—all our desires were fulfilled. And if anyone happened to have a wish left, this was satisfied as soon as he entered the house of the maggid. But if there was one among us whose soul was still churned up with wanting—he was at peace when he looked into the face of the maggid.

Effect

A number of disciples once went to the maggid. "We are not going to stay," they said to one another. "We only want to look into his face." They told the coachman to wait in front of the house. The maggid at once told them a story which consisted of twenty-four words. They listened, bade him farewell, and said to the coachman: "Drive on slowly. We'll catch up with you." They walked behind the carriage and talked about the story they had heard. For the rest of that day and the whole of the night, they walked after the carriage. At dawn the coachman stopped, looked back, and said crossly: "Isn't it bad enough that yesterday you forgot the Afternoon and the Evening Prayer! Are you going to skip the Morning Prayer too?" He had to repeat this four times before they even heard him.

In the Maggid's House

Rabbi Shneur Zalman used to say: "What of prophecies! What of miracles! In the house of my teacher, the holy maggid, you drew up holy spirit by the bucketful, and miracles lay around under the benches, only that no one had the time to pick them up!"

In a certain year, on the eve of Shavuot, the feast of the Revelation, the rabbi of Rizhyn sat at his table and said no word of the teachings to his disciples, as he usually did at this hour. He was silent and wept. It was the same the second evening of the feast. But after grace he said:

"Many a time, when my ancestor, the holy maggid, taught at table, his disciples discussed what their teacher had said, on the way home, and each quoted him differently, and each was positive he had heard it in this, and no other way, and what they said was quite contradictory. There was no possibility of clearing up the matter because when they went to the maggid and asked him, he only repeated the traditional saying: 'Both, these and those are words of the living God.' But when the disciples thought it over, they understood the meaning of the contradiction. For at the source, the Torah is one; in the worlds her face is seventyfold. If, however, a man looks intently at one of these faces, he no longer has need of words or of teachings, for the features of that eternal face speak to him."

In Exile

The maggid of Mezritch said: "Now, in exile, the holy spirit comes upon us more easily than at the time the Temple was still standing.

"A king was driven from his realm and forced to become a wayfarer. When, in the course of his wanderings, he came to the house of poor people, where he was given modest food and shelter, but received as a king, his heart grew light and he chatted with his host as intimately as he had done at court with those who were closest to him.

"Now, that He is in exile, God does the same."

God's Fatherhood

Concerning the verse in the Scriptures: "But from thence ye will seek the Lord thy God, and thou shalt find Him," the maggid of Mezritch said: "You must cry to God and call him father until he becomes your father."

103

The maggid of Mezritch said:

Nothing in the world can change from one reality into another, unless it first turns into nothing, that is, into the reality of the between-stage. In that stage it is nothing and no one can grasp it, for it has reached the rung of nothingness, just as before creation. And then it is made into a new creature, from the egg to the chick. The moment when the egg is no more and the chick is not yet, is nothingness. And philosophy terms this the primal state which no one can grasp because it is a force which precedes creation; it is called chaos. It is the same with the sprouting seed. It does not begin to sprout until the seed disintegrates in the earth and the quality of seed-dom is destroyed in order that it may attain to nothingness which is the rung before creation. And this rung is called wisdom, that is to say, a thought which cannot be made manifest. Then this thought gives rise to creation, as it is written: "In wisdom hast Thou made them all."

The Last Miracle

The maggid of Mezritch said:

The creation of Heaven and earth is the unfolding of Something out of Nothing, the descent from above to below. But the zaddikim who in their work disengage themselves from what is bodily, and do nothing but think about God, actually see and understand and imagine the universe as it was in the state of nothingness before creation. They change the Something back into the Nothing. This is more miraculous: to begin from the lower state. As it is said in the Talmud: "Greater than the first miracle is the last."

The Strong Thief

The maggid of Mezritch said:

"Every lock has its key which is fitted to it and opens it. But there are strong thieves who know how to open without keys. They break the lock. So every mystery in the world can be unriddled by the particular kind of meditation fitted to it. But God loves the thief who breaks the lock open: I mean the man who breaks his heart for God."

Said the maggid to Rabbi Zusya, his disciple: "I cannot teach you the ten principles of service. But a little child and a thief can show you what they are.

"From the child you can learn three things:

He is merry for no particular reason;

Never for a moment is he idle;

When he needs something, he demands it vigorously.

The thief can instruct you in seven things:

He does his service by night;

If he does not finish what he has set out to do, in one night, he devotes the next night to it;

He and those who work with him, love one another;

He risks his life for slight gains;

What he takes has so little value for him, that he gives it up for a very small coin;

He endures blows and hardship, and it matters nothing to him;

He likes his trade and would not exchange it for any other."

The Rabbi and the Angel

The first time—it was on a Friday—that Rabbi Shmelke, the rav of Nikolsburg, and his brother Rabbi Pinhas, the rav of Frankfort-on-the-Main, went to the house of the Great Maggid, they were deeply disappointed. They had expected a long and elaborate welcome, but he dismissed them after a brief greeting and devoted himself to preparing for another, a more distinguished guest: the sabbath. At the three sabbath meals, they were all agog to hear learned and intricate speeches. The maggid said only a few words at each, and without a great show of intellect. At the third, in particular, he did not speak at all like a teacher to his disciples who are avid to learn, but like a good father, united with his sons at a meal only a little more solemn than usual. This was why they took leave of Rabbi Baer the very next day and then went to the House of Study to bid his disciples goodbye. There they saw one whom they had not met: Rabbi Zusya. When they entered, he looked

105

at them for a long time, first at one, then at the other. Finally he fixed his eyes on the floor and said without greeting or any transitional phrase: "Malachi says: 'For the priest's lips should keep knowledge, and they should seek the teaching from his mouth; for he is an angel of the Lord of hosts.' Our sages expounded this as follows: 'If the rabbi resembles an angel, you shall seek the teachings from his lips.' How are we to understand this? Has any one of us ever seen an angel, so that we could compare the rabbi with him? But that is just what is meant! You have never seen an angel, yet, if he stood before you, you would not ask him questions, or examine him, or demand a sign, but believe and know he was an angel. It is the same with the true zaddik. If there is someone who makes you feel such as this—from his lips you shall seek the teachings."

When Rabbi Zusya had ended, the brothers, in their hearts, had already joined the disciples of the maggid.

The Ball

Before the maggid began to teach the two brothers, Shmelke and Pinhas, he told them how to conduct themselves throughout the day, from the moment of waking to falling asleep. His directions took into account all their habits, confirming them or modifying them, as though he knew the whole of their lives. In closing he said: "And before you lie down at night, you add up everything you have done during the day. And when a man calculates his hours and sees that he has not wasted a moment in idleness, when his heart beats high with pride, then—up in Heaven—they take all his good works, crush them into a ball, and hurl it down into the abyss."

Body and Soul

When Rabbi Shmelke returned from his first trip to the Great Maggid, and they asked him what his experience had been, he replied: "Up to that time I had mortified my body so that it might endure the soul. But now I have seen and learned that the soul can endure the body and need not separate from it. This is what we are told in the holy Torah: 'And I will set My abiding presence among you, and My soul shall not abhor you.' For the soul shall not abhor the body."

Its Own Place

Once Rabbi Mikhal of Zlotchov took his young son Yitzhak on a visit to the Great Maggid. The maggid left the room for a short time and while he was absent the boy picked up a snuff box lying on the table, looked at it from every angle, and put it back again. The moment the maggid crossed the threshold he looked at Yitzhak and said to him: "Everything has its own place; every change of place has a meaning. If one does not know, one should not do."

To Say Torah and to Be Torah

Rabbi Leib, son of Sarah, the hidden zaddik who wandered over the earth, following the course of rivers, in order to redeem the souls of the living and the dead, said this: "I did not go to the maggid in order to hear Torah from him, but to see how he unlaces his felt shoes and laces them up again."

How to Say Torah

The maggid once said to his disciples:
"I shall teach you the best way to say Torah. You must cease to be aware of yourselves. You must be nothing but an ear which hears what the universe of the word is constantly saying within you. The moment you start hearing what you yourself are saying, you must stop."

The Stokers' Discussion

The Great Maggid accepted only chosen men as his disciples. Of these he said that they were noble tapers which need only to be lit to burn with a pure flame. Some scholars he rejected because—so he said—his way was not suited to them. But several young men who were not yet considered worthy of being his disciples, remained with him and performed services for him and his disciples. They went by the name of "stokers," because tending the stoves was part of their duties.

One night, as he was about to fall asleep, one of the disciples, Shneur Zalman, the later rav of Northern White Russia, heard three of these young men working at a stove in the adjoining room. They were talking about the sacrifice of Isaac. One of them said: "Why do people make such a great to-do about Abraham? Who would not do as he did, if God himself commanded it! Just think of all those who threw away their lives without such a command, solely to sanctify the Name! What do you think of it?"

The other said: "I see it this way. The children of Israel have within them the heritage of the holy fathers, and so it is no particular virtue for them to give up what they treasure most. But Abraham was the son of a worshipper of idols."

The first of the three stokers answered: "What did that matter at the moment that God, God himself, spoke to him?"

Now the second said: "You must not forget that he rose at early dawn and immediately prepared for the journey without delaying at home with his son even for an hour!"

The first rejected this reason also. "If God spoke to me now," he said, "I should not wait until morning. I should do his bidding right in the middle of the night."

Then the third who had been silent up to this time, said: "In the Scriptures it is written: 'For now I know,' and further on: 'Thou hast not withheld thy son, thine only one, from Me.' You might think that the words 'from Me' were unnecessary. But we learn something just from them: that when the angel held back his hand, Abraham did not rejoice because Isaac was to live, but still—even at this moment—rejoiced more than ever that the will of God was fulfilled by him. That is why it is written, 'for now I know'—*now*, when the angel had already arrested Abraham's hand."

The first of the three stokers did not reply, and the two others were also silent. All Rabbi Shneur Zalman heard was the crackling of the faggots and the hiss of the flames.

How to Become Spiritual

In the days of the Great Maggid, a well-to-do merchant, who refused to have anything to do with hasidic teachings, lived in

Mezritch. His wife took care of the shop. He himself spent only two hours a day in it. The rest of the time he sat over his books in the House of Study. One Friday morning, he saw two young men there whom he did not know. He asked them where they were from and why they had come, and was told they had journeyed a great distance to see and hear the Great Maggid. Then he decided that for once he too would go to his house. He did not want to sacrifice any of his study time for this, so he did not go to his shop on that day.

The maggid's radiant face affected him so strongly that from then on he went to his home more and more frequently and ended up attaching himself to him altogether. From this time on, he had one business failure after another until he was quite poor. He complained to the maggid that this had happened to him since he had become his disciple. The maggid answered: "You know what our sages say: 'He who wants to grow wise, let him go south; he who wants to grow rich, let him go north.' Now what shall one do who wants to grow both rich and wise?" The man did not know what to reply. The maggid continued: 'He who thinks nothing at all of himself, and makes himself nothing, grows spiritual, and spirit does not occupy space. He can be north and south at the same time." These words moved the merchant's heart and he cried out: "Then my fate is sealed!" "No, no," said the maggid. "You have already begun."

The List of Sins

During his stay in Mezritch, the rav of Kolbishov saw an old man come to the Great Maggid and ask him to impose penance on him for his sins. "Go home," said the maggid. "Write all your sins down on a slip of paper and bring it to me." When the man brought him the list, he merely glanced at it. Then he said. "Go home. All is well." But later the rav observed that Rabbi Baer read the list and laughed at every line. This annoyed him. How could anyone laugh at sins!

For years he could not forget the incident, until once he heard someone quote a saying of the Baal Shem: "It is well-known that no one commits a sin unless the spirit of folly possesses him. But what does the sage do if a fool comes to him? He laughs at all this folly, and while he laughs, a breath of gentleness is wafted through the world. What was rigid, thaws, and what was a burden becomes light." The rav reflected. In his soul he said: "Now I understand the laughter of the holy maggid."

From Where?

They tell:

A disciple of the Gaon of Vilna saw his dead father appear to him every night in a dream and ask him to give up his faith and become a Christian. Since Vilna was far away from where he lived, and Mezritch near, he decided to ask the Great Maggid for counsel and aid, in spite of the fact that a serious quarrel had broken out between the two schools. "Open your father's grave," said the maggid. "In it you will find two pieces of wood lying so that they form a cross. Take them out and you will soon have peace again." And everything was just as the maggid had said.

When the man went to Vilna, years later, he told the whole matter to his teacher. The Gaon said: "This is touched on in the Palestinian Talmud. But it is astonishing that the maggid of Mezritch understood the passage."

When, after a time, the man visited Rabbi Baer, he repeated the Gaon's words to him. "Your teacher," said the maggid, "knows it from the Palestinian Talmud, and I know it from where that work knows it."

Failure

Once the maggid concentrated all the force of his being on the coming of redemption. Then a voice asked from Heaven: "Who is trying to hasten the end, and what does he consider himself?"

The maggid replied: "I am the leader of my generation, and it is my duty to use all my strength for that purpose."

Again the voice asked a question. "How can you prove this?" "My holy congregation," said the maggid, "will rise and testify for me."

110

"Let them rise!" cried the voice.

Then Rabbi Baer went to his disciples and said: "Is it true that I am the leader of my generation?" But all were silent. He repeated his question and still no one said, "It is true." Not until after he had left them, did the numbness leave their minds and tongues, and they were startled at themselves.

Conjuring

During the last years of the maggid's life, the mitnagdim were so hostile to the hasidim that they came to regard them as the builders of the Tower of Babel, reborn, and as such banned them, forbade association with them, marriage, eating of their bread and drinking of their wine. The disciples of the maggid complained of this on each of the three meals of the sabbath. But all three times he was silent as though he had not heard. So, at the close of the sabbath, his disciples, ten in number, formed a congregation of their own and opened the House of Prayer. There, with secret rites, they turned the ban back on those who had banned them. By the third hour after midnight, the thing was done, and they went to the room where they slept. Around the fourth hour, they heard the maggid's crutches drag over the floor. He had been using them for several years because of his weak feet. They rose, washed their hands, and stood before their master. He said: "Children, what have you done?" They replied: "We no longer had the strength to endure it!" He said: "You have done a foolish thing and you have forfeited your head." In that very year the Great Maggid died.

At the Pond

After the maggid's death, his disciples came together and talked about the things he had done. When it was Rabbi Schneur Zalman's turn, he asked them: "Do you know why our master went to the pond every day at dawn and stayed there for a little while before coming home again?" They did not know why. Rabbi Zalman continued: "He was learning the song with which the frogs praise God. It takes a very long time to learn that song."

111

The Left Foot

It is known that the Great Maggid used crutches. Many years after his death, his great disciple, Rabbi Shneur Zalman, once heard his own disciples arguing about who should be called "the zaddik of the generation." "What is there to argue about!" he cried. "The zaddik of the generation is my master, the holy maggid of Mezritch, and none other! 'Let us make man in our image' is written about him, for he was a perfect man. You will object and say: 'How is that possible? His feet were crippled!' But I tell you he *was* perfect, and you know what is said of the perfect man: that with each of his limbs he moves all the worlds, as it is written in the Book of Splendor: 'Mercy—that is the right arm, rigor is the left.' That was why he dragged his left foot. He offered it up, lest he waken rigor within the world!"

From the Look-Out of Heaven

At a time of great anguish for Israel, Rabbi Elimelekh brooded more and more on his griefs. Then his dead master, the maggid of Mezritch, appeared to him. Rabbi Elimelekh cried out: "Why are you silent in such dreadful need?" He answered: "In Heaven we see that all that seems evil to you is a work of mercy."

ABRAHAM, THE ANGEL

The Mothers

They tell:

In the days when the Great Maggid was still poor and unrecognized, it happened on a winter evening that his wife set out for the bath, for her monthly purification. But she was caught in a savage snow-storm, lost her way, and groped about for a long time until finally, at dead of night, she found the bath. When she knocked at the door, the bath-master called to her from within, grumbled that she had waked him from his sleep, and refused to let her in. The woman stood outside in the icy night, but she would not go away. At midnight she heard carriage-bells and the snorting of horses. A fine carriage drove up to the bath-house. Four women got out. They knocked at the door and called. The bath-master came with a light, looked at the women with awe, and admitted them. But before they entered, they took the wife of the maggid between them. They all bathed together. When they had done, they asked her into their carriage and drove her home. She got out and looked around, but the carriage was gone. Softly she entered the room. "So you bathed with the Mothers!" the maggid said. That night she conceived her son Abraham.

Origin

They say that the Great Maggid had purified and unified his body and spirit so utterly that his body was as his spirit, and his spirit was as his body. Therefore in the hour he begot his son, a pure spirit from the world of angels entered his wife's womb, and from there it was born for a brief space into the world of man.

The Face

Sometimes Rabbi Abraham looked so great and awe-inspiring that men could not bear to look at him. One zaddik, who was performing some holy rite, did look at him and forgot whether or not he had said the blessing. On his return home, he refused both food and drink. Another martialled his courage four whole weeks, but when he crossed the threshold, and saw Rabbi Abraham binding on his phylacteries, he trembled and turned away, and did not again venture into his presence.

Barukh and Efraim, the grandsons of the Baal Shem Tov, once said to each other: "Why do you suppose people call the son of the maggid an angel? Let us have a look at him." But when they reached the street in which he lived, and saw Rabbi Abraham's face in the window, they fled in such haste that Efraim dropped his book of psalms.

Marriage

When Rabbi Abraham, the Angel, entered the room on his wedding-night, his face was more awe-inspiring than ever before, and his lips uttered dark sounds of lament. His appearance and his voice terrified the bride to the secret core of her being, and she fell fainting to the ground. Until morning she lay in a fever.

When he entered the room on the following night, his wife's heart filled with heroic strength and she endured his terrible greatness.

Rabbi Abraham begot two sons. After that he lived apart as before.

His Wife's Dream

His wife had a dream. She saw a vast hall and in it thrones, set in a semi-circle. On each throne sat one of the great, and one said: "Let us summon him home." The others nodded in chorus. The woman came forward. She stood before the great on the thrones and pleaded and fought for her husband's life on earth. Her words burned with intensity. The great listened in silence. Finally one said: "Give him to her for twelve earthly years." The others nodded in chorus. The dream melted away. When the maggid said the morning greeting, he laid his hands on the head of his son's wife.

114

Anniversary

On the eve of the ninth of Av, the day of the burning of the Temple, the men sat on the floor of the dark room of prayer, mourning the destroyed sanctuary, and the reader began: "How doth the city sit solitary, that was full of people!" Rabbi Abraham, the Angel, sitting among the men, cried aloud, "How . . ." and fell silent, his head between his knees. The reader ended the lament. Everyone went home. Rabbi Abraham remained, his head between his knees. They found him in the same position the following day, and he did not rise until he had experienced the destruction to the very end.

Strategic Retreat

Rabbi Abraham said:
"I have learned a new form of service from the wars of Frederick, king of Prussia. It is not necessary to approach the enemy in order to attack him. In fleeing from him, it is possible to circumvent him as he advances, and fall on him from the rear until he is forced to surrender. What is needed is not to strike straight at Evil but to withdraw to the sources of divine power, and from there to circle around Evil, bend it, and transform it into its opposite."

Inheritance

It is told:
After his death, the maggid appeared to his son and—invoking the commandment to honor one's parents—ordered him to give up his life of perfect seclusion, for whoever walks a way such as this, is in danger. Abraham replied: "I do not recognize a father in the flesh. I recognize only one merciful Father of all that lives."
"You accepted your inheritance," said the maggid. "With that you recognized me as your father even after my death."
"I renounce my father's inheritance," cried Rabbi Abraham, the Angel. At that very moment, fire broke out in the house and consumed the few small things the maggid had left his son—but nothing besides.

A short time after the fire in which the clothing and utensils the maggid had left his son were burned, Rabbi Abraham's brother-in-law made him a present of a robe of white silk the maggid had worn on high holidays, the famous "white *pekeshe.*" On the eve of the Day of Atonement, Abraham put it on to honor his father. The lights in the House of Prayer had already been lit. With a fervent gesture the zaddik leaned over to one of them. The robe caught fire. They snatched it from his body. With a long look of understanding, he watched it crumble to ash.

The Mountain

Once Rabbi Abraham visited his father-in-law in Kremnitz. The most distinguished members of the congregation assembled to welcome the holy man. But he turned his back on them and looked out of the window at the mountain at whose foot the city lay. Among those waiting for him was a man very much aware of his own learning and intent on his own importance. He said impatiently: "Why do you keep staring at the mountain? Have you never seen anything like it before?"
The rabbi answered: "I look and am amazed to see how such a lump of earth made much of itself until it grew into a tall mountain."

Without God

Rabbi Abraham said:
"Lord of the world, if it were possible to imagine a fraction of a second without your influence and providence, of what avail to us were this world, and of what avail to us were that other world? Of what avail to us were the coming of the Messiah, and of what avail to us the resurrection of the dead? What would there be to delight in, in all of this, and what would it be there for?"

The Full Stature

Rabbi Abraham said:
"We say in our prayers: 'Every stature shall bow before thee.' When man reaches the highest rung, when he reaches his full

stature, only then does he become truly humble in his own eyes, and knows what it is: to bow before you."

The Other Dream

In the night after the seven days of mourning for Rabbi Abraham, his wife had a dream. She saw a vast hall, and in it thrones, set in a semi-circle. On each throne sat one of the great. A door opened, and one who looked like those others, entered. It was Abraham, her husband. He said: "Friends, my wife bears me a grudge because in my earthly life I lived apart from her. She is right, and therefore I must obtain her forgiveness." His wife cried out: "With all my heart I forgive you," and awoke comforted.

Sanctified

Rabbi Israel of Rizhyn told:
A few years after the death of Rabbi Abraham, the Angel, his widow, my blessed grandmother, received an offer of marriage from the great zaddik Rabbi Nahum of Tchernobil. But the Angel appeared to him in a dream and looked at him threateningly. So he let her be.
My blessed grandmother lived in want. When the Rabbi of Tchernobil had taken her son, my father, into his house, she went to the Land of Israel. She told no one there who she was. She took in washing and supported herself with the money she got for this. She died in the Land of Israel. If only some one could tell me where she lies buried!

PINHAS OF KORETZ AND HIS SCHOOL*

The Black Melammed

In his young years, Rabbi Pinhas earned his livelihood as a melammed, that is, as a teacher of children, in Koretz, where he was generally known as the "Black Melammed." He concealed his true nature from everybody. The only one who knew about him was the rav of Koretz. This rav had a special room in the bath-house and his own bath. Rabbi Pinhas asked his permission to bathe there any time he pleased, day or night, and the rav told the bath-master to admit him at any hour whatsoever.

Once Rabbi Pinhas came after midnight and woke up the bath-master. But he refused to open because, the day before, he had bought some geese and was keeping them in just that room overnight. But the "Black Melammed" would not take no for an answer. He knocked a few shingles out of the roof, climbed through the opening, dipped into the bath, and was going out the same way, when a piece of the wall broke off, and struck him on the head with such force that he lost his footing and fell. He lay on the ground unconscious for several hours. In the morning, people found him and thought he was dead. When the rav heard of it, he said no one must touch him. He himself, however, did not go there, but to the House of Prayer, and prayed: "Lord of the world, keep him alive! Lord of the world, keep this zaddik alive for your own sake!" Then he went to the place where Pinhas was still lying motionless. He shook him and said: "Pinhasel, get up! Go, teach your pupils! Remember, you are a hired man who has his day's work to do!" And Rabbi Pinhas got up and went to his school.

---

* Here I have made an exception to the practice of limiting each chapter to one zaddik. Because the school of Pinhas of Koretz continues and complements his personality and teachings, I am representing it in this chapter in the person of Rabbi Rafael.

118

Blood-Letting

When Rabbi Pinhas visited the Baal Shem for the first time, his host looked at him for quite a while and then sent for the doctor to let his guest's blood. But before he began, the Baal Shem warned him to be careful to do it right, for, so he said: "That is holy blood, preserved ever since the six days of creation. If you are not quite sure your hand is steady," he added jestingly, "better tap my vein!"

When the Citron Came

When the Baal Shem Tov lay dying, his disciple Rabbi David of Ostrog came to him and said: "Rabbi, how can you leave us behind alone!" The zaddik whispered to him: "The bear is in the woods, and Pinhas is a sage." His disciple knew that these words referred to Rabbi Baer of Mezritch and Rabbi Pinhas of Koretz, although Pinhas did not belong to the group of disciples. But he had come to the Baal Shem twice—the second time just before his death—and the Baal Shem had been to see him twice as well.

After the master's death, Rabbi Baer taught in his place. But Rabbi Pinhas continued to lead an anonymous existence. In the House of Study, he said his prayers behind the stove and no one paid any attention to him.

Now, Rabbi David of Ostrog, who was a well-to-do man, was in the habit of buying two exceptionally fine citrons every year before the Feast of Tabernacles, one for the Baal Shem, the other for himself. The year the master died, he brought three beautiful fruits instead of two before the holiday, one for himself, one for Rabbi Baer, and one for Rabbi Pinhas.

That year citrons were very scarce, and not a single one had gotten to Koretz. On the first day of the feast, the congregation waited with praying to see whether one would perhaps be brought from a neighboring town to which they had sent for it. Finally the heads of the congregation decided that the daily Morning Prayer should be said; that, in the meantime, a messenger might still arrive. But the Morning Prayer was ended, and no one had come. So the reader was asked to begin the liturgy proper to that day. Hesitatingly he went up to the pulpit. He had not yet said the blessing, when the "Black Melammed" came out from behind the stove, walked to the reader, and said to him: "Do not begin yet!" Then he returned to his place behind the stove. The people had not noticed anything, but when they asked the reader why he did not begin, and he referred them to Rabbi Pinhas, they were annoyed and asked for an explanation. "At the right time," he told them, "the citron will be here."

"What do you mean?" they shouted. "What do you mean by 'the right time'?"

"In an hour."

"And if it has not come by then, you'll have to put up with a kick or so, won't you?"

"I have nothing against that," he replied.

Before the hour was up, they reported that a peasant had come on horseback to bring something to Rabbi Pinhas. It was the citron and a letter. Everyone crowded around to read it. The recipient was addressed as the "Head of all the sons of the Diaspora." The writer of the letter was known to many as a holy man. Rabbi Pinhas took the citron, had them bring the palm fronds, and spoke the blessing. They asked him to give them to the reader, so that he might recite the Hallel Psalms. "I shall recite them," he said. He went to the pulpit and prayed before the congregation.

Without a Guest

It is told:

When Rabbi Pinhas had become known, and more and more hasidim came to him with their concerns, he was alarmed to see how much all this diverted him from the service of God and the study of the Torah. The only solution he could think of was that people must stop bringing their problems to him—and his prayer was granted. From that time on, he did not live with his fellow-men—except when he prayed with the congregation—but kept himself apart and devoted himself solely to the service of his Lord.

When the Feast of Tabernacles approached, he had to let a non-Jew make his holiday booth, for the Jews refused to help him. Since he lacked the proper tools, he sent his wife to borrow them from a neighbor, but it was only with the greatest difficulty that she could get what was needed. When he was in the House of Study on the evening of the feast, he asked some wayfarers to dine with him, as he did every year, but he was so thoroughly hated far and wide, that no one would accept his invitation and he had to go home alone. When he had said the words bidding the holy guests, the patriarchs, to enter the booth that evening, he saw our Father Abraham standing outside like someone who has come to a house he is accustomed to visit, and only just sees that it is not the house he thought, and pauses in surprise. "What wrong have I done?" Rabbi Pinhas cried.

"It is not my custom to enter a house where no wayfarers have come as guests," our Father Abraham replied.

From then on, Rabbi Pinhas prayed he might find favor in the eyes of his fellow-men, and again his prayer was granted.

The Breaking of the Vessels

Rabbi Pinhas said: "We all know that very long ago, when God was building worlds and tearing them down, the vessels broke because they could not endure the abundance poured into them. But through this, light penetrated to the lower worlds and they did not remain in darkness. It is the same with the breaking of vessels in the soul of the zaddik."

The Teaching of the Soul

Rabbi Pinhas often cited the words: " 'A man's soul will teach him'," and emphasized them by adding: "There is no man who is not incessantly being taught by his soul."

One of his disciples asked: "If this is so, why don't men obey their souls?"

"The soul teaches incessantly," Rabbi Pinhas explained, "but it never repeats."

The Pupil

Rabbi Pinhas said: "Ever since I began giving true service to my Maker, I have not tried to get anything, but only taken what God gave me. It is because the pupil is dark, that it absorbs every ray of light."

Sefirot

Rabbi Pinhas said:

"Every word and every action contains all the ten Sefirot, the ten powers emanating from God, for they fill the entire world. And it is not the way people think: that mercy is a principle in itself and rigor is a principle in itself. For all the ten creative powers are contained in every single thing. Whoever drops his hand, does so in the secret of the efflux of light. Whoever lifts his hand, does so in the secret of the reflux of light. The completed motion of lowering and lifting, houses the secret of mercy and rigor.

"There are no words which, in themselves, are useless. There are no actions which, in themselves, are useless. But one can make useless both actions and words by saying or doing them uselessly."

Hiding

Rabbi Rafael of Bershad, the favorite disciple of Rabbi Pinhas, told:

"On the first day of Hanukkah, I complained to my teacher that in adversity it is very difficult to retain perfect faith in the belief that God provides for every human being. It actually seems as if God were hiding his face from such an unhappy being. What shall he do to strengthen his faith?

"The rabbi replied: 'It ceases to be a hiding, if you know it is hiding.'"

The Doubter

A disciple of Rabbi Pinhas was tormented by doubt, for he could not see how it was possible for God to know all his thoughts, even the vaguest and most fleeting. He went to his teacher in great anguish to beg him to dispel the confusion in his heart. Rabbi Pinhas was standing at the window and saw his visitor arrive. He entered, greeted his master, and was about to tell him his troubles, when the zaddik said: "My friend, I know. And why should God not know?"

On the Throne

Rabbi Pinhas said: "At New Year's, God is in that concealment which is called 'the sitting on the throne,' and everyone can see him, everyone according to his own nature: one in weeping, one in prayer, and one in the song of praise."

Before the Ram's Horn Was Sounded

One New Year's Day, just before the ram's horn was sounded, Rabbi Pinhas said:

"All creatures renew themselves in sleep, even stones and streams. And if man wants to renew his life over and over, then before falling asleep, he must put from him his shape, and commend his naked soul to God. It will ascend and receive new life. But today is the day of the great renewal, and deep sleep falls on all spiritual creatures, on angels, and holy names, and the letters of the Scriptures. This is the meaning of the great judgment in which the spirit is renewed. And so today, man shall be destroyed in deep sleep, and the renewing hand of God will touch him." After these words, he raised the ram's horn to his lips.

On the Day of Destruction

They asked Rabbi Pinhas: "Why should the Messiah be born on the anniversary of the destruction of the Temple—as the tradition has it?"

"The kernel," he replied, "which is sown in earth, must fall to pieces so that the ear of grain may sprout from it. Strength cannot be resurrected until it has dwelt in deep secrecy. To doff a shape, to don a shape—this is done in the instant of pure nothingness. In the husk of forgetting, the power of memory grows. That is the power of redemption. On the day of destruction, power lies at the bottom of the depths, and grows. That is why, on this day, we sit on the ground. That is why, on this day, we visit graves. That is why, on this day, the Messiah is born."

For the Sake of Renewal

Rabbi Pinhas said: "Solomon, the preacher, says: 'Vanity of vanities, all is vanity,' because he wants to destroy the world, so that it may receive new life."

The Miracle of the Light

Rabbi Pinhas said: "Listen, and I shall tell you the meaning of the miracle of the light, at Hanukkah. The light which was hidden since the days of creation was then revealed. And every year, when the lights are lit for Hanukkah, the hidden light is revealed afresh. And it is the light of the Messiah."

A Man on Earth

They asked Rabbi Pinhas: "Why is it written: 'in the day that God created a man on earth,' and not 'in the day that God created Man on earth'?"

He explained: "You should serve your Maker as though there were only one man on earth, only yourself."

The Place of Man

They asked Rabbi Pinhas: "Why is God called 'makom,' that is, place? He certainly is the place of the world, but then he ought to be called that, and not just 'place.'"

He replied: "Man should go into God, so that God may surround him and become his place."

The Easy Death

Once they asked Rabbi Pinhas why, when he prayed, they could hear no sound and see no movement, so that he seemed to lack the fervor which shook the other zaddikim from head to foot.

"Brothers," he answered, "to pray means to cling to God, and to cling to God means to loose oneself from all substance, as if the soul left the body. Our sages say that there is a death which is as hard as drawing a rope through the ring on the mast, and there is a death as easy as drawing a hair out of milk, and this is called the death in the kiss. This is the one which was granted to my prayer."

Concerning the words in the Scriptures: "He is thy psalm and
He is thy God," Rabbi Pinhas said the following:
"He is your psalm and he also is your God. The prayer a man
says, the prayer, in itself, is God. It is not as if you were asking
something of a friend. He is different and your words are
different. It is not so in prayer, for prayer unites the principles.
When a man who is praying thinks his prayer is something
apart from God, he is like a suppliant to whom the king gives
what he has begged from him. But he who knows that prayer
in itself is God, is like the king's son who takes whatever he
needs from the stores of his father."

The Prayerbook

In the days of Rabbi Pinhas, the prayer-book which is based
on the kavvanot of letters, and bears the name of Rabbi Isaak
Luria, the great Kabbalist, had just been published. The zaddik's disciples obtained his permission to pray from that book,
but after a time they came to him and complained that since
they were using it for their prayers, they had lost the sense of
intensified life which prayer had always given them. Rabbi
Pinhas told them: "You have put all the strength and pur-
posefulness of your thinking into the kavvanot of the holy
names, and the combinations of the letters, and have deviated
from the essential: to make your hearts whole and dedicate
them to God. That is why you have lost the live feeling of
holiness."

In Praise of Song

Rabbi Pinhas always spoke in high praise of music and song.
Once he said: "Lord of the world, if I could sing, I should
not let you remain up above. I should harry you with my song
until you came down and stayed here with us."

The One Thing

Once they told Rabbi Pinhas of the great misery among the
needy. He listened, sunk in grief. Then he raised his head.

"Let us draw God into the world," he cried, "and all need will be quenched."

Valid Prayer

Rabbi Pinhas said: "A prayer which is not spoken in the name of all Israel, is no prayer at all!"

When Two Sing

Rabbi Pinhas said: "When a man is singing and cannot lift his voice, and another comes and sings with him, another who can lift his voice, then the first will be able to lift his voice too. That is the secret of the bond between spirit and spirit."

The Ear That Is No Ear

Rabbi Pinhas said: "In the book *The Duties of the Heart*, we read that he who conducts his life as he ought, should see with eyes that are no eyes, hear with ears that are no ears. And that is just how it is! For often, when someone comes to ask my advice, I hear him giving himself the answer to his question."

The Quickening

They asked Rabbi Pinhas: "Why is it, that a person who sees his friend after an interval of more than twelve months, says the blessing: 'Who quickenest the dead.'"
He answered: "Every human being has a light in Heaven. When two meet, the lights fuse, and a new light shines out of them. This is called a begetting, and the new light is an angel. But this angel cannot live longer than twelve months, unless those two beings meet on earth again before the time is up. But if they meet after the twelve months have passed, they can quicken the angel again for a time. That is why they say that blessing."

Differences

Rabbi Rafael asked his teacher: "Why is no face like any other?" Rabbi Pinhas replied: "Because Man is created in the image of God. Every human being sucks the living strength of God from another place, and all together they make up Man. That is why their faces all differ from one another."

In Everyone

Rabbi Pinhas said: "In everyone there is something precious, which is in no one else. That is why it is said: 'Despise not any man.'"

And this is how he expounded the saying in the Talmud, that every just man "will burn himself with the baldachin of his neighbor." With the secret core of his neighbor, that is, with the precious thing hidden in the being of his neighbor, and—among all men—only in him.

The Water Carrier

The wife of Rabbi Pinhas once scolded her servant. This annoyed the rabbi and he said to her: "One should never hurt a Jew. A Jew is precious, very precious!" He pointed to a water carrier by the name of Hirsh, who was just taking a pail into the house. The man was very simple-minded, and still unmarried although he was about forty years old. The rabbi said to his wife: "I tremble before Hershele—because he is so precious!"

Country Houses

Rabbi Pinhas said: "God's relationship to the wicked may be compared to that of a prince who, besides his magnificent palaces, owns all manner of little houses hidden away in the woods and in villages, and visits them occasionally to hunt or to rest. The dignity of a palace is no greater than that of such a temporary abode, for the two are not alike, and what the lesser accomplishes, the greater cannot. It is the same with the righteous man. Though his value and service be great, he cannot accomplish what the wicked man accomplishes in the hour he prays, or does something to honor God, and God who is watching the worlds of confusion, rejoices in him. That is why the righteous man should not consider himself better than the wicked."

Concerning Anger

Rabbi Pinhas once said to a hasid: "If a man wishes to guide the people in his house the right way, he must not grow angry at them. For anger does not only make one's soul impure; it transfers impurity to the souls of those with whom one is angry."

Another time he said: "Since I have tamed my anger, I keep it in my pocket. When I need it, I take it out."

Gog

In the intermediate days of the Feast of Tabernacles, Rabbi Pinhas expounded the passage from Ezekiel which is read that week, and which deals with the coming of Gog and Magog. He said: "According to the tradition, the main battle in the wars of Gog falls within the days of the Feast of Tabernacles. People have a way of saying about persons or nations: 'He is as great as Gog; it is as great as Gog.' And why? Because Gog is great in arrogance and brutality. And that is the battle which we must fight at the Feast of Tabernacles: the battle against our own pride."

Endless Struggle

Rabbi Rafael, who was humble all of his days, and avoided being honored, begged his teacher over and over to tell him how he could wholly fend off pride, but received no answer. Again he pressed his master: "O rabbi—pride, pride!"

"What do you want?" said Rabbi Pinhas. "This is a piece of work with which a man must wrestle all his years, and which he can never finish. For pride is the garment of God, as it is written: 'The Lord is king; he is clothed in pride.' But God is boundless, and he who is proud, injures the garment of the unbounded. And so the work of self-conquest is without bounds."

Out of the Net

This was Rabbi Pinhas' comment on the verse in the psalm: "Mine eyes are ever toward the Lord; for he will bring forth my feet out of the net."

"As the bird-catcher baits the net, and the bird comes and pecks at it and tangles his foot in the cord, so the Evil Urge confronts men with all the good they have done: learning, charities, and all manner of devout actions, in order to snare them in the net of pride. But if he succeeds in this, man can free himself no more than the captive bird. Then nothing can save him except the help of God."

The Bees

Rabbi Rafael of Bershad said: "They say that the proud are reborn as bees. For, in his heart, the proud man says: 'I am a writer, I am a singer, I am a great one at studying.' And since what is said of such men is true: that they will not turn to God, not even on the threshold of hell, they are reborn after they die. They are born again as bees which hum and buzz: 'I am, I am, I am.'"

A Boon to God

Rabbi Rafael said:
"What a boon that God prohibited pride! If He had bidden us be proud, how could I possibly do God's commandment!"

What You Pursue

Rabbi Pinhas used to say: "What you pursue, you don't get. But what you allow to grow slowly in its own way, comes to you. Cut open a big fish, and in its belly you will find the little fish lying head down."

The Greater Strength

He also used to say: "The strength of him who accepts reproof is greater than his who reproves. For if a man humbles himself to accept reproof and to recognize the truth of it, then God's words apply to him: 'I dwell in the high and holy place, with him also that is of a contrite and humble spirit.'"

More Love

When Rabbi Pinhas and his disciples discussed wicked or hostile persons, they recalled the advice the Baal Shem Tov once gave to the father of a renegade son: that he should love him more. "When you see," they said, "that someone hates you and does you harm, rally your spirit and love him more than before. That is the only way you can make him turn. For the whole of Israel is a vehicle for holiness. If love and unity prevail among them, then the Divine Presence and all holiness is about them. But if—God forbid!—there should be a schism, a rift appears, and through the opening holiness falls down into the 'shells.' And so, if your neighbor grows remote from you in spirit, you must approach him more closely than before—to fill out the rift."

* * *

Rabbi Shemuel told this about Rabbi Rafael of Bershad: "When he was going on his summer trip, he called me and asked me to share his carriage with him. I said: 'I am afraid I should crowd you.' Then he said to me in the manner he always used to express special affection: 'Let us love each other more and we shall have a feeling of spaciousness.' And after we had prayed, he said to me: 'God is a great-hearted friend.' "

* * *

Rabbi Rafael said: "Measured behavior is a dreadful evil. It is a dreadful evil when a man measures his behavior to his fellow-men. It is as if he were always manipulating weights and measures."

* * *

Once Rabbi Rafael was ill, and thought he was going to die. Then he said: "Now all merits must be set aside, lest they separate my heart from the heart of any Jew in the world."

* * *

Rabbi Pinhas said: "We should also pray for the wicked among the peoples in the world; we should love them too. While we do not pray like this, while we do not love like this, the Messiah will not come."

* * *

He used to say: "My Rafael knows how to love the most wicked evil-doers!"

Concerning the words of the prayer: "He who maketh peace in his high places, may he make peace for us . . ." Rabbi Pinhas said: "We all know that Heaven (shamayim) came into being when God made peace between fire (esh) and water (mayim). And he who could make peace between the utmost extremes, will surely be able to make peace between us."

* * *

Rabbi Rafael of Bershad was very eager to make peace. He often went into the homes of the hasidim and addressed their wives, so that the readiness to keep peace with their husbands might grow in their hearts.

Once, on the ninth day of Av, the anniversary of the destruction of the Temple, he happened to be in a community whose members had for a long time been nursing a quarrel which grew more and more involved and difficult to end. One of the factions approached him with the request to arbitrate. "But the rabbi," so they said, "will probably not want to bother with our affairs in this period of mourning."

"No day is better than this," he replied. "For it was because of an idle quarrel that the city of God was destroyed."

* * *

On the sabbath, when the first chapter in the Scriptures, the story of creation, is read, the hasidim in Bershad sit in a circle all day, and sing over and over: "Sabbath of creation, all in one! sabbath of creation, all in one!"

The Most Important Quality

Rabbi Pinhas used to say: "I am always afraid to be more clever than devout." And then he added: "I should rather be devout than clever, but rather than both devout and clever, I should like to be good."

For Truth

Rabbi Pinhas told his disciples: "I have found nothing more difficult than to overcome lying. It took me fourteen years. I broke every bone I had, and at last I found a way out."

He also said: "For the sake of truth, I served twenty-one

years. Seven years to find out what truth is, seven to drive out falsehood, and seven to absorb truth."

* * *

Once, when Rabbi Pinhas was at the desk, reciting the Evening Prayer, and came to the words: "Who guardest thy people Israel," he screamed aloud from the very bottom of his soul. The countess who owned the region happened to be passing the House of Prayer. She leaned over one of the low window-sills and listened. Then she said to those around her: "How true that scream was! How without any admixture of falsehood!" When they repeated her remark to Rabbi Pinhas, he said with a smile: "Even the peoples of the world know the truth when they hear it."

* * *

On a certain eve of the Day of Atonement, before praying "All Vows," the assembled congregation recited the psalms in noisy confusion. Rabbi Pinhas turned to them and said: "Why do you exert yourselves so much? Probably because you feel that your words are not mounting upward. And why not? Because you have told nothing but lies the entire year. He who lies throughout the year, gets a lying tongue. And how can a lying tongue shape true words which mount to Heaven? I, who am talking to you, know all about it, because I myself had a hard time with this matter. So you can believe me: You must assume the burden of not telling lies. Then you will get a truthful tongue, and the words it shapes will fly to God."

With the Evil Urge

Once, when Rabbi Pinhas entered the House of Study, he saw that his disciples, who had been talking busily, stopped and started at his coming. He asked them: "What were you talking about?"

"Rabbi," they said, "we were saying how afraid we are that the Evil Urge will pursue us."

"Don't worry," he replied. "You have not gotten high enough for it to pursue you. For the time being, you are still pursuing it."

132

What Is Punishable

A certain zaddik died and soon after appeared in a dream to Rabbi Pinhas, who had been his friend. Rabbi Pinhas asked him: "What is the attitude toward the sins of youth?" "They are not taken seriously," said the dead man. "Not if a man has atoned. But false piety—that is punished with great severity."

The Pulpit

Once Rabbi Pinhas came into the House of Study and his glance fell on a pulpit. "This pulpit too," he said, "is judged on New Year's Day: whether it is to break or to be preserved."

The Barrier

Rabbi Pinhas said:

"On the sabbath, people come to hear words of teaching. They are full of fervor—and on the very first week-day everything is exactly as it was. For just as the senses, so memory too meets with a barrier. As soon as the holiness of the sabbath is over, all are a thousand miles away from it, and no one remembers it any more. It is as when a madman recovers: he is unable to remember what happened in the days of his madness."

The Pin in the Shirt

Once some women came to Rabbi Pinhas from a nearby town and bothered him with their trivial concerns. When he saw them at his door again on the following morning before prayer, he fled to his son's house and cried: "If only the Messiah came, so that we might get rid of the zaddikim, 'the good Jews.'" After a while, he added: "You think that it is the wicked who delay the coming of the Messiah. Not so—it is 'the good Jews' who are delaying it. A nail somewhere in the wall—what has that to do with me! But a pin sticking in my shirt—that's what pricks!"

Fame

The "Spola grandfather" said:
"To be famous is not a good thing.
"Once I went from town to town with the poor wayfarers. In

our wanderings we came to a town in which Rabbi Pinhas of Koretz was living at that time. There was feasting in his house and a large table was spread with food for the poor. I entered with the rest and sat down. Rabbi Pinhas himself went from one man to the next and gave each a cake. When he came to me, he raised me from the bench until I was level with his face, and kissed me on the forehead.

"When I was beginning to grow famous, I drove to his town to spend the sabbath with him. Dressed in a splendid robe, after the fashion of the famous, I approached and greeted him. He merely glanced at me and asked: 'Where are you from?'

"To be famous is not a good thing."

The Man Who Denies God

Rabbi Pinhas said: "Whoever says that the words of the Torah are one thing and the words of the world another, must be regarded as a man who denies God."

Dreams

Rabbi Pinhas said: "Dreams are a secretion of our thoughts and, through them, our thought is purified. All the wisdom in the world is a secretion of the Torah, and through it the Torah is purified. That is why we read: 'When the Lord brings back those that returned to Zion, we will be like unto them that dream.' For then it will be revealed that wisdom exists only that the Torah may be purified, and exile only that the thought of Israel may be purified, and all will be like a dream."

The Tongue of Tongues

They asked Rabbi Pinhas: "How are we to understand that before the building of the Tower of Babel, all men spoke one tongue in common, but that when God confounded their language, each group of people spoke its own tongue? How was it possible for each people suddenly to speak and understand a language of its own, instead of the tongue which had been common to them all?"

Rabbi Pinhas explained: "Before the building of the tower, all peoples had in common the holy tongue, but each people had its own language besides. That is why it is written: 'And the whole earth was of one language,' that is, the holy language, and 'of one speech' means that besides the holy language they had in common, each people had its own special tongue. This they used to communicate with one another, while the holy tongue was used between different peoples. When God punished them, he took from them the holy tongue."

Originality

Rabbi Pinhas said: "When a man embarks on something great, in the spirit of truth, he need not be afraid that another may imitate him. But if he does not do it in the spirit of truth, but plans to do it in a way no one could imitate, then he drags the great down to the lowest level—and everyone can do the same."

The Eunuchs

Once Rabbi Shmelke and his brother, who subsequently became the rabbi of Frankfort, drove to Rabbi Pinhas of Koretz in order to savor the true taste of the sabbath. They arrived on Friday and found the zaddik in the kitchen where, in honor of the holy hours to come, he was supervising the cooking of the fish. He greeted his guests with the words: "Isaiah says: 'Thus saith the Lord . . . concerning the eunuchs,' that is, those who cannot enjoy holy delight, 'let them keep my sabbaths.' Keep the sabbath and you will savor its full taste."

All Joys

Rabbi Pinhas said: "All joys hail from paradise, and jests too, provided they are uttered in true joy."

The Watchers

A wedding was once celebrated in the house of Rabbi Pinhas. The feasting went on for days, and the number of guests did not lessen, yet during all that time, nothing was damaged, not the smallest flask was broken. When the people expressed surprise at this, the rabbi said: "Why are you astonished? The dead are good watchers!" Now they understood why—while the dance was going on—he had called out: "You dead, you have nothing to do. Watch well that no damage is done!"

The Parting

Rabbi Leib, son of Sarah, the wandering zaddik, used to visit Rabbi Pinhas several times a year. They did not agree concerning worldly matters, because Rabbi Leib did his work all over the world, in a secret manner, while Rabbi Pinhas believed no one could do his work well except in that place which was appointed for him. But at parting he always said to his friend: "We shall never agree, but your work has Heaven for its goal, and my work has Heaven for its goal, and so we are united, and what we do is one and the same thing." Once Rabbi Leib came to Ostrog for the Day of Atonement. At the close of the service, he went to Rabbi Pinhas to exchange wishes for the coming year with him. The two closed the door and talked with each other for a time. When Rabbi Pinhas came out, his cheeks were wet and the tears still streamed from his eyes. As he accompanied Rabbi Leib out, the hasidim heard him say: "What can I do since it is your will to go first?" That year Rabbi Leib died toward the end of the winter, in the month Adar, and Rabbi Pinhas toward the end of summer, in the month Elul.

Mourning

In after years the hasidim related this incident. At the last bend in the road which leads to the west wall of the Temple, the "wailing wall," a zaddik saw a tall woman one evening. She was veiled from head to foot and wept softly to herself. Then his own eyes filled with tears and, for an instant, he could not see. When he looked up, the woman had vanished. "For whom can the Divine Presence be mourning, if not for Rabbi Pinhas!" he exclaimed to his soul, tore his robe, and said the blessing for the dead.

Testimony

Rabbi Rafael of Bershad was known far and wide for his integrity.

Once his testimony was to be the deciding factor in condemning a Jew who had been accused of a crime. Rabbi Rafael knew that the man was guilty. The night before the court was to assemble, he did not go to bed but struggled with himself in prayer until the dawn of day. Then he lay down on the floor, closed his eyes, and died on the instant.

YEHIEL MIKHAL OF ZLOTCHOV

The Want

In early life, Rabbi Yehiel Mikhal lived in great poverty, but not for an hour did happiness desert him.

Someone once asked him: "Rabbi, how can you pray day after day, 'Blessed be thou . . . who has supplied my every want?' For surely you lack everything a man has need of!" He replied: "My want is, most likely, poverty, and that is what I have been supplied with."

On Two Rungs

When Rabbi Mikhal was still poor and taught children in the city of Brusilov, a man who was fond of joking came to him on a Friday, toward evening, and asked him the following question: "How much effort and trouble must a poor man go through before he gets together what he needs for the sabbath! For the well-to-do burgher, on the other hand, it is no trouble at all. But when the sabbath arrives, and the poor man begins to study the tractate for the sabbath, the first thing he reads about are the circumstances under which a poor man who takes, becomes guilty of desecrating the sabbath, while the rich burgher who gives, is considered blameless. Why does it begin with the guilt of the poor man?"

In asking this, the man had nothing in mind but to make a jest, but Rabbi Mikhal took the question seriously. "Come and take the evening meal with me," he said. "I shall think it over until then." After the meal, he repeated the question and gave this answer: "The guilt of the poor man is mentioned in the beginning, because it is he who first stretched out his hand to take."

* * *

Many years later, while Rabbi Mordecai of Neskhizh was visiting his teacher Rabbi Mikhal, the maggid of Zlotchov, a devout and learned man came and asked for a little money. The maggid told Rabbi Mordecai to give him a small sum. A short time after this, a tramp who looked common and coarse also asked for alms. Rabbi Mikhal himself gave him something. When he was asked why he behaved differently in these two instances, he said: "Every act of charity can bring about a sacred union, if the hand of him who gives touches that of him who takes. But when the receiver is a man of slight value, then it is more difficult to accomplish this union."

The Cow

It is told:

During the years when the holy maggid of Zlotchov was still unrecognized, he was so poor that his wife had no shoes and went around in slippers she had made with her own hands. At that time he often fasted from one sabbath to the next, and did not come home from the House of Study the entire week. Each morning, his wife sold the milk of the one cow they owned, and with the proceeds supported herself and her children. One Friday morning the cow gave no milk, lay down, and did not move. After several hours, when all attempts to revive her had failed, the woman gave up in despair and hired a peasant to flay the animal. Before he had started on the job, Rabbi Mikhal came home. When he saw the cow lying in the courtyard he tapped her gently with his stick and said: "Hey there, get up! You have to provide for us!" And the cow got up.

The Baal Shem's Messenger

Before he was recognized, Rabbi Yehiel Mikhal lived in the city of Yampol, not far from Mezbizh, the city of the Baal Shem Tov. At that time the Baal Shem's hasidim included a cattle-dealer who used to come to his master before setting out on a business trip, in order to spend the sabbath near him. Once, when he was taking leave after a visit of this kind, the Baal Shem said to him: "When you get to Yampol, give Rabbi Mekhele my greetings."

But when he got to Yampol, the man asked around in vain

for a rabbi by that name. Finally he went to the House of Study and inquired there. "No," they said, "we have never heard of that rabbi." But someone added: "We do have a Mekhele here, but no one has ever called him 'rabbi.' As a matter of fact, the children call him 'the crazy man,' and no one except the children ever bothers about him. For how can one deal with a man who beats his head against the wall while he prays, until the blood spurts out!"

"I want to talk to him," said the cattle-dealer.

"That will not be so easy," they told him. "When he is at home and sitting over his books, he will not let anyone disturb him. But if you go up to him and whisper: 'I should like something to eat,' he will jump up to get food for his guest, and then you can talk to him."

The dealer asked the way to the "crazy man." He lived in a tumble-down house and ragged children were huddled at his door. Rabbi Mikhal was sitting at the table before an open book of the Kabbalah. He did not look up when his visitor entered. The man went up to him and said in a low tone: "I should like something to eat." Instantly the rabbi rose, looked around, and went through drawers and cupboards, but everything was empty. He picked up a book, ran out with it, took it to the store as a pledge, and brought back bread and herring. While his visitor ate, he said: "The Baal Shem Tov told me to give you his greetings." Rabbi Mikhal bowed his head in silence.

Later the cattle-dealer said: "Rabbi Mekhele, I see that you are a holy man, and since this is so, all you need do is to pray for wealth and you will have it. Why do you live in such want?"

"A king," replied the rabbi, "had made preparations for the wedding of his beloved daughter and invited all the people in the city where he lived into his palace. And inscribed on each invitation was the menu of the wedding-feast. But suddenly the princess fell ill. No doctor could do anything for her, and a few hours later she died. Quietly the people who had gathered for the celebration dispersed. They were full of sorrow for the death of their dear and lovely princess. Only one guest stayed. Holding his invitation in his hand, he asked to be served the entire menu, and they did as he asked. There he sat and smacked his lips over his food in shameless pleasure. Shall I behave as he, now that the Divine Presence, which is the Community of Israel, is in exile?"

Refusal

The people of a certain city begged the Baal Shem Tov to induce his disciple Yehiel Mikhal to accept the position of rabbi, which they had offered him. The Baal Shem Tov urged him to accept, but he persisted in his refusal. "If you do not listen to me," said his master, "you will lose this world and the coming world too."
"Even if I lose both worlds," answered his disciple, "I shall not accept what does not befit me."
"Then, receive my blessing, my son," said the Baal Shem, "that you have withstood temptation."

The Revealed Secret

Rabbi Hayyim, the famous head of the Talmudic Academy in Brody, heard of the powerful effect the exhortations of young Rabbi Mikhal had on his hearers. Since the number of evil-doers in Brody was increasing, he asked him to speak in the great House of Prayer on the coming sabbath, and ordered the entire congregation to attend. Rabbi Mikhal ascended the pulpit and put his head down on the desk. For a good while he stood in that position. The congregation became impatient, and the worst of the ne'er-do-wells were most indignant that so young a man had the impudence to make them wait. Some of them went up to him to snatch him from the pulpit, but they did not dare carry out their purpose when they saw the director of the Talmudic Academy leaning against a pillar of the pulpit and clasping it with his hands. At last Rabbi Mikhal raised his head: "It is written," he said: " 'The secret counsel of the Lord is with them that fear Him.' Secret transgressions He reveals to those who fear him, that their warning

may strike straight into the hearts of the transgressors."
Everyone in the House of Prayer heard these words, although
they were uttered in a low voice, and there was not one who
could keep back the tears welling in his eyes.

Through the Hat

Once Rabbi Mikhal visited a city where he had never been
before. Soon some of the prominent members of the congregation came to call on him. He fixed a long gaze on the forehead of everyone who came, and then told him the flaws in his
soul and what he could do to heal them. It got around that
there was a zaddik·in the city who was versed in reading faces,
and could tell the quality of the soul by looking at the forehead. The next visitors pulled their hats down to their noses.
"You are mistaken," Rabbi Mikhal said to them. "An eye
which can see through the flesh, can certainly see through the
hat."

The Time Rabbi Elimelekh Was Frightened

In his later years, Rabbi Elimelekh of Lizhensk, who was on
a journey, met a young man with a knapsack on his back.
"Where are you bound for?" he asked him.
"I am going to the holy maggid of Zlotchov," was the reply.
"When I was young," said Rabbi Elimelekh, "I heard one day
that Rabbi Yehiel Mikhal was visiting a town not far from
Lizhensk. I immediately started on my way there. When I
arrived, I looked for a place to stay, but all the houses were
empty. Finally I found a very old woman busy at her stove.
This is what she told me: 'Everyone has gone to the House of
Prayer. There's a rabbi there who has made the day into a
Day of Atonement. There he stands and is telling everyone his
sins, and praying forgiveness for everyone.' When I heard
that, I was frightened and went back to Lizhensk."

Heavy Penance

There was once a man who had desecrated the sabbath against
his will because his carriage had broken down, and although

he walked and almost ran, he did not reach the town before the beginning of the holy hours. For this, young Rabbi Mikhal imposed a very harsh and long penance on him. The man tried to do as he had been told with all his strength, but he soon found that his body could not endure it. He began to feel ill, and even his mind became affected. About this time he learned that the Baal Shem was traveling through this region and had stopped in a place nearby. He went to him, mustered his courage, and begged the master to rid him of the sin he had committed. "Carry a pound of candles to the House of Prayer," said the Baal Shem, "and have them lit for the sabbath. Let that be your penance." The man thought the zaddik had not quite understood what he had told him and repeated his request most urgently. When the Baal Shem insisted on his incredibly mild dictum, the man told him how heavy a penance had been imposed on him. "You just do as I said," the master replied. "And tell Rabbi Mikhal to come to the city of Chvostov where I shall hold the coming sabbath." The man's face had cleared. He took leave of the rabbi. On the way to Chvostov, a wheel broke on Rabbi Mikhal's carriage and he had to continue on foot. Although he hurried all he could, it was dark when he entered the town, and when he crossed the Baal Shem's threshold, he saw he had already risen, his hand on the cup, to say the blessing over the wine to introduce the day of rest. The master paused and said to Rabbi Mikhal who was standing before him numb and speechless: "Good sabbath, my sinless friend! You had never tasted the sorrow of the sinner, your heart had never throbbed with his despair—and so it was easy for your hand to deal out penance."

To Himself

In a sermon which Rabbi Mikhal once gave before a large gathering, he said: "My words shall be heeded." And he added immediately: "I do not say: 'You shall heed my words,' I say: 'My words shall be heeded.' I address myself too! I too must heed my words!"

143

They asked the maggid of Zlotchov: "All the commandments are written in the Torah. But humility, which is worth all the other virtues put together, is not stated in it as a commandment. All we read about it is the words in praise of Moses, saying that he was more humble than all other people. What is the significance of this silence concerning humility?"

The rabbi replied: "If anyone were humble in order to keep a commandment, he would never attain to true humility. To think humility is a commandment is the prompting of Satan. He bloats a man's heart telling him he is learned and righteous and devout, a master in all good works, and worthy to think himself better than the general run of people; but that this would be proud and impious since it is a commandment that he must be humble and put himself on a par with others. And a man who interprets this as a commandment and does it, only feeds his pride the more in doing so."

The Help Meet

The maggid of Zlotchov was asked by one of his disciples: "The Talmud says that the child in the womb of his mother looks from one end of the world to the other, and knows all the teachings, but that the instant it comes in contact with the air of earth, an angel strikes it on the mouth, and it forgets everything. I do not understand why this should be: first know everything and then forget it?"

"A trace is left behind in man," the rabbi answered, "by dint of which he can re-acquire knowledge of the world and the teachings, and do his service."

"But why must the angel strike him?" asked the disciple. "If this were not so, there would be no evil."

"Quite true," the rabbi answered. "But if there were no evil, there would be no good, for good is the counterpart of evil. Everlasting delight is no delight. That is how we must interpret what we are taught: that the creation of the world took place for the good of its creatures. And that is why it is written: 'It is not good that the man'—that is to say the primal man

God created—'should be alone,' that is, without the counter-effect and the hindrance of the Evil Urge, as before the creation of the world. For there is no good, unless its counterpart exists. And further on we read: 'I will make him a help meet for him'—the fact that evil confronts good gives man the possibility of victory: of rejecting evil and choosing good, and only then does the good exist truly and perfectly."

Man and the Evil Urge

This is what Rabbi Mikhal said concerning the verse in the Scriptures: "Let us take our journey, and let us go, and I will go before thee."

"That is what the Evil Urge says to man secretly. For this Urge is to become good and wants to become good by driving man to overcome it, and to make it good. And that is his secret request to the man he is trying to seduce: 'Let us leave this disgraceful state and take service with the Creator, so that I too may go and mount with you rung by rung, although I seem to oppose, to disturb, and hinder you.' "

Multiply

A disciple tells:
Once, when my teacher Rabbi Yehiel Mikhal was in his prayer room in Brody, he heard a man reciting the six hundred and thirteen commandments. He said jestingly: "Why are you reciting the commandments? They were given to do, not to recite!" I asked him what he meant by this, whether we are not supposed to teach and learn the commandments too. "In the case of every commandment," he said, "we should try to discover how it can be done. Let us begin with the first of all commandments: 'Be fruitful and multiply.' Why do you think two verbs are used here instead of one?" I was silent because I was ashamed to speak, but when he repeated his question, I said: "Rashi interprets it in this way: If it only said 'be fruitful,' we might think that one man should always beget only one child." "But then," he objected, "it would be enough to say merely: 'multiply.' "

145

The son of Rabbi Zusya of Hanipol, who was also saying his prayers there, pointed out that in another passage, it is written: "And I will . . . make you fruitful and multiply you," that here also two verbs were used.

"This too is difficult," said Rabbi Mikhal and again put his question to me. I mentioned that Rashi refers the words 'and will multiply you' to the upright posture which distinguishes man from animals.

"But what has it to do with upright posture?" asked the rabbi. I did not know what to say. He said: "This is the way Rabbi Mendel of Primishlan expounded the verse in the Mishnah: 'He who rides the ass shall dismount and pray,' that is, 'he who masters the animal within him, need not suppress it, since—in an eternal prayer—he is devoted and consecrated to God in all that he does, and has become freed of his body.' Thus man can perform bodily acts in this world. He can cohabit, and though—seen from the outside—his movements may be those of an animal, within he is free as an angel, for in what he does, he is devoted and consecrated to God. And this is what is meant by the commandment: 'Be fruitful,' not like animals—but 'multiply,' and that means be *more* than they! Do not walk bent over, but upright, and cling to God as the bough clings to the root, and consecrate your cohabitation to him. This is the will of God; not only to make us fruitful, but to multiply our powers."

Learn from All

They asked Rabbi Mikhal: "In the Sayings of the Fathers we read: 'Who is wise?' He who learns from all men, as it is said, 'From all my teachers I have gotten understanding.' Then why does it not say: 'He who learns from every teacher'?"

Rabbi Mikhal explained: "The master who pronounced these words, is intent on having it clear that we can learn not only from those whose occupation is to teach, but from every man. Even from one who is ignorant, or from one who is wicked, you can gain understanding as to how to conduct your life."

146

Rabbi Yehiel Mikhal said:

"The words in the Scriptures: 'But ye that cleave unto the Lord your God are alive every one of you this day,' is expounded as follows: 'Cleave to his qualities.' But this must be properly understood. Emanating from God are ten qualities and these come in twos which oppose each other like two colors, one of which is apparently in direct contrast to the other. But seen with the true inner eye, they all form one simple unity. It is the task of man to make them appear a unity to the true outer eye, as well. Perhaps one man finds it difficult to be merciful, because his way is to be rigorous, and another finds it difficult to be rigorous because his way is merciful. But he who binds the rigor within him to its root: to the rigor of God, and the mercy which is in him to its root: to the mercy of God, and so on in all things, such a man will unite the ten qualities within himself, and he himself will become the unity they represent, for he cleaves to the Lord of the world. Such a man has become wax into which both judgment and mercy can set their seal."

Imitation of the Fathers

The maggid of Zlotchov was asked by one of his disciples: "In the book of Elijah we read: 'Everyone in Israel is in duty bound to say: When will my work approach the works of my fathers, Abraham, Isaac and Jacob.' How are we to understand this? How could we ever venture to think that we could do what our fathers could?"

The rabbi expounded: "Just as our fathers invented new ways of serving, each a new service according to his own character: one the service of love, the other that of stern justice, the third that of beauty, so each one of us in his own way shall devise something new in the light of the teachings and of service, and do what has not yet been done."

Not for Wages

They asked the maggid of Zlotchov: "It is written: 'If ye walk in My statutes, and keep My commandments, and do them;

then I will give your rains in their season, and the land shall yield her produce, and the trees of the field shall yield their fruit.' How is it that God promises us wages for serving him? For our sages have told us that we shall not be like servants who serve their master on condition that they receive wages." The zaddik made this reply: "It is true that whoever does a commandment for the sake of gain, even if it be gain in the coming world, gets nothing, for all he wanted to do was serve himself. But he who does a commandment out of the true fear and love of God, his doing shines out into the world and draws an abundance of blessings down upon it. Thus the favor of Heaven and earth is a sign of right doing, not for sake of gain, but for the sake of God himself. That is why it is written: 'I have set before thee life and death, the blessing and the curse; therefore choose life that thou mayst live, thou and thy seed!' Choose the deed of life which brings abundance of life into the world!"

With

This is what Rabbi Mikhal said concerning the verse in the psalm, "Thou hast dealt well with thy servant":
"What you have done, O Lord, can be designated by the word 'with.' When your servant does your commandment, you are acting along with him. But you give him credit for doing it, as though he had acted alone, without your help."

The Nature of the Teachings

No matter what book Rabbi Mikhal was reading, whether a book of the open or the hidden teachings, everything he read seemed to him to point to the service of God. When one of his disciples asked him how this was possible, he replied: "Could there be anything in the teachings which does not point out to us, how to serve God?"

Our Disgrace

Rabbi Mikhal said: "This is our disgrace, that we fear anyone besides God. That is what is said of Jacob in the words: 'Then

Jacob was afraid and he was distressed.' We must be distressed because of our fear of Esau."

Keeping the Law

Disciples asked the maggid of Zlotchov: "In the Talmud we read that our Father Abraham kept all the laws. How could this be, since they had not yet been given to him?"

"All that is needful," he said, "is to love God. If you are about to do something and you think it might lessen your love, then you will know it is sin. If you are about to do something and think it will increase your love, you will know that your will is in keeping with the will of God. That is what Abraham did."

Between

Concerning the verse in the Scriptures: "I stood between the Lord and you," Rabbi Mikhal of Zlotchov said: "The 'I' stands between God and us. When a man says 'I' and encroaches upon the word of his Maker, he puts a wall between himself and God. But he who offers his 'I'—there is nothing between him and his Maker. For it is to him that the words refer: 'I am my beloved's and his desire is toward me.' When my 'I' has become my beloved's, then it is toward me that his desire turns."

Sanctification of God

The disciples of the maggid of Zlotchov asked him: "Concerning the words in the Scriptures: 'Ye shall be holy; for I the Lord your God am holy,' the Midrash comments: 'My holiness is beyond your holiness.' But who does not know this? What do we learn through this?"

He expounded: "This is what is meant: My holiness, which is the world, depends upon your holiness. As you sanctify my name below, so is it sanctified in the heights of Heaven. For it is written: 'Give ye strength unto God.'"

The Praying Rabbi

They asked Rabbi Yehiel Mikhal why he was delaying the prayer. He answered: "We are told that the tribe of Dan went last of all the wandering tribes and gathered up everything they had lost. The children of Dan gathered up all the prayers which had been said by the sons of Israel without true fervor, and, therefore, were lying on the ground. That is just what I am doing."

* * *

He expounded the passage in the Talmud which states that the first hasidim waited for a time before they began to pray, in order to concentrate their hearts on God: "During the time they were waiting, they prayed to God to help them concentrate their hearts on him."

* * *

Before beginning to pray, he was in the habit of saying: "I join myself to all of Israel, to those who are more than I, that through them my thought may rise, and to those who are less than I, so that they may rise through my thought."

* * *

Concerning the heading of the psalm, "A prayer of the afflicted when he fainteth," he said: "Join yourself to the prayer of the afflicted and you will cleave to God."

* * *

The Evil Urge once came to him while he was praying. "Go away," he said to it, "and come back when I am eating. While one is praying, there must be no arguments."

* * *

His disciples asked him: "Why is 'every knee shall bow to thee,' mentioned first in the prayer? Why does 'every stature shall prostrate itself before thee alone,' come second? Why is the word 'alone' used only in the one case and not in the other?" He explained: "Knees must be bowed before a king of flesh and blood, so that the gesture of homage can be seen. But only before the King of Kings, only before Him who examines the heart, can what is upright remain upright and yet, in reality, be bowed before Him."

* * *

To Rabbi Wolf of Zbarazh, one of his five sons, Rabbi Mikhal once said: "When I had risen in prayer, and was standing in the hall of truth, I begged God to grant me that my reason might never proceed against his truth."

The Rich Man

Once when Rabbi Mikhal was in the city of Brody on a long visit, he made a habit of praying in the "Klaus" which went by the name of "Hasidim-Study" although many opponents of the hasidic teachings attended the daily service there. Now Rabbi Mikhal did not arrive in the House of Prayer until noon, and even after he had put the prayer shawl over his shoulder, he waited for quite a while before he put it on, bound on the phylacteries, and commenced to pray. His learned enemies were annoyed at this but did not venture to question him themselves. After much reflection and considerable discussion, they sent a rich man, by the name of Zalman Perles, to the rabbi. He went up to the zaddik and asked in respectful tones: "We do not quarrel with the fact that you do not come to the House of Prayer until noon, for, most likely, you are not ready in your heart before then. But what does surprise us is that when you have come, you stand there for such a long time before you finally begin to pray. Why do you do this, and what does it mean?"

Rabbi Mikhal asked in his turn: "Is there no one more learned than you here, to put this question to me?"

"Yes, indeed!" answered Perles. "There are men here, so learned, that I do not reach even to their ankles."

"And why," said the zaddik, "don't they ask me?"

"Well," the other replied, "they are poor, and they have broken hearts—as poor men have. But I am rich and my heart is sound."

"Well, then," said the rabbi, "you yourself admit that the teachings do not ask me why I delay my prayer; only sixty thousand rubles are asking me. But sixty thousand rubles shall not have the pleasure of hearing me reveal why I delay my prayer."

The Great Chorus

Rabbi Mordecai of Kremnitz, the son of Rabbi Mikhal, related: "My father used to intone the verse in the psalm: 'My mouth shall speak the praise of the Lord,' as a question. 'We ask ourselves,' he explained to me, 'how our mouth can speak the praise of God. For do not the seraphim and the hosts of Heaven tremble and grow faint at the greatness of his name? To this the Scriptures reply: And let all flesh bless His holy name. All flesh, all that is living—just because it is flesh, it is called upon to praise Him. We read in the Section of Songs that even the smallest earthworm chants a song to Him. All the more man, who has been granted the power to think up more and more new ways of praising his Maker.' "

Participation

This was Rabbi Mikhal's comment on the words of Hillel, "If I am not for myself, who will be for me? And if I am for myself, what am I?" " 'If I am not for myself,' that is, if I do not work for myself alone, but continually participate in the congregation, 'who will be for me?' In that case, whatever 'who,' that is, whatever any member of the congregation does in my place, counts just as though I had done it myself. But if I am 'for myself'—if I do not participate with others, if I do not join with them, 'what am I?' Then everything in the way of good works which I have wrought alone is less than nothing in the eyes of God, who is the source of all good."

The Naming

They asked the maggid of Zlotchov: "We read in the Scriptures that God brought the animals to Adam that he might name them. And why does it say that whatsoever the man called a creature, according to its living soul, that was to be his name. What is meant by 'living soul'?"
He replied: "You know that every being has the root of its soul, from which it receives its life, in the upper worlds. Now Adam knew the soul-roots of all creatures and gave each its right name, each according to its living soul."

Dubious Faith

A disciple asked the maggid of Zlotchov: "The words in the Scriptures that Noah went into the ark 'because of the waters of the flood' Rashi interprets to the effect that Noah had small faith. He believed, and yet he did not believe, and not until the waters of the flood compelled him, did he go into the ark. Shall we really count Noah, that righteous man, among those who were small of faith?"

The zaddik replied: "There are two sorts of faith: simple faith, which accepts the word and waits to see it fulfilled, and working faith whose power contributes to the fulfillment of that which is to be. With all his heart Noah feared to believe in the coming of the flood, so that his faith might not make that coming more sure. And so he believed and did not believe, until the waters compelled him."

Up the Mountain

Rabbi Yehiel Mikhal said: "It is written: 'Who shall ascend into the mountain of the Lord? And who shall stand in His holy place?' For the sake of comparison, let us take a man who rides up a mountain in his carriage, and when he is half-way up, the horses are tired and he must stop and give them a rest. Now, whoever has no sense at this point, will roll down. But he who has sense will take a stone and put it under the wheel while the carriage is standing. Then he will be able to reach the top. The man who does not fall, when he is forced to interrupt his service, but knows how to pause, will get to the top of the mountain of the Lord."

Temptation

Rabbi Mikhal said: "When the Evil Urge tries to tempt man to sin, it tempts him to become all too righteous."

The Hair Shirt

Rabbi Yudel, a man known for his fear of God and the harsh penances he imposed on himself, once came to visit the maggid of Zlotchov. Rabbi Mikhal said to him: "Yudel, you are wearing a hair shirt against your flesh. If you were not given to sudden anger, you would not need it, and since you are given to sudden anger, it will not help you."

His Sleep

The Rabbi of Apt told, "When my teacher, Rabbi Yehiel Mikhal slept, he looked like one or the other of the angel-beings of the chariot of God: sometimes he had the face of the spiritual animals and sometimes that of the holy wheel-beings; the one when he wanted to mount to the firmament, the other when a call from the firmament reached him."

The Sabbath of Rest

A hasid asked the maggid of Zlotchov: "Rashi, our teacher, says: 'What was lacking in the created world? Nothing but rest. Came the sabbath, and so rest came.' Why does he not just say: 'The world lacked rest until the sabbath came?' For the words 'sabbath' and 'rest' mean exactly the same thing."

"Sabbath," replied the rabbi, "means the homecoming. On that day all the spheres return to their true place. That is what Rashi refers to: during the week, the spheres find no rest because they have been lowered from the place which is theirs. But on the sabbath they find rest because they are allowed to go home."

Satan's Hasidim

In his old age, Rabbi Mikhal fasted on many occasions. Finally one of his disciples ventured to ask him the reason for this self-mortification. The rabbi answered: "I must tell you that Satan has made up his mind to rid the world of hasidim. First he tried to harass us: he instigated persecutions; he had us maligned and denounced. He fanned the flames of enmity in houses and alleys, and thought that in these ways he could make us despair, that we should grow exhausted, and become renegades. But when he realized that his plan had miscarried, and that the ranks he had wanted to weaken, were strengthened, he thought up something new. He decided to make hasidim of his own. Soon after, thousands of Satan's hasidim spread over the land and joined forces with the true hasidim, so that truth was mixed with falsehood. That is why I fasted. I thought I could thwart this plan of his too. But now I shall not fast any more, for I see that I cannot keep Satan from continuing to make his own hasidim. But those who consecrate and truly dedicate themselves to the service of God—those God will separate from the false hasidim. He will light their eyes with the light of His face, so that for them truth will not be mixed with lies."

The Suns and the Earth

Rabbi Mikhal said:
"In every generation there are great zaddikim who shirk the work of salvation by devoting themselves to the Torah. As they fulfil the commandments, each of them ponders on what holy place his soul came from, and is intent on having it go home to that place after its earthly journey is accomplished, to rejoice in the light of heavenly wisdom. That is why to such a man the things of this earth are as nothing. And though he is saddened by the misery among men and the bitter exile of Israel, this is not enough to move his heart to dare in prayer what must be dared. All his great longing is directed solely to his own homecoming, as it is written: 'One generation passeth away, and another generation cometh; and the earth abideth forever. The sun also riseth and the sun goeth down, and hasteth to his place where he ariseth.' Suns rise and go down and let the misery on earth endure."

Banishment and Salvation

A disciple asked the maggid of Zlotchov: "God said to Moses: 'Now shalt thou see what I shall do to Pharaoh; for by a strong hand shall he let them go, and by a strong hand shall he drive them out of his land.' Need the thrall who is freed from heavy servitude be driven into freedom? Will he not hasten from it as the bird from the snare?"

"When Israel is banished," said the maggid, "it is always because it has put the ban on itself, and only when Israel dissolves this self-imposed ban, does it attain to salvation. When it overcomes the power of evil within itself, the demonic power of evil is broken, and instantly the rulers of earth also lose their power to subjugate Israel. Because Israel in Egypt was not will-

155

ing to return from spiritual exile, Moses said to the Lord: '. . . neither hast thou delivered thy people at all.' This means: 'It is not you who can deliver them.' But God replies: 'Now shalt thou see . . .' And he, who is more powerful than all the powers, keeps the covenant. He casts his great light on the demonic power of Egypt and dazzles it. But the holy sparks which were banned into it, awake; each finds its kin. The sparks behold the primal light and flame toward it, until the demonic power cannot endure them any longer and is forced to drive them out. And the moment this happens above, it also happens below in Israel and in Pharaoh. This is the significance of the plagues."

The Blessing

Rabbi Mikhal once said to his sons: "My life was blessed in that I never needed anything until I had it."

Love for Enemies

Rabbi Mikhal gave this command to his sons: "Pray for your enemies that all may be well with them. And should you think this is not serving God, rest assured that more than all prayers, this is, indeed, the service of God."

Willing

In the last two years before his death, Rabbi Mikhal fell into a trance of ecstasy time after time. On these occasions, he went back and forth in his room, his face aglow with inner light, and one could see that he was clinging to a higher life rather than to earthly existence, and that his soul had only to make one small step to pass into it. That is why his children were always careful to rouse him from his ecstasy at the right moment. Once, after the third sabbath meal, which he always had with his sons, he went to the House of Study as usual, and sang songs of praise. Then he returned to his room and walked up and down. At that time, no one was with him. Suddenly his daughter, who was passing his door, heard him repeat over and over: "Willingly did Moses die. Willingly did Moses die." She was greatly troubled and called one of her brothers. When he entered, he found his father lying on the floor on his back, and heard him whisper the last word of the confession "One," with his last breath.

From World to World

Many years after Rabbi Mikhal's death, young Rabbi Zevi Hirsh of Zhydatchov saw him in a dream. The dead man said to him: "Know, that from the moment I died, I have been wandering from world to world. And the world which yesterday was spread over my head as Heaven, is today the earth under my feet, and the Heaven of today is the earth of tomorrow."

"After He Had Gone in to Bath-sheba"

To Rabbi Aaron Leib of Primishlan, a disciple of the maggid of Zlotchov, came a man on whose face he read signs of having comitted adultery. When he had talked with his caller for a time, he said to him: "It is written: 'A Psalm of David; when Nathan the prophet came unto him, after he had gone in to Bath-sheba.' What can this mean? It means that Nathan chose the right way to move David to turn to God. Had he confronted him publicly and as his judge, he would only have hardened his heart. But he came to censure David in secrecy and love, just as David himself had gone in to Bath-sheba. And then his censure went to the king's heart and melted and recast it, and from it mounted the song of one recast and turned to God." When Rabbi Aaron Leib finished speaking, the man confessed his sin and turned wholly to God.

ZEV WOLF OF ZBARAZH

In the Last Hour

On a certain New Year's night, the maggid of Zlotchov saw a
man who had been a reader in his city, and who had died a
short time ago. "What are you doing here?" he asked.

"The rabbi knows," said the dead man, "that in this night, souls
are incarnated anew. I am such a soul."

"And why were you sent out again?" asked the maggid.

"I led an impeccable life here on earth," the dead man told
him.

"And yet you are forced to live once more?" the maggid went
on to ask.

"Before my death," said the man, "I thought over everything I
had done and found that I had always acted in just the right
way. Because of this, my heart swelled with satisfaction and in
the midst of this feeling I died. So now they have sent me back
into the world to atone for my pride."

At that time a son was born to the maggid. His name was Rabbi
Wolf. He was very humble.

His Tears

In his childhood, Rabbi Zev Wolf, the youngest of Rabbi Yehiel
Mikhal's five sons, was a wild and self-willed boy. It was in
vain that his father tried to curb him. When he was almost thirteen years old and about to become a "son of commandment"
who would be responsible for himself and establish his own
relation toward the will of God, the zaddik ordered the verses
from the Scriptures written for the phylacteries the boy was to
wear from this time on. Then he bade the scribe bring him the
two empty boxes together with the verses from the Scriptures.
The scribe brought them. Rabbi Mikhal took the boxes in his
hand and looked at them for a long time. He bowed his head

over them and his tears flowed into them. Then he dried the boxes and put into them the verses from the Scriptures. From the hour the boy Wolf put on the phylacteries for the first time, he grew tranquil and was filled with love.

The Servant

Rabbi Wolf's wife had a quarrel with her servant. She accused the girl of having broken a dish and wanted her to pay for the damage. The girl, on the other hand, denied having done what she was accused of, and refused to replace the article. The quarrel became more and more heated. Finally the wife of Rabbi Wolf decided to refer the matter to the court of arbitration of the Torah, and quickly dressed for a visit to the rav of the town. When Rabbi Wolf saw this, he too put on his sabbath clothes. When his wife asked him why, he told her that he intended accompanying her. She objected to this on the grounds that this was not fitting for him, and that besides, she knew very well what to say to the court. "You know it very well," the zaddik replied. "But the poor orphan, your servant, in whose behalf I am coming, does not know it, and who except me is there to defend her cause?"

The Radish Eater

At the third meal on the sabbath, an intimate and holy gathering, the hasidim at Rabbi Wolf's table carried on their conversation in a low voice and with subdued gestures so as not to disturb the zaddik who was deep in thought. Now, it was Rabbi Wolf's wish and the rule in his house that anyone could come in at any time, and seat himself at his table. On this occasion too, a man entered and sat down with the rest, who made room for him although they knew that he was an ill-bred person. After a time, he pulled a large radish out of his pocket, cut it into a number of pieces of convenient size, and began to eat with a great smacking of lips. His neighbors were unable to restrain their annoyance any longer. "You glutton," they said to him. "How dare you offend this festive board with your taproom manners?"

Although they had tried to keep down their voices, the zaddik soon noticed what was going on. "I just feel like eating a really good radish," he said. "I wonder whether anyone here could get me one?" In a sudden flood of happiness which swept away his embarrassment, the radish eater offered Rabbi Wolf a handful of the pieces he had cut.

The Coachman

On a freezing cold day, Rabbi Wolf drove to the celebration of a circumcision. When he had spent a little time in the room, he felt sorry for the coachman waiting outside, went to him, and said: "Come in and get warm."

"I cannot leave my horses alone," the man replied, moved his arms, and stamped his feet.

"I'll take care of them until you get warm and can relieve me again," said Rabbi Wolf. At first the coachman refused to consider such a thing, but after a while he allowed the rabbi to persuade him, and went into the house. There everyone who came, regardless of rank or whether or not he was known to the host, got all the food and drink he wanted. After the tenth glass, the coachman had forgotten who was taking his place with the horses, and stayed hour after hour. In the meantime, people had missed the zaddik but told themselves that he had had something important to attend to, and would return when he was through. A good deal later, some of the guests left. When they came out on the street, where night was already falling, they saw Rabbi Wolf standing beside the carriage, moving his arms and stamping his feet.

The Horses

When Rabbi Wolf drove out in a carriage, he never permitted the whip to be used on the horses. "You do not even have to shout at them," he instructed the coachman. "You just have to know how to talk to them."

The Quarrelers

Rabbi Wolf saw no evil in any man and regarded all human beings as righteous. Once, when two persons were quarreling,

160

and Rabbi Wolf was asked to side against the one who was guilty, he said: "According to me, one is as good as the other —and who would venture to come between two righteous men?"

The Gamblers

A hasid complained to Rabbi Wolf that certain persons were turning night into day, playing cards. "That is good," said the zaddik. "Like all people, they want to serve God and don't know how. But now they are learning to stay awake and persist in doing something. When they have become perfect in this, all they need do is turn to God—and what excellent servants they will make for him then!"

The Thieves

One night, thieves entered Rabbi Wolf's house and took whatever they happened to find. From his room the zaddik watched them but did not do anything to stop them. When they were through, they took some utensils and among them a jug from which a sick man had drunk that very evening. Rabbi Wolf ran after them. "My good people," he said, "whatever you have found here, I beg you to regard as gifts from me. I do not begrudge these things to you at all. But please be careful about that jug! The breath of a sick man is clinging to it, and you might catch his disease!"

From this time on, he said every evening before going to bed: "All my possessions are common property," so that—in case thieves came again—they would not be guilty of theft.

Renegades

A number of zaddikim met in Lwow and discussed the corrupt ways of the new generation. There were many who were giving up the holy customs, wearing shorter robes, cutting their beards and the curls at their temples, and would soon backslide spiritually as well. They thought it imperative to do something to stop the stones from crumbling, or else—on a day none too far off—the entire lofty structure would be bound to collapse. And so those who had met to confer on this matter resolved to set up solid bounds, and to make a beginning by forbidding renegades to appeal to the court of arbitration. But they agreed not to make this decision effective until they had the consent of Rabbi Wolf of Zbarazh. Several zaddikim reported to him the results of the meeting and made their request. "Do you think I love you more than them?" he asked. The decision was never put into effect.

Assistance

While Rabbi Wolf was on a journey, a poor young hasid came up to him and asked for financial assistance. The zaddik looked in his purse, put back a large coin he had happened to find, fetched out a smaller one and gave it to the needy young man. "A young man," he said, "should not have to be ashamed, but neither should he expect Heaven knows what." The hasid went from him with bowed head.

Rabbi Wolf called him back and asked: "Young man, what was that you were just thinking?"

"I have learned a new way to serve God," the other replied. "One should not be ashamed, and one should not expect Heaven knows what."

"That is what I meant," said the zaddik and accorded him help.

MORDECAI OF NESKHIZH

What Does It Matter

Before Rabbi Mordecai of Neskhizh had recognized his vocation, he ran a small business. After every trip he took to sell his wares, he set aside a little money to buy himself a citron for the Feast of Tabernacles. When he had managed to collect a few rubles in this way, he drove to the city and on the way there thought only of whether it would be vouchsafed him to buy the finest of the citrons for sale. Suddenly he saw a water vendor standing in the middle of the road and lamenting his horse which had collapsed. He left his carriage and gave the man all the money he had to buy himself another. "What does it matter?" he said to himself as he turned to go back home. "Everybody will say the blessing over the citron; I shall say mine over this horse!" But when he reached his house, he found a beautiful citron which friends, in the meantime, had brought him as a gift.

With the Prince of the Torah

To those who came to him to share the sabbath meal, Rabbi Mordecai rarely said words of teaching, and then only a very few. When one of his sons once ventured to ask him the reason for this restraint, he replied: "One must unite with the angel-prince of the Torah in order to receive in one's heart the word of teaching. Only then, does what one says enter the heart of one's hearers so that each receives what he requires for his own particular needs."

The Promise

Rabbi Mordecai used to say: "Whoever has eaten of my sabbath meal will not leave the world without having turned to God."

163

At Dawn

Once Rabbi Mordecai sat with his disciples all night until break of day. When he saw the light of dawn, he said: "We have not transgressed the bounds of day. Rather has day transgressed our bounds and we need not cede to it."

The Standard

Rabbi Mordecai of Neskhizh said to his son, the rabbi of Kovel: "My son, my son! He who does not feel the pains of a woman giving birth within a circuit of fifty miles, who does not suffer with her, and pray that her suffering may be assuaged, is not worthy to be called a zaddik."

His younger son Yitzhak, who later succeeded him in his work, was ten years old at the time. He was present when this was said. When he was old he told the story and added: "I listened well. But it was very long before I understood why he had said it in my presence."

Why People Go to the Zaddik

Rabbi Mordecai said: "People go to the zaddikim for many different reasons. One goes to the zaddik to learn how to pray with fear and love; another to acquire strength to study the Torah for its own sake. Still another goes because he wants to mount to a higher rung of spiritual life, and so on. But none of these things should be the true purpose of going, for each of them can be attained, and then it is no longer necessary to toil for it. The only, the true purpose, should be to seek the reality of God. No bounds are set to this, and it has no end."

The Fish in the Sea

Rabbi Yitzhak of Neskhizh told:

"Once my father said to one of his friends, in the month of Elul: 'Do you know what day this is? It is one of the days when the fish tremble in the ocean.'"

One of the men standing near Rabbi Yitzhak, observed: "People usualy say, 'when the fish tremble in the waters.'"

"The way my father said it," Rabbi Yitzhak replied, "that is the only way it expresses the secret of what occurs between God and the souls."

The Offering

This is how Rabbi Mordecai of Neskhizh expounded the words in the Scriptures: "And in your new moons ye shall present a burnt-offering unto the Lord."

If you want to renew your doing, offer up to God the first thought you have on awaking. God will help him who accomplishes this, to be bonded to Him the whole day, and to bind everything to that first thought.

Seeing and Hearing

A rabbi came to the zaddik of Neskhizh and asked: "Is it true, what people say, that you hear and see all things?"

"Think of the words of our sages," he replied, " 'a seeing eye, and a hearing ear.' Man has been so created that he can see and hear whatever he wants to. It is only a question of his not corrupting his eyes and his ears."

The Skull Cap

It is told:

A woman came to Rabbi Mordecai of Neskhizh and begged him with many tears to find out the whereabouts of her husband who had left her years ago and gone to a foreign country. "What makes you think I could help you?" said the zaddik. "Is he here? Is he perhaps in the water-barrel over there?"

Now, because her faith was great, the woman went to the water-barrel and looked in. "There he is!" she cried. "There he is, sitting in the water!"

"Has he a hat on?" asked the rabbi.

"Only his skull cap."

"Then fetch it."

The woman reached for it and drew it out. At the very same moment her husband, who was carrying on his tailor's trade in a far-away land, was sitting at the window of the house of a lord for whom he happened to be sewing, when a storm-wind rose and blew the cap off his head. The man shook in every limb. The core of his heart trembled and he started on his way home.

Lilith

They tell:

A man of whom Lilith had taken possession traveled to Neskhizh, where he wanted to beg Rabbi Mordecai to free him. The rabbi divined that this man was on the way to him and gave orders throughout the city to have all doors closed at nightfall, and to admit no one. When the man reached the city at dusk, he could not find a lodging, and had to lie down on some hay in a loft. Instantly Lilith appeared and said: "Come down to me."

He asked: "Why do you want to do that? Usually it is you who come to me."

"In the hay, on which you are lying," she replied, "is an herb which prevents me from coming near you."

"Which is it?" he asked. "I shall throw it away and then you will be able to come to me."

He showed her one herb after another, until she said: "That's the one!" Then he bound it to his breast and was free.

The Special Thing

The rabbi of Lublin once asked the rabbi of Apt, who was a guest in his house: "Do you know the old rabbi of Neskhizh?" "I do not know him," he replied. "But tell me: what is there so special about him that you asked me this?"

"The minute you made his acquaintance, you would know," said the rabbi of Lublin. "With him everything: teaching and prayers, eating and sleeping, is all in one piece, and he can elevate his soul to its origin."

Then the rabbi of Apt decided to go to Neskhizh. His carriage was at the door, when he heard that he had been denounced to the authorities and found it necessary to go to the official magistrate of the district. By the time he returned, it was two weeks before Passover and he again postponed his journey. After the holidays, he was told that the rabbi of Neskhizh had died in the week before Passover.

166

FROM THE CIRCLE OF THE BAAL SHEM TOV

Two Candle Holders

For many years Rabbi Moshe Hayyim Efraim, a grandson of the Baal Shem, and his wife lived in great poverty. On the sabbath eve she put the candles into a holder she herself had made out of clay. Later they grew wealthy. One sabbath eve when the rabbi entered the room on his return from the House of Prayer, he saw his wife looking at her wide-branched silver candelabra with joy and pride. "Now it all looks bright to you," he said. "But to me all looked bright in the days gone by."

When the Sabbath Was Over

Rabbi Barukh, a grandson of the Baal Shem told:
"A 'maggid,' a prophetic spirit, used to appear to the rav of Polnoye and teach him. But when the rav attached himself to my grandfather, the Baal Shem Tov, he took that maggid from him and gave him another, one of the Maggidim of Truth.

"Once Rabbi Pinhas of Koretz and I spent the sabbath with the rav of Polnoye. At the close of the sabbath, a messenger arrived to ask Rabbi Pinhas to go home at once, because of some urgent matter. The rav had retired to a room he always went to when he wished to give himself up to meditation. But Rabbi Pinhas could not bear to go away without taking leave of him. So he begged me to tell the rav of the message which had come, but I too hesitated. In the end both of us went to the door and listened. Inadvertently I touched the broken knob and the door flew open. Rabbi Pinhas fled in fright, but I stayed, stood still, and did not turn my eyes away."

So Be It

Rabbi Jacob Joseph, the rav of Polnoye, was once invited to a circumcision which was to take place in a nearby village.

167

When he arrived, one man was still lacking to make up the quorum of ten. The zaddik was very much annoyed that he was forced to wait. Waiting always displeased him. A heavy rain had been falling since early morning, and so they could not get hold of a passerby for quite a while. At last they saw a beggar coming down the street. When they asked him to attend the ceremony as the tenth man, he said: "So be it," and entered. When they offered him warm tea, he said: "So be it." After the circumsicion they invited him to the meal, and he gave the same reply. Finally his host asked him: "Why do you always say the same thing?" The man answered: "For it is written: 'Happy is the people with whom it is so!'" And with that he vanished before the eyes of all.

That night the rav could not sleep. Over and over he heard the beggar say "So be it," until it became manifest to him that it could have been none but Elijah who had come to reprove him for his tendency to grow annoyed. "Happy is the people that is in such a case," he whispered and instantly fell asleep.

The Book

The son of the rabbi of Ostrog told:

When the rav of Polnoye's book "The Genealogies of Jacob Joseph" appeared in print and my father got hold of it, he kept reading and re-reading it. Especially passages which begin: "This I heard from my teacher," he read until he knew them by heart. This went on for a year or even longer. Once, when he was again reading one of these passages, he realized that he did not understand it fully after all. He had the horses harnessed and drove to Polnoye. I was a boy at that time, and he took me with him. He found Rabbi Jacob Joseph ill and wretched. He was lying in his bed which was soon after to be his death-bed. The rav asked my father why he had come. When he was told the reason, he held the book in his arms and spoke in a voice full of strength, and his face was all spirit and flame. Before my very eyes his bed rose up from the ground.

168

It is told:

Rabbi Leib, son of Sarah, wandered about all the days of his life and never stayed in one place for any length of time. He often stopped in woods and caves, but he also came to cities and there secretly associated with certain intimate friends of his. He also never failed to appear wherever a large market was held. On such occasions, he rented a booth and stood in it from the beginning to the end of the market. Over and over his disciples begged him to tell them the purpose of this strange habit. Finally he yielded to their importunities.

A man with a heavy load on his shoulders was just passing by. Rabbi Leib called him and whispered in his ear for a while. Then he told his disciples to follow the man and observe him. They saw him go up to one of the merchants, set down his load, and heard him say that he did not want to be a servant any longer. The merchant shouted angrily at him and refused to pay him his due wages, but the man went silently away. Then the disciples who were following him saw that he was wearing a shroud. They ran up to him and adjured him to reveal his secret to them. "Hasty and transitory was my sojourn in the world of chaos," he said to them. "I did not know that I have been dead long since. Now the rabbi told me and has given me redemption."

To Expound Torah and to Be Torah

This is what Rabbi Leib, son of Sarah, used to say about those rabbis who expound the Torah: "What does it amount to— that they expound the Torah! A man should see to it that all his actions are a Torah and that he himself becomes so entirely a Torah that one can learn from his habits and his motions and his motionless clinging to God, that he has become like Heaven itself, of which it is said: 'There is no speech, there are no words, neither is their voice heard. Their line is gone out through all the earth, and their words to the end of the world.' "

Rabbi Arye of Spola, called the "Spola grandfather," had in his youth known the Baal Shem. One Passover, before the seder, he had his little son recite the mnemotechnical sentence in which the ritual actions are enumerated. When the boy was asked to explain the meaning of the word "kaddesh," "sanctify," he gave the customary response: "When the father returns from the House of Prayer, he should at once say kiddush, that is, say the benediction over the wine," and there he stopped.

The father asked him: "Why do you not add why he should at once say kiddush?"

"My teacher did not tell me anything more," said the boy. So his father taught him to add the words: "so that the little children may not fall asleep but ask the question they are supposed to: 'Why is this night different from all other nights?'"

The next day, when the children's teacher was a guest at the seder, the rabbi asked him why he did not teach the children to follow the word "kaddesh" by giving the reason for saying kaddesh, since this was the traditional sequence. The teacher replied that he had regarded this as superfluous because the rule did not hold only for those fathers who had little children in the house. "That is a grave error on your part," said the rabbi. "You are altering an old custom whose significance you have not plumbed. This is what it signifies: 'When the father returns from the House of Prayer,' that is, when our Father has seen and heard how everyone in Israel, no matter how tired he may be from the preparations for the Passover, said the Evening Prayer full of fervor, and when he now returns to his Heaven, 'he should at once say kiddush,' he should at once renew the holy marriage contracted when he said to Israel: 'And I will betroth thee unto Me for ever,' and redeem us in this very night 'the night of watching,' so that the little children, the people of Israel, may not fall into the deep sleep of despair, but receive a motive for asking their Father in Heaven: 'Why is the night of this exile different from all other nights?' " When the rabbi had said these words, he wept, raised his hands to Heaven, and cried: "Father, father, lead us from our exile, while that which is written still holds for us: 'I sleep, but my earth waketh!' Let us not fall utterly asleep!" All wept with him. But after a while, he roused himself and cried: "Now let us delight our Father and show him that his children can dance, even though they are in darkness." He gave orders to play a merry tune and began to dance.

The "Grandfather's" Dance

When the "Spola grandfather" danced on a sabbath and on feast-days, his feet were as light as those of a four-year-old. And not a single one of those who saw his holy dance failed to turn to God at that very instance, and with his whole soul, for he stirred the hearts of all who beheld him, to both tears and ecstasy.

Once Rabbi Shalom Shakhna, the son of Abraham the Angel, was his guest on a Friday evening. They had just made peace with each other after waging a long dispute. Rabbi Shalom sat there as always on the night of the sabbath, wholly surrendered to his clinging to God. The "grandfather" looked around joyfully as always, and both were silent. But when they had finished eating, Rabbi Arye Leib said: "Son of the Angel, can you dance?"

"I cannot dance," Rabbi Shalom replied.

Rabbi Arye Leib rose. "Then watch the Spola grandfather dance," he said. His heart immediately lifted his feet and he danced around the table. When he had moved once this way and once that, Rabbi Shalom jumped up. "Did you see how the old man can dance!" he called to the hasidim who had accompanied him. He remained standing and kept his eyes fixed on the feet of the dancer. Later he said to his hasidim: "You may believe me: he has made all his limbs so pure and so holy, that with every step he takes, his feet accomplish holy unifications."

Purim Games

At the Purim festival, the "Spola grandfather" was in the habit of organizing a special kind of games. He had a number of hasidim, carefully chosen and directed by him, disguise themselves, one as the "King of Purim," the rest as his princes and counsellors. These sat together in solemn session, in counsel or in judgment, had dicussions, and made resolutions and decisions. Sometimes the "grandfather" himself took part in the masquerade.

The hasidim tell that these games had a powerful effect which traveled through space: that they set at nought doom or the threat of doom decreed for Israel.

Leah and Rachel

In the days when young Nahum, later the Rabbi of Tchernobil, was privileged to live near the Baal Shem, Rabbi Israel ben Eliezer undertook one of his usual journeys. Nahum, who wanted very much to go too, kept walking around the waiting carriage. When the Baal Shem got in, he said to him: "If you can tell me the difference between that sequence of prayer in the Lamentations at Midnight, which bears Leah's name and that which bears Rachel's, you may come with me." Nahum replied without hesitation: "What Leah effects with her tears, Rachel effects with her joy." The Baal Shem at once asked him to get into the carriage.

The Zaddik and His Hasidim

Rabbi Yitzhak of Skvira, a grandson of Rabbi Nahum's, told: "In a small town, not far from Tchernobil, several hasidim of my grandfather's were seated together at the conclusion of the sabbath. They were all honest and devout men and at this meal of 'the escort of the queen,' they were casting the accounts of their souls. They were so humble and so full of the fear of God, that they thought they had sinned very greatly and agreed that there was no hope for them, and that their only consolation was that they were utterly devoted to the great zaddik Rabbi Nahum, and that he would uplift and redeem them. Then they decided that they must immediately go to their teacher. They started out right after the meal and together they went to Tchernobil. But at the end of that same sabbath, my grandfather was sitting in his house and casting the accounts of his

172

soul. Then in his humility and fear of God, it seemed to him that he had sinned very greatly, and that there was no hope for him except one: that those hasidim, so earnest in the service of God, were so deeply devoted to him, and that they would now comfort him. He went to the door and gazed in the direction his disciples lived, and when he had stood there a while, he saw them coming.

At this instant—so Rabbi Yitzhak ended his story—two arcs fused to a ring.

Words of Comfort

Several disciples of Rabbi Nahum of Tchernobil came to him and wept and complained that they had fallen prey to darkness and depression and could not lift up their heads either in the teachings or in prayer. The zaddik saw the state of their hearts and that they sincerely yearned for the nearness of the living God. He said to them: "My dear sons, do not be distressed at this seeming death which has come upon you. For everything that is in the world, is also in man. And just as on New Year's Day life ceases on all the stars and they sink into a deep sleep, in which they are strengthened, and from which they awake with a new power of shining, so those men who truly desire to come close to God, must pass through the state of cessation of spiritual life, and 'the falling is for the sake of the rising.' As it is written that the Lord God caused a deep sleep to fall upon Adam, and he slept and from his sleep he arose, a whole man."

The Quality of God

A Lithuanian once came to Rabbi Nahum of Tchernobil and complained that he had no money to marry off his daughter. The zaddik just happened to have fifty gulden put aside for another purpose. He let the poor man have the money and also gave him his silk robe, so that he might cut a fine figure at the wedding. The man took everything, went straight to an inn and began to drink vodka.

Some hours later, hasidim went to the inn and found him lying on the bench, thoroughly drunk. They took the rest of the money and the silk robe away from him, brought it all back to

Rabbi Nahum, and told him how his confidence had been abused. But the rabbi cried out angrily: "I just caught hold of the tail end of this quality of God's: 'He is good and beneficient to the wicked and to the good,' and you want to snatch it from my hands! Take everything back at once!"

The Rider in the Hen
It is told:
In the course of a journey, Rabbi Nahum was a guest in the house of another zaddik. They had a hen killed in his honor, and served it at the meal. He looked at it for a while and said: "In this fowl, I can see an armed man on horseback." They called the ritual slaughterer and he confessed that at the moment of slaughtering, he had been startled by an armed officer who came riding by, and that from then on he had thought of nothing but that.

Fire Against Fire
It is told:
Once, when the Baal Shem was on a journey, and stopped at the house of one of his disciples, Rabbi David Leikes, a government order was proclaimed to the effect that on a certain day, at noon, the Talmud was to be burned wherever a volume was found. On the morning of that day, Rabbi David hid his Talmud under the wash-tub. At twelve o'clock the bells began to chime. Pale as death he came into the room and saw his teacher calmly walking up and down. "With your fire," said the Baal Shem, "you have put out their fire." The order was rescinded.

The Rope Dancer
Once Rabbi Hayyim of Krosno, a disciple of the Baal Shem's, was watching a rope dancer together with his disciples. He was so absorbed in the spectacle that they asked him what it was that riveted his gaze to this foolish performance. "This man," he said, "is risking his life, and I cannot say why. But I am quite sure that while he is walking the rope, he is not thinking of the fact that he is earning a hundred gulden by what he is doing, for if he did, he would fall."

174

MENAHEM MENDEL OF VITEBSK

His Childhood

From the time he was eleven years old, Menahem studied in the house of the Great Maggid and was dear to him. One sabbath, after the midday meal, the maggid saw him walking up and down the room with a mischievous expression, his cap atilt on his head. He went to the threshold, put his hand on the door-knob, and asked: "How many pages of the Gemara did you learn today?"

"Six," said the boy.

"If," said the maggid, "after six pages, the cap slides to the edge, how many pages do you think are necessary to make it fall off?" Then he closed the door.

Menahem beat against it and said in tears: "Open, rabbi, and tell me what I must do."

The maggid opened the door. "I shall take you to my teacher, the holy Baal Shem," he said.

They arrived in Mezbizh on a Friday. The maggid at once went to the house of Baal Shem Tov. Menahem dressed himself and combed his hair with the greatest care, for this was a habit of his and remained so to his dying day. In the House of Prayer the Baal Shem Tov stood in front of the desk and waited with praying until the boy came. But he did not summon Menahem to him until after the conclusion of the sabbath. The maggid and Rabbi Jacob Joseph of Polnoye, the other great disciple of the Baal Shem, stood in front of their master. He called the boy, looked at him for a long time, and then told him a story about oxen and a plough. His listeners soon realized that it was a parable foretelling the life of Menahem, but the boy understood just so much of it as he had experienced up to this time. The rabbi of Polnoye understood half, and the maggid all.

Later the Baal Shem Tov said to the maggid: "This mischievous boy is full of reverence through and through."

More

On New Year's Day the Great Maggid did not blow the ram's horn himself. This was the office of his disciple Rabbi Menahem Mendel, and the maggid called out what he was to blow. In the last period of his life, when he could no longer walk about on his sore feet, he did this from his room. Once Rabbi Menahem Mendel was absent and Rabbi Levi Yitzhak was to take his place. He put the ram's horn to his lips, but when the maggid called out the first blast, Levi Yitzhak saw a dazzling light and fainted away. "What is the matter with him?" asked the maggid. "Mendel sees much more and still he is not afraid."

Pursued by Honors

The maggid of Mezritch once sent his disciple Rabbi Menahem on a journey to various communities. He was to speak in public and waken desire to study the Torah for its own sake. In one of the towns he visited, a number of learned men came to see Rabbi Mendel at his inn, and showered him with special honors. While talking to them, he brought up the question why it is said that when a man flees from honors, honors pursue him. "If it is good and seemly to be honored," he said, "why is he who flees from honors rewarded for his unseemly fears by having honors pursue him? But if it is wrong to be honored, why should this pursuit punish him for praiseworthy flight? The fact is that the honest man should avoid honors. But—just like everybody else—he is born with a desire for them and must fight against it. Only after a long time, during which he has studied the Torah zealously and for its own sake, will he succeed in overcoming that reprehensible desire and no longer feel satisfaction at being called 'rabbi,' or the like. But the desire for honor which he had in his youth, and which he has conquered, still clings in the very bottom of his soul, and though he knows that now he is free, it pursues him like a tenacious memory, and confuses him. That is the taint of the primeval serpent, and of this too he must cleanse himself."

176

The Worm

Rabbi Mendel said: "I do not know wherein I could be better than the worm. For see: he does the will of his Maker and destroys nothing."

Vocation

Several hasidim from White Russia came to the Great Maggid and complained that the distance to Mezritch was so great, they could not come as often as they needed to, and in the intervals they were without a teacher and guide. The maggid gave them his belt and his staff and said: "Take this to the man called Mendel, in the city of Vitebsk."

On their arrival in Vitebsk, they inquired for a Rabbi Mendel in every street and alley, but they were told that there was no rabbi by that name. A woman who had been watching them, asked whom they were looking for. "Rabbi Mendel," they replied.

"We haven't a rabbi by that name," she said. "But we certainly have more than enough Mendels. My own son-in-law's name is Mendele."

Then the hasidim knew that this was the man they had been sent to find. They followed the woman to her house and gave her son-in-law the belt and staff. He clasped the belt around him and closed his hand over the knob of the staff. They looked at him and scarcely recognized him. Another man stood before them, a man garbed in the power of God, and the fear of God lifted their hearts.

The Document

The document through which the congregation of Minsk invested Rabbi Mendel with the office of preacher began with the address: "To the holy zaddik, the aloof and holy light," and so forth. It was signed by more than a hundred prominent persons. When Rabbi Mendel had it in hand and read all the encomia and honorary titles, he said: "This would be a fine document to take with one into the World of Truth! But when they question me, I shall have to tell the truth anyway. And the confession of the accused weighs more than the words of a hundred witnesses. So what will all this praise avail me?"

Once Rabbi Menahem fell seriously ill and could not speak. His hasidim surrounded his bed and wept. He rallied his strength and whispered: "Do not be afraid. From the story which the holy Baal Shem once told me, I know that I shall go to the Land of Israel."

Before going on his journey to the Land of Israel, Rabbi Menahem visited the rabbi of Polnoye, who asked him: "Do you remember the story of the oxen and the plough?"

"I remember," he replied.

"And do you know," the rabbi of Polnoye continued, "what point in it you have reached in your life?"

With a little sigh, Rabbi Menahem said: "I've reeled off the greater half of it."

The Heap of Cinders

Before leaving for the Land of Israel, Rabbi Menahem Mendel paid a visit to old Rabbi Jacob Joseph of Polnoye, the great disciple of the Baal Shem Tov. He arrived at the inn in a troika, and this in itself was enough to annoy the hasidim in Polnoye, whose master insisted on a simple life. But when Rabbi Mendel left the inn and went to the zaddik's house hatless and beltless, a long pipe in his mouth, they all thought that Rabbi Jacob Joseph, who was known for his violent temper, would refuse to receive his guest because of this careless and lax behavior. But the old man welcomed him on the threshold with a great show of love, and spent several hours talking to him. When Rabbi Mendel had gone, the disciples asked their master: "What is there to this man who had the impudence to enter your house with only the cap on his head, with silver buckles on his shoes, and a long pipe in his mouth?"

The zaddik said: "A king who went to war hid his treasures in a safe place. But he buried his most precious pearl, which he loved with all his heart, in a heap of cinders because he knew that no one would look for it there. And so that the powers of evil might not touch it, Rabbi Mendel buries his great humility in the cinder-heap of vanity."

A Comparison

Rabbi Israel of Rizhyn said:

"Rabbi Mendel's journey to the Holy Land was like the journey of our Father Abraham. Its purpose was to pave the way for God and Israel."

For Azazel

When someone asked Rabbi Israel of Rizhyn why he did not go to the Land of Israel, he said: "What has a rough fellow like myself to do in the Land of Israel! Now Rabbi Mendel of Vitebsk—he had something to do with the Land of Israel, and the Land of Israel with him." And he went on to tell: "Before Rabbi Mendel set out for the Land of Israel, he invited the officers of the king to dinner in the city of Vitebsk. And they brought their wives with them, as is their custom. Rabbi Mendel had posted several of his young hasidim near the gate, so that they might help the guests, both men and women, from their carriages, a courtesy which officers of the king expect. And he promised the young men that not a shadow of desire should graze their hearts when they lifted those lovely women from the coach. And so it is: If you want to go to the Land of Israel, you must first concentrate your soul on the secret of the goat which is sent into the wilderness for Azazel. That is what Rabbi Mendel meant with that dinner of his. He could do it! But I, who am such a rough fellow—if I came to the Land of Israel, they would ask me: 'Why have you come without your Jews?'"

At the Window

While Rabbi Menahem was living in the Land of Israel, a foolish man climbed the Mount of Olives unobserved. When he got to the top, he blew the ram's horn. The people were startled and soon a rumor sprang up that this was the blowing of the ram's horn which was to precede redemption. When this was reported to Rabbi Menahem, he opened his window, looked out into the world, and said: "This is no renewal!"

179

The Air of That Land

Rabbi Menahem used to say: "It is true that the air of the Land of Israel makes a man wise. Before I was in that land, all my thoughts and desires were intent on saying a prayer just once in exactly the right way. But since I am in this land, all I want is just once to say 'Amen' in the right way."

Another thing he said, was: "This is what I attained in the Land of Israel. When I see a bundle of straw lying in the street, it seems to me a sign of the presence of God, that it lies there lengthwise, and not crosswise."

The Signature

When Rabbi Menahem wrote letters from the Land of Israel, he always signed himself: "He, who is truly humble."

The rabbi of Rizhyn once was asked: "If Rabbi Menahem were really humble, how could he call himself so?"

"He was so humble," said the rabbi of Rizhyn, "that just because humility dwelt within him, he no longer regarded it as a virtue."

The Ride to the Leipzig Fair

Among the hasidim who went to the Land of Israel with Rabbi Menahem Mendel was a wise man who had been a great merchant and had become so attached to the zaddik that he gave up his business in order to accompany him to the Holy Land. When after a time it became necessary to send a reliable messenger to the hasidim who had stayed at home, to ask them for financial assistance, this man was entrusted with the errand. But while he was on the ship he suddenly fell ill and died. No one in the Land of Israel knew about it. But after his death, he himself felt as if he were riding in a carriage bound for the fair in Leipzig and talking to an old servant he used to take with him on such trips, and also to the coachman who looked very familiar. And all the while he had a great longing for his teacher. The desire to see him grew stronger and stronger until he decided to turn back and go to him. When he told his two companions of his resolve, they argued vehemently against it: it would be foolish to give up the important business transaction in hand for a mere whim! But he insisted on having his way in the face of all their objections. Finally they told him that he was dead, and that they were evil angels to whom he had been entrusted. Instantly he summoned them before the court of Heaven, and they could not refuse. The verdict was that the angels were to take him to Rabbi Mendel. When he reached the city of Tiberias and entered the zaddik's house, one of the angels went in with him in his true and terrible form. The rabbi was startled at the sight of the angel but bade him wait until he had finished his work. For a whole week he wrought at the soul of the man until it was in the right shape.

This is the story that Rabbi Nahman of Bratzlav told his hasidim.

All the Candles

The hasidim who studied in the "Klaus" of the rabbi of Lubavitch, the son-in-law of Rabbi Shneur Zalman's son, used to light a candle before everyone who sat over his books in the House of Study. But when they had finished their evening work and began to tell one another stories about the zaddikim, they put out all the candles except one, which they left burning. Once, when they were seated around the one burning candle, the rabbi came into the room to fetch a book. He asked them whom they were talking about. "Rabbi Mendel of Vitebsk," they said.

"In his honor," he told them, "you must light all the candles. For when he expounded the teachings, all feeling of self was blotted from his heart, and 'the other side' had no way of getting at him. And so, when you talk about him, you must light all the candles—as if you were studying the holy Torah."

SHMELKE OF NIKOLSBURG

David's Harp

When Rabbi Shmelke and his brother Rabbi Pinhas, later the rabbi of Frankfort, were in Mezritch, they rented an attic room so that they might be undisturbed in their studies. Once, after the conclusion of the sabbath, they were sitting and studying late at night, when they heard a strange weeping in which they could clearly detect the voices of both a man and a woman. They looked out of the window and there, on a bench, in the alley, they saw the servant and the maid of the house, both in tears. When they asked them the reason, they said that they had been employed there for a long time and had been waiting to get married for years, but the master of the house was against it, and had managed to prevent it again and again.

At that the brothers declared that all that was necessary was to set up the marriage canopy; everything else, including the consent of the master of the house, would then come of itself. They left at once to wake the cantor who immediately fetched ten men, opened the House of Prayer, and set up the canopy. The wedding was duly celebrated. Rabbi Shmelke beat time with a piece of branch, and Rabbi Pinhas clinked two candelabras so that they gave forth a beautiful sound. Then the maggid came in. At the "Feast of King David" he had sat there with that remoteness of the soul which sometimes overtook him. Suddenly he jumped up and ran to the House of Prayer. "Don't you hear David's harp?" he cried.

New Melodies

Rabbi Moshe Teitelbaum, the disciple of the "Seer" of Lublin, said: "When Rabbi Shmelke prayed on a sabbath and on feast-days, but especially on the Day of Atonement when he performed the service of the high priest, the mystery became manifest in the sound of music carrying from word to word, and he sang new melodies, miracle of miracles, which he had never heard and which no human ear had ever heard; and he did not even know what he was singing and what melody he was singing, for he clung to the upper world."

*   *   *

A very old man who had sung in Rabbi Shmelke's choir when he was a boy, used to tell this: "It was the custom to lay out the notes for each text, so that it would not be necessary to fetch them when the praying before the pulpit began. But the rabbi paid no attention to the notes and sang utterly new melodies which no one had ever heard. We singers all fell silent and listened to him. We could not understand from where those melodies came to him."

In Nikolsburg

When Rabbi Shmelke was called to be the rav of Nikolsburg, he prepared an impressive sermon which he intended to preach to the Talmud scholars of Moravia. On the way, he stopped over in the city of Cracow and when the people there begged him to preach to them, he asked his disciple Moshe Leib, later the rabbi of Sasov, who had accompanied him: "Well, Moshe Leib, what shall I preach?"

"The rabbi has prepared a splendid sermon for Nikolsburg. Why should he not preach that here as well?" answered Moshe Leib.

Rabbi Shmelke took his advice. Now a number of men had come from Nikolsburg to Cracow in order to welcome him, and these heard the sermon. So when the zaddik arrived in Nikolsburg, he asked his disciple: "Well, Moshe Leib, now what shall I preach on the sabbath? I cannot dish up the same sermon over again to the men who heard me speak in Cracow."

"We must take some time," said Moshe Leib, "and discuss a problem of the law in preparation for a sermon."

But up to Friday they did not have a moment's time to open a book. Finally Rabbi Shmelke asked: "Well, Moshe, what shall we preach?"

"On Friday evening, they must surely give us a little free time," said Moshe Leib.

They held in readiness a very large candle which was to burn right through the night, and, when the crowd had gone home, they sat down before the book. Then a hen flew in at the window and the whirr of her wings put out the light. Said Rabbi Shmelke: "Well, Moshe Leib, now what are we to preach?"

"Surely," Moshe Leib replied, "there will be no preaching until the afternoon and so in the morning, after prayer, let us go into our room, lock the door, let no one in, and talk over a subject." In the morning they went to prayer. Before the chapter for the week was read, the desk was moved in front of the Ark and the head of the congregation came and asked Rabbi Shmelke to give his sermon. The House of Prayer was filled with the Talmud scholars of Moravia. Rabbi Shmelke had them bring him a volume of the Gemara, opened it at random, posed a problem from the page before him, and asked the scholars to discuss it. Then he too, so he said, would say his say. When they had all spoken, he put the prayer shawl over his head and remained like this for about a quarter of an hour. Then he organized the questions they had raised, one hundred and thirty in number, and gave the replies, seventy-two in number, and there was nothing that was not answered, and solved, and quelled.

Noting Down

When Rabbi Shmelke was called to Nikolsburg in Moravia, a certain custom prevailed in that congregation. Every new rav was asked to note down in the chronicle some new regulation which was to be followed from that time on. He too was asked to do this, but put it off from day to day. He looked at each and every one and postponed noting anything in the book. He looked at them more and more closely and over and over, and put off writing until they gave him to understand that the delay was becoming unduly long. Then he went to where the chronicle lay and wrote down the ten commandments.

The Seven Worldly Wisdoms

When Rabbi Shmelke assumed office in Nikolsburg, he preached on the seven worldly wisdoms on the first seven sabbath-days, one wisdom on each sabbath. From week to week, the congregation grew more surprised at this peculiar choice of subject for a sermon, but no one ventured to question the zaddik about it. On the eighth sabbath he began by saying: "For a long time I did not understand the words of Solomon, the preacher: 'It is better to hear the rebuke of the wise than for a man to hear the song of fools.' Why is it not written: 'than the song of fools'? This is the meaning. It is good to hear the rebuke of a wise man who has heard and understood the song of fools, that is, the seven worldly wisdoms, which—compared to the teachings of God—are a song of fools. To another man the foolish worldly sages could say: 'It is easy for you to scorn our wisdoms, for you have not tasted of their sweetness! If you knew it, you would not want to know anything else!' But he who has studied the seven wisdoms and passed through their inmost core, only to choose the wisdom of the Torah—if such a man cries out: 'Vanity of vanities,' no one can gainsay him."

The Messiah and Those Who Pray

On the first day of the New Year festival, Rabbi Shmelke entered the House of Prayer before the ram's horn was sounded, and prayed, with tears in his eyes: "Alas! Lord of the world! All the people are crying to you, but what of all their clamor! They are thinking of nothing but their own needs, and not of the exile of your glory!" On the second day he again came before the blowing of the ram's horn and wept and said: "It is written in the first book of Samuel: 'Wherefore cometh not the son of Jesse to eat bread, neither yesterday nor today?' Why did the King Messiah not come, not yesterday on the first day of the New Year, and not today, on the second? It is because today, just as yesterday, all their prayers are for nothing but bread, for nothing but the satisfaction of bodily needs!"

The Tears of Esau

Another time he said: "In the Midrash it is written: 'Messiah son of David, will not come before the tears of Esau have ceased to flow.' The children of Israel, who are God's children, pray for mercy day and night, and shall they weep in vain, as long as the children of Esau shed tears? But 'the tears of Esau'—that does not mean the tears which the peoples weep and you do not weep; they are the tears which all human beings weep when they ask something for themselves, and pray for it. And truly: Messiah son of David will not come until such tears have ceased to flow, until you weep because the Divine Presence is exiled, and because you yearn for its return."

A Sermon for Atonement

On the eve of the Day of Atonement, Rabbi Shmelke of Nikols-burg put on his prayer shawl and went to the House of Prayer. On his way from the entrance to the Ark, he called aloud the words of the Scriptures: ". . . for on this day shall atonement be made for you, to cleanse you," and after that he quoted Rabbi Akiba's words from the Mishnah: "Before whom do you atone, and who cleanses you: Your Father in Heaven." All the people burst into tears.

When he stood in front of the Ark, he said: "Brothers of my heart, you must know that the core of turning is the offering up of life itself. For we are of the seed of Abraham who offered his life for the sanctification of the blessed Name and let them cast him into a lime-kiln; we are of the seed of Isaac who offered his life and laid his neck on the stone of the altar—they are surely pleading to our Father in Heaven in our behalf on this holy and awful day of judgment. But let us too walk in their tracks and imitate their works: let us offer up our own lives for the sanctification of the Name of Him who is blessed. Let us unite and sanctify His mighty Name with fervent love and with this as our purpose, let us say together: 'Hear, O Israel!' " And weeping, all the people said: "Hear, O Israel: The Lord our God, the Lord is one."

Then he went on to say: "Dear brothers, now that it was vouch-safed us to unite and sanctify His Name in great love, now that we have offered our lives, and our hearts have become cleansed for the service and fear of the Lord, we must also unite our souls. All souls come from one root, all are carved from the throne of His splendor, and so they are a part of God in Heaven. Let us be united on earth too, so that the branches again may be as the root. Here we stand, cleansed and pure, to unite our souls. And we take upon us the commandment: 'Love thy neighbor as thyself.' " And all the people repeated aloud: "Love thy neighbor as thyself." And he continued: "Now that it has been vouchsafed us to unite His Great Name, and to unite our souls, which are a part of God in Heaven, let the holy Torah plead in our behalf before our Father in Heaven. Once God offered it to all peoples and to all languages, but we alone accepted it and cried: 'All that the Lord hath spoken will we do,' and only then did we say: 'We hear.' And so it is fitting that the Torah ask our Father in heaven for mercy and grace for us on this holy and awful day of judgment." And he opened the doors of the Ark.

Then, in front of the open Ark, he recited the confession of sins, and all the people repeated it after him word for word, and as they did so, they wept. He took out the scroll and, holding it high in his hands, spoke to his congregation about the sins of man. But in the end he said: "You must know that the weeping we do on this day is unblest if it is filled with gloom, for the Divine Presence does not dwell in heaviness of heart, but only in rejoicing in the commandments. And, see, no joy is greater than the joy on this day, when it is granted to us to drive all evil impulses from our hearts, through the power of turning, to come close to our Father in Heaven whose hand is outstretched to receive those who turn to Him. And so, all the tears we shed on this day, should be tears of joy, as it is written: 'Serve the Lord with fear and rejoice with trembling.' "

Sleep

Rabbi Shmelke did not want to interrupt his studies for too long a time, and so he always slept sitting up, his head resting on his arm. In his fingers he held a lit candle which roused him when it guttered and the flame touched his hand. When Rabbi Elimelekh visited him and recognized the power of the holiness which was still locked within him, he prepared a couch for him and with great difficulty persuaded him to lie down for a little while. Then he closed and shuttered the windows. Rabbi Shmelke slept until broad daylight. It did not take him long to notice this, but he was not sorry he had slept, for he was filled with a hitherto unknown sunny clearness. He went to the House of Prayer and prayed before the congregation as usual. But to the congregation it seemed that they had never heard him before. They were entranced and uplifted by the manifest power of his holiness. When he recited the verses about the Red Sea, they gathered up the hems of their kaftans for fear the waves towering to the left and right might wet them with salty foam. Later Shmelke said to Elimelekh: "Not until this day did I know that one can also serve God with sleep."

The Rap

In Apt there was a servant of the House of Prayer whose duty it was to go through the town and, with his hammer, rap at the door of every Jewish house, for the men to come and pray, or learn, or recite psalms. He had only to rap ever so lightly and instantly the sleepers started up, even if it was midnight, and dressed quickly, and hurried to the House of Prayer, and long after he had rapped, the rap of their eager hearts echoed the rap of the hammer. The man had been granted this gift as a boy, when he had served Rabbi Shmelke of Nikolsburg with a heart that was awake and full of devotion.

The Clean Freethinkers

A number of freethinkers in Nikolsburg were carrying on an argument with Rabbi Shmelke. "But you will have to admit," they said in conclusion, "that we, on our part, have virtues which the Poles lack. Our clothing, for instance, is spotlessly clean, and that is more than you can say for that of the Poles, who ignore the bidding of the sages: 'The wise man shall not wear a spotted robe.'"
The rabbi laughed and replied: "You are right. Your clothes are clean, and those of the Poles are not. That is because—according to what the Talmud says of the gradation of virtues—

cleanliness leads to purity, purity to aloofness, and so on higher and higher to the rung of the holy spirit. Now, when the Poles set about beginning with cleanliness, the Evil Urge does all he possibly can to dissuade them from it, for he fears they will rise from rung to rung and attain to the holy spirit. And even when they try to fend off the Evil Urge and assure him that they do not intend to do any such thing, he does not believe them, and will not stop until he has talked them out of cleanliness. But when the Evil Urge takes exception to your cleanliness, you need only assure him that you do not intend to rise, and he instantly takes you at your word, and lets you be just as clean as you like."

The Enemy

A rich and distinguished man in Nikolsburg was hostile to Rabbi Shmelke and tried to think of some way to make him seem ridiculous. On the eve of the Day of Atonement, he came to him and begged him that on this day, when each man forgives his neighbor, they too might become reconciled with each other. He had brought the rabbi a jar of very old and strong wine, and urged him to drink, for he thought that, since the zaddik was unused to drinking, he would become drunk and appear before his congregation in this condition. For the sake of reconciliation, Rabbi Shmelke drank one glass after another and the rich man thought he had accomplished his purpose and went home well-satisfied.

But when evening fell, and the hour of prayer drew near, the shudder of the day of judgment took hold of the rabbi, and in a moment every vestige of the effect of the wine had left him. After the Evening Prayer, Rabbi Shmelke remained in the House of Prayer all night, in the company of other devout people. Just as every year, he sang the psalms and the congregation joined in. When, in the forty-first psalm, he came to the verse: "By this I know that Thou delightest in me: mine enemy will not triumph over me," he repeated it over and over, and translated it, but not in the usual way but freely and boldly: "By this I know that you delight in me: my enemy will suffer no ill because of me." And he added: "Even though there are persons who are hostile to me and try to make me an object of ridicule, forgive them, Lord of the world, and let them not suffer because of me." And he said this in a voice so full of power, that all those who were praying, burst into tears, and each repeated his words from the bottom of his heart. But among them was that rich and distinguished man. In this hour he turned to God and all his malice dropped from him. From this time on, he loved and honored Rabbi Shmelke above all other people.

The Commandment to Love

A disciple asked Rabbi Shmelke: "We are commanded to love our neighbor as ourself. How can I do this, if my neighbor has wronged me?"

The rabbi answered: "You must understand these words aright. Love your neighbor like something which you yourself are. For all souls are one. Each is a spark from the original soul, and this soul is wholly inherent in all souls, just as your soul is in all the members of your body. It may come to pass that your hand makes a mistake and strikes you. But would you then take a stick and chastise your hand, because it lacked understanding, and so increase your pain? It is the same if your neighbor, who is of one soul with you, wrongs you for lack of understanding. If you punish him, you only hurt yourself."

The disciple went on asking: "But if I see a man who is wicked before God, how can I love him?"

"Don't you know," said Rabbi Shmelke, "that the original soul came out of the essence of God, and that every human soul is a part of God? And will you have no mercy on him, when you see that one of his holy sparks has been lost in a maze, and is almost stifled?"

The Ring

A poor man came to Rabbi Shmelke's door. There was no money in the house, so the rabbi gave him a ring. A moment later, his wife heard of it and heaped him with reproaches for throwing to an unknown beggar so valuable a piece of jewelry, with so large and precious a stone. Rabbi Shmelke had the poor man called back and said to him: "I have just learned that the ring I gave you is of great value. Be careful not to sell it for too little money."

The Messengers

A man came to Rabbi Shmelke and complained that he could not make a living, but had to keep on asking kind people to help him. He repeated the words of the prayer: "'Let us not be in need of the gift of flesh and blood. . .'" Rabbi Shmelke said: "You must not read 'gift' but 'gifts,' for there is one God, but many messengers to do his bidding. And that is what the verse means. Let us not be in need of the gifts we can consider only as the gifts of men. In the hour we take them, let us recognize the givers as your messengers."

Poor Man and Rich Man

Rabbi Shmelke said: "The poor man gives the rich man more than the rich gives the poor. More than the poor man needs the rich man, the rich is in need of the poor."

Be Holy

A man once asked Rabbi Shmelke: "It is written: 'Ye shall be holy, for I the Lord your God am holy. Ye shall fear every man his mother and his father.' How can the lump of clay which is the habitation of evil lusts, strive to acquire a quality which is God's? And what connection is there between this summons to the superhuman, and the commandment to fear father and mother, which is a human law for humans?"
The rabbi replied: "According to the words of our sages, three are concerned with the creation of every child: God, father, and mother. God's part is all holy. The other parts can be sanctified and made as much like it as possible. That is what is meant by the commandment. You are holy and yet you shall become holy. You must, therefore, shun the heritage of your father and mother, which you have within you, and which is opposed to holiness. You must not yield to it, but master it and shape it."

Preparation

A disciple of Rabbi Shmelke's begged his master to teach him how to prepare his soul for the service of God. The zaddik told him to go to Rabbi Abraham Hayyim, who—at that time—was still an innkeeper. The disciple did as he was bidden and lived in the inn for several weeks without observing any vestige of holiness in the innkeeper who from the Morning Prayer till night devoted himself to his business. Finally he asked him what he did all day. "My most important occupation," said Rabbi Abraham, "is to clean the dishes properly, so that not the slightest trace of food is left, and to clean and dry the pots and pans, so that they do not rust." When the disciple returned home and reported to Rabbi Shmelke what he had seen and heard, the rabbi said to him: "Now you know the answer to what you asked me."

The Test

They asked Rabbi Shmelke: "Why is the sacrifice of Isaac considered so glorious? At that time, our Father Abraham had already reached a high rung of holiness, and so it was no wonder that he immediately did as God asked him!"
He answered: "When man is tried, all the rungs and all holiness are taken from him. Stripped of everything he has attained, he stands face to face with Him who is putting him to the test."

Rather Not

Rabbi Shmelke once said: "If I had the choice, I should rather not die. For in the coming world, there are no Days of Awe, and what can the soul of man do without the Days of Judgment?"

Our Generation

Once they asked Rabbi Shmelke: "Some find it difficult to believe that the Messiah could suddenly come in this, our trivial day and age. And how could our generation bring about what the tannaim and amoraim, the 'generations of knowledge,' and the generations after them could not accomplish?"
The zaddik replied: "For many years the host of a king besieged a well-fortified city. All kinds of troops, under the command of expert generals, advanced on the fortress again and again with all the force of which they were capable, until finally

they conquered. Then an army of workers was ordered to clear away the enormous amount of débris, so that a new beginning could be made, so that in the city he had vanquished a new palace could be built for the victorious king. That is our generation."

Thieves' Luck

With regard to Rashi's comment: "He whose ear heard 'Thou shalt not steal' on Mount Sinai and then went and stole, his ear shall be pierced," Rabbi Shmelke said:
"Before God gave his commandments down from Mount Sinai, every one took good care that his property was not stolen from him. And because the thieves knew this, they did not try to steal. But after God spoke the words, 'Thou shalt not steal,' and men felt secure, the trade of thieving began to thrive."

The Brothers

Rabbi Shmelke of Nikolsburg was once entertaining his brother, Rabbi Pinhas, the rav of Frankfort, as his guest. Now, Rabbi Shmelke had always eaten in moderation, but in his old age he ate only a very little food and drank only a little water. When Rabbi Pinhas, who had not seen him for many years, noticed this, he said: "Here are two brothers of one father and mother. The one gobbles and guzzles like a beast, the other is like an angel of the Lord: he needs neither food nor drink, but savors the radiance of divine glory." Rabbi Shmelke replied: "Here are two brothers of one father and of one mother. The one is like a high priest, the other like a good house-father. The high priest eats, and his eating is part of the sacrifice which shrives the house-father."

The Ride on the Danube

It is told:
Dangerous plots against the Jews were brewing in the emperor's palace. Then Rabbi Shmelke and his disciple Moshe Leib of Sasov set out for Vienna to put an end to such plans. But it was freezing weather, and the Danube was full of ice-floes. They boarded a narrow boat which could not hold more than two

193

men. They stood up in it and Rabbi Shmelke started singing the song which had been sung beside the Red Sea, and Moshe Leib sang the bass. And the little boat moved safely between the floes. In Vienna the people ran down to the shore and stood there open-mouthed. Soon the news of these strange arrivals reached the court. On the very same day the empress received Rabbi Shmelke and granted his requests.

The Amen to the Blessing

When Rabbi Shmelke felt he was going to die, he said to his hasidim: "I did not want to tell you up to now, but now I must tell it while there is still time. You know that I have always been careful to say grace and blessings before eating and drinking and the like, in a place where there was someone who said 'Amen.' For each blessing begets an angel, and the angel is incomplete unless someone says 'Amen.' But once, on a journey, I had to say a blessing in a lonely place, when—after attending to my bodily needs—I washed my hands at a well, and there was no one anywhere around who could say 'Amen.' Hardly had I begun to feel troubled about this, when two men stood close before me, and before I had time to marvel at their size and grandeur, I was saying the blessing, and they answered 'Amen' with overwhelming sweetness. But when I wanted to look at them more closely, a cloud carried them off."

The Soul of Samuel

On the second day of Iyyar of the year 5538, Rabbi Shmelke summoned his disciples. He was sitting very erect in his big chair, his face was radiant, and his eyes as unclouded as always. He said to them: "Today, you must know, is the day of my death." They began to weep, but he bade them stop, and continued: "You must know that the soul of the prophet Samuel is within me. For this there are three outward signs: my name is Samuel; I am a Levite, as he was; and my life has lasted fifty-two years, just as his. But he was called Samuel, and I Shmelke, and so I remained Shmelke." Soon after this, he told his weeping disciples to leave him, leaned back, and died.

AARON OF KARLIN

The Moment

In his youth, Rabbi Aaron of Karlin was fond of wearing fine clothes, and every day he went driving in a carriage. But a moment came when, as he was leaning back in his carriage, holy insight overwhelmed him and he knew that he must leave this way of his, and enter upon another. He leaned forward; his spirit surged up within him. He set foot on the carriage-step and was flooded with the gift. He set foot on the earth, and all the firmaments were under the sway of his power.

A Whisper

On a Friday evening, after eating in the house of the maggid of Mezritch, Rabbi Aaron returned to his inn and began to recite the Song of Songs in a whisper. Soon after, the maggid's servant came and knocked at his door. He said the maggid could not sleep because the Song of Songs came roaring through his room.

The Long Sleep

Once, when Rabbi Aaron was in the house of the Great Maggid along with other disciples, he was suddenly overcome with weariness. Without realizing what he was doing, he went into his teacher's room and lay down on his bed. Here he slept that whole day and all the following night. His companions wanted to wake him, but the maggid would not let them. He said: "Now he is putting on the phylacteries of Heaven."

Delights

A zaddik told this: The delights of all the worlds wanted to reveal themselves to Rabbi Aaron, but he only shook his head. "Even if they are delights," he said at last, "before I enjoy them, I want to sweat for them."

Rabbi Aaron traveled through all of Russia, from one Jewish city to the next, in search of youths worth bringing his teacher, the Great Maggid, as disciples, so that through them the hasidic teachings might spread through the world. Once he came to the city of Amdur. Now he had heard that, beyond the town, in a lonely wood, lived a devout and learned man, Rabbi Hayke, who kept aloof from the world and from men, and mortified his flesh. In order to bring him to the town, Rabbi Aaron preached in the House of Prayer a number of times, and his words had a powerful effect, but it took a long time for the hermit to hear of it. When the hour for the next sermon drew near, something drove him to the House of Prayer. When Rabbi Aaron heard he had come, he did not preach his sermon, but said only these words: "If a man does not grow better, he grows worse." Like a poison which rouses the very core of life against itself, these words bit into the mind of the ascetic. He ran to the rabbi and begged him to help him out of the maze of error in which he had lost his way. "Only my teacher, the maggid of Mezritch can do that," said Rabbi Aaron.

"Then give me a letter to him," said the man, "so that he may know who I am."

His request was granted, and he started out on his journey confident that before he spoke freely to the maggid, the famous teacher would know that he had before him one of the great men of his generation. The maggid opened the letter and—obviously with deliberate intent—read it aloud. It said that the man who was delivering it did not have a particle of sound goodness in him. Rabbi Hayke burst into tears. "Now, now," said the maggid. "Does what the Lithuanian writes really matter so much to you?"

"Is it true or isn't it?" asked the other.

"Well," said the maggid, "if the Lithuanian says so, it is, very probably, true."

"Then heal me, rabbi!" the ascetic begged him.

For a whole year, the maggid worked over him and healed him. Later, Rabbi Hayke became one of the great men of his generation.

The King

Rabbi Aaron was once reciting the Morning Prayer in the House of Prayer at Mezritch. As he was about to call out God as the "King," tears gushed from his eyes and he could not continue. After prayers, they asked him what had happened. He explained: "At that moment I thought of how Rabbi Yohanan ben Zakkai said to Vespasian: 'Peace be with you, O king. Peace be with you, O king.' And the Roman said to him in anger: 'You deserve the death penalty on two scores. First, I am not the king, yet you called me king. Secondly, supposing I was the king, why did you not come to me before now?' As yet, God is not really king over the world, and I have a part in the blame that this is not so, for why have I still not accomplished the turning; why have I still not come to him?"

The Chandelier

Rabbi Aaron of Tehernobil, son of a daughter of Aaron of Karlin, born long after he died and named after him, was denounced to the authorities and saved only by dint of bribes which the hasidim had given against his will. When he learned of this, he said: "Alas! How weak is my generation! If I stood on the rung of my grandfather, Rabbi Aaron the Great, wrong judgment could have been averted without resorting to bribery." And he went on to tell:

"Once the Haidamaks in the Ukraine and Russia conspired against the Jews and resolved to kill them and seize their property. When word of this reached Mezritch, the heads of the community went to the holy maggid and asked him what to do. Since he saw that Satan had succeeded in gaining the upper hand, he bade all, men, women, and children, hide in the woods around the town, and take with them as much of their possessions as they could carry.

"One group of men hurried to the House of Prayer to save the sacred utensils. From the ceiling hung a large pewter chandelier with thirty-six branches. My grandfather, Rabbi Aaron the Great, had acquired it with the money he had collected, kopek by kopek, among his disciples and the hasidim of the maggid. Every Friday, the holy maggid himself used to light all the branches of this chandelier. It was the only thing left in the House of Prayer. All the other utensils had been removed. My grandfather had been standing at a window, without paying any attention to what was happening around him. Suddenly he noticed them getting at the chandelier. In a moment he was in the middle of the hall. 'Don't touch it!' he cried in a loud voice.

"Messengers went to the maggid to tell him of the incident and find out what he wanted done. The maggid listened to what they had to say and was silent for a time. Then he said: 'All the men, women, and children shall gather in the House of Prayer.' When my grandfather saw the entire community gathering in the House of Prayer, he sent word to the maggid to beg him to come and take pity on him. The maggid gave no reply. Again my grandfather sent to implore him to give him aid of any kind. The maggid did not reply.

"The House of Prayer was filled with the Jews of the community of Mezritch. They were all there: men, women, and children. Only the maggid was missing. Then a man, who had been keeping watch outside, came and reported to my grandfather that the Haidamaks were in the city. My grandfather went out and placed himself in the entrance to the House of Prayer. When the Haidamaks advanced toward him, he hurled the words of the psalm at them in a voice of thunder: 'Why are the nations in an uproar?'

"The leader of the Haidamaks was seized with madness and began to hit out at his own people. They scattered and fled."

On the Earth

This is what Rabbi Aaron of Karlin said concerning the words in the Scriptures: ". . . a ladder set up on the earth, and the top of it reached to Heaven."

"If a man of Israel has himself firmly in hand, and stands solidly on the earth, then his head reaches up to Heaven."

Nothing at All

They asked Rabbi Aaron what he had learned from his teacher, the Great Maggid. "Nothing at all," he said. And when they pressed him to explain what he meant by that, he added: "The nothing-at-all is what I learned. I learned the meaning of nothingness. I learned that I am nothing at all, and that I Am, notwithstanding."

The Little Fear and the Great Fear

Rabbi Shneur Zalman told this about his friend, Rabbi Aaron of Karlin, who died young:

"His fear of God was like the fear of a man who is going to be shot, and stands at the wall and sees the muzzle of the gun pointed at his heart, and looks straight into the muzzle, full of fear and yet undaunted. But this was only his little fear of God, his every-day fear. When the great fear of God came over him —no comparison suffices to describe that!"

Unworthiness and the Hearing of Prayers

They asked Rabbi Aaron: "Concerning Moses' prayer to God to pardon his people, the commentary says: 'that they may not say I was unworthy to plead for mercy in their behalf.' Is not this contrary to the testimony in the Scriptures that Moses was meek above all other men?"

"Just because he was so meek," the zaddik replied, "he said to God: 'Hear my prayer, though I am not worthy of it, so that they may not say that the unworthiness of man became manifest through me, and stop pleading to you with all the strength of their hearts, but rather that they may realize that you hear the prayer of any mouth at all.'"

"I"

A disciple of the Great Maggid had received instruction from him for several years and was now starting on his journey home. On the way, he decided to stop in Karlin to visit Rabbi Aaron, who for a time had been his companion in the maggid's House of Study. It was nearly midnight when he reached the city, but his desire to see his friend was so great that he at once went to his house and knocked at the lit window. He heard the dear, familiar voice ask, "Who is it?" and—certain that

199

his own voice would be recognized—he answered nothing but the word: "I!" But the window remained closed and no other sound came from within, though he knocked again and again. At last he cried out in distress: "Aaron, why don't you open for me?" Then his friend replied, but his voice was so grave and solemn that it sounded almost strange to him: "Who is it that dares call himself 'I' as befits only God himself!" When the disciple heard this, he said to himself: "I have not learned nearly enough," and without delaying he returned to Mezritch.

Conversion

Rabbi Aaron once came to the city where little Mordecai, who later became the rabbi of Lechovitz, was growing up. His father brought the boy to the visiting rabbi and complained that he did not persevere in his studies. "Leave the boy with me for a while," said Rabbi Aaron. When he was alone with little Mordecai, he lay down and took the child to his heart. Silently he held him to his heart until his father returned. "I have given him a good talking-to," he said. "From now on, he will not be lacking in perseverance."

Whenever the rabbi of Lechovitz related this incident, he added: "That was when I learned how to convert men."

The Greeting

A grand-nephew of Rabbi Aaron related: "At the close of the sabbath, when I sat at his table while they said the Elijah-song, I noticed that he and his son Rabbi Asher clasped hands under the table, at the words: "Hail to Him who greeted him, and to him whom He greeted.' And I understand what this meant: Elijah had assumed the shape of the Father, and the Father wanted to accord his son the grace of the greeting."

Permission

It is told:

Passover was coming, and Rabbi Aaron, who was in Mezritch, wanted to go home for the holidays. He asked and received the maggid's permission. But hardly had he left the house, when the maggid called some of his disciples and said to them: "Go

to Aaron's inn at once, and talk him out of going to Karlin."
They went and tried to persuade their friend to celebrate the
festival with them. When they failed to make any impression
on him, they gave away that it was the maggid himself who had
sent them.

Immediately Aaron hurried to him and said: "Rabbi, it is very
necessary for me to go home, and now I am told that you wish
me to spend the holidays with you—is that so?"

"I shall not keep you," said the rabbi. "If it is necessary for
you to go, go in peace." But when Aaron had left, he again said
to his disciples: "Don't let him go!" This recurred one more
time, but since the maggid did not give him instructions to the
contrary, Rabbi Aaron would not listen to what seemed sheer
foolery, and left for Karlin. When he entered his house, he had
to lie down, and he died three days later. He was thirty-six
years old.

When the maggid heard of his death, he quoted the saying of
our sages: "When Aaron died, the clouds of glory vanished,"
and he added: "He was our weapon. What are we to do in the
world now!"

The disciples reproached their maggid for allowing this radiant
and holy man to go to his death. "Why didn't you tell him?"
they asked.

"What was given a man to administer, he must faithfully administer," he said.

The maggid died the following autumn.

The Foolish Thing

Rabbi Asher, son of Rabbi Aaron, told:
"When I went to see Rabbi Pinhas of Koretz, I did not tell him
who I was, but he said: 'Your father is walking behind you.'
After a while, he added: 'Your father has done a foolish thing.'
I was frightened, for I knew that whatever Rabbi Pinhas said
about a zaddik—and even if he had been in the upper world
these five hundred years—reached the ears of heavenly judgment. 'The foolish thing your father has done,' he went on to
say, 'was not to live longer than he did.'"

When Rabbi Israel of Rizhyn betrothed his son Rabbi Abraham Jacob, later the rabbi of Sadagora, to a daughter of Rabbi Aaron of Karlin, a grandson of the great Rabbi Aaron, and the engagement contract was being written, he said: "It is our custom, at a time such as this, to recite the genealogy of the bride's father. The great Rabbi Aaron was the truth of the world. His son, Rabbi Asher, the grandfather of the bride, has always been close on the track of truth. And the father of the bride—if he knew that a crumb of truth was hidden under a floor-board, he would tear up the floor with his bare hands."

LEVI YITZHAK OF BERDITCHEV

He Who Was Also There

When Levi Yitzhak was young, a rich man chose him for his son-in-law because of his amazing gifts—for such was the custom. As a mark of respect for his prominent father-in-law, they honored him in the first year of his marriage, by asking him to recite the passage, "Unto thee it was shown . . ." before the congregation in the House of Prayer, on the Day of Rejoicing in the Law. He went to the pulpit and, for a while, stood motionless. Then he put out his hand to take his prayer shawl, but laid it down again and stood without moving as before. The heads of the community bade the servant whisper to him not to weary the assemblage, but to begin. "Very well," he said and took the prayer shawl in his hand. But when he had almost covered his shoulders, he laid it back. His father-in-law was ashamed before the congregation, especially since he had often boasted of the excellent young man he had gained for his house. Angrily he sent him a message either to begin the prayer or leave the pulpit. But even before Levi Yitzhak was told these words, his voice suddenly rang through the hall: "If you are versed in the teachings, if you are a hasid," he said, "then speak the prayer!" And with this he returned to his place. His father-in-law said nothing.

But when they were at home and Levi Yitzhak sat opposite him at the festive board, his face bright with the joy befitting the day, he could contain himself no longer and shouted: "Why did you bring this disgrace upon me?"

The rabbi replied: "When I first put out my hand to draw the prayer shawl over my head, the Evil Urge came and whispered in my ear: 'I want to say "Unto thee it was shown . . ." with you!' I asked: 'Who are you that you regard yourself worthy to do this?' And he: 'Who are you that you regard yourself worthy to do this?' 'I am versed in the teachings,' I said. 'I too am versed in the teachings,' he replied. I thought to put an end to this idle talk and said contemptuously: 'Where did you study?' 'Where did you study?' he countered. I told him. 'But I was right there with you,' he murmured laughingly. 'I studied there in your company!' I pondered for a moment. 'I am a hasid,' I informed him triumphantly. And he, unperturbed: 'I too am a hasid.' I: 'To what zaddik did you travel?' And he, again echoing me: 'To whom did you travel?' 'To the holy maggid of Mezritch,' I replied. Whereupon he laughed still more derisively. 'But I tell you that I was there with you and became a hasid just as you did. And that is why I want to say with you, "Unto thee it was shown. . . ." ' Then I had enough of it. I left him. What else could L have done?"

In Tanners' Alley

On one of his journeys, as night was falling, Levi Yitzhak came to a little town where he knew no one at all, nor could he find a lodging until finally a tanner took him home with him. He wanted to say the Evening Prayer, but the smell of the hides was so penetrating that he could not utter a word. So he left and went to the House of Study which was quite empty, and there he prayed. And then, suddenly, he understood how the Divine Presence had descended to exile and now—with bowed head—stood in Tanners' Alley. He burst into tears and wept and wept until he had cried his heart out over the sorrow of the Divine Presence, and he fell in a faint. And then he saw the glory of God in all its splendor, a dazzling light ranged in four-and-twenty rungs of divers colors, and heard the words: "Be strong, my son! Great suffering will come upon you, but have no fear, for I shall be with you."

In Transport

On the morning of the Feast of Tabernacles, when Rabbi Levi Yitzhak was about to reach into the chest where the citron and the sheaf of palm, myrtle and willows of the brook awaited the blessing, he thrust his hand through the glass lid, and did not mark that he had cut himself.

At the Feast of Hanukkah, when he saw the holy lights burning, he was impelled to put his bare hand into the flame, yet felt no hurt.

At the Feast of Purim, before the book of Esther was read, he danced during the benediction, danced on the desk, and almost on the scroll itself.

When he had drawn water for the baking of the unleavened bread, he was so enraptured at fulfilling this holy rite, that he fell into the well.

When at the seder he said the word "matzah," that is, unleavened bread, he was so moved with fervor that he threw himself under the table and tipped it over with the seder-bowl, unleavened bread, and the wine, so that all had to be prepared anew. He donned the fresh clothing they brought him, and—like one savoring an exquisite morsel—said: "Ah! Ah! this matzah!"

The Bath

It is told:

When Rabbi Levi Yitzhak had become rav in Berditchev, those who opposed his teachings beset him with hostilities. Among these was a group, so unfalteringly faithful to the memory of the great Rabbi Liber who had lived and taught in Berditchev, and died fifteen years before, that they did not want to have anything to do with the innovator. Once Rabbi Levi Yitzhak had them come to him and told them that he intended to immerse himself in Rabbi Liber's bath. Now Rabbi Liber had never had a true bath. What they called his bath was nothing but a roof on four posts, and under it a pit full of water. In winter Rabbi Liber used to break the ice with an axe and then immerse himself for his holy ablutions. After his death, the roof had caved in and mud gathered in the pit. And so the zaddik was told that to bathe in it was impossible. But he was firm in his purpose and hired four workingmen who dug for a whole day. So it went for a number of days. His enemies laughed at this curious new rav. It was quite obvious—so they said—that Rabbi Liber did not wish his bath to be used.

Rabbi Levi Yitzhak asked all those of his intimates who had known Rabbi Liber to assemble early the following morning.

He himself went to the bath with them, and once more the work-men began to dig. After two hours one of them cried out: "I see water!" Soon they reported that more water had collected. "There is no need to dig any further," said the rabbi. He took off his clothes and, keeping only his cap on his head, went down into the pit. When he stepped into the water, everyone there saw that it barely lapped his ankles, but in a moment it had risen to his mouth. Then he asked: "Is there anybody here who remembers Rabbi Liber in his youth?" They answered that in the new part of the city lived a beadle who was a hundred and sixteen years old, and had served Rabbi Liber when he was young. The zaddik sent for him and waited in the water which reached to his mouth. At first the old man refused to come. But when he was told what had happened, he went with the man who had come to fetch him.

"Do you still remember the beadle," the rabbi asked him, "who hanged himself from the chandelier in the House of Prayer?" "Surely I remember him," the old man answered in surprise. "But how are you concerned with him? All that was a good seventy years ago, long before you were born!"

"Tell us about it," said the rabbi.

The old man told: "He was a simple man, but he was very devout. And he had his own way of doing things. On Wednesday of every week he began to polish the great chandelier, hanging from the ceiling, for the sabbath, and while he did this he always said: 'I do this for the sake of God.' But one Friday afternoon, when people came to the House of Prayer, they found him hanging from the chandelier in a noose knotted of his belt."

The rabbi said: "That time—on the day before the sabbath—when everything had been cleaned and polished, and there was nothing more to be done, the simple beadle asked himself: 'What more can I do in honor of God? What more can I do in his honor?' His poor, weak mind grew confused, and because of all the great things in the world, to him the chandelier had always been greatest, he hanged himself from it in honor of God. And now that seventy years have passed since that day,

Rabbi Liber appeared to me in a dream and told me to do whatever could be done to release the soul of that simple man. Therefore I had the holy bath restored and immersed myself. Now tell me: Is the hour come for the release of that poor soul?"

"Yes, yes, yes!" they all called as if with a single voice.

"Then I too say: 'Yes, yes, yes!'" said the rabbi. "Go in peace." With that he came out of the water, and the water sank so that it would barely have lapped his ankles.

Rabbi Levi Yitzhak had a bath-house built in that place, and had the old bath restored; for himself he had another dug next to it. Only when he was about to prepare for some difficult work did he use the bath of Rabbi Liber. Even today the house with the two baths still stands in the old part of the city, near the "Klaus," and they still call the one that of Rabbi Liber, and the other that of Rabbi Levi Yitzhak.

Passover Night

Soon after Rabbi Levi Yitzhak had been received as rav by the community of Berditchev, he prayed with great ardor on the first evening of the Feast of Passover, and this lasted for so many hours that the congregation grew tired of waiting, finished their prayers, and went home to prepare the seder meal. Only one man remained, one of those poor wayfarers from another place who, according to the custom, was to take the festive meal at the house of one of the burghers. He had been told that the Jew just reading the prayer was to be his host, and because he was weary with the day's journey he lay down on a bench and was soon fast asleep. Meantime, the rabbi had finished the silent Prayer of Benedictions. When he saw that all the people had gone home, he cried: "O angels, angels on high! Descend on this holy day in praise of the Lord, blessed be He!" At this the stranger half woke from a deep sleep. Still drowsy and dazed, he heard a rushing sound surge through the house and was terrified to the core of his being. But the rabbi recited the hymns in great happiness. Then he caught sight of the stranger and asked him why he alone had remained. The man, who was now fully awake, told him how it had come about, and the rabbi asked him to go to the seder with him. But the stranger was timid and dared not accept. He seemed to fear that—in lieu of food—secret words that work magic would fall to his share. "Calm yourself," said the rabbi. "You will eat at my house just what you would eat at the table of other burghers." Then the man decided to go with him.

The Doubting Innkeeper

The owner of a tavern in Berditchev, where mead was dispensed, was not in favor of the hasidic way of life, but liked to listen when hasidim told each other of the deeds of their leaders. On one such occasion he heard them speak of the praying of Rabbi Levi Yitzhak. In the sabbath service, when—so they told—the rabbi came to the words: "Holy, holy, holy," in the chanting of which denizens of heaven unite with men, the angels came to listen to what his lips were saying.

"Do you really think that this is so?" asked the innkeeper.

"Yes, it is so," they said.

"And where do the angels go after that?" he inquired. "Do they remain floating in air?"

"No," they answered him. "They fly down and stand around the rabbi."

"And where do you go in the meantime?"

"When the rabbi begins to sing mightily, and dances so mightily through all the house, there is no room for us inside."

"Well," said the innkeeper, "I shall see this matter for myself. He won't get me to budge from the spot!"

At the Feast of the New Moon, when the rabbi began to burn with ecstasy, the innkeeper came up close behind him. The rabbi —in his great fervor—turned around, seizing him by the coat-tails, shook him, pushed him, and thus, shaking and pushing him alternately, dragged him from one end of the house to the other, and back again. The innkeeper hardly knew what was happening to him. He was almost out of his mind. There was a roaring in his ears as of a tremendous surge. Rallying the last shreds of his strength, he wrenched himself free from the hands of the zaddik and fled. From that time on, he too believed that other powers were involved than merely those of this earth.

For Israel

Before reciting the Prayer of Benedictions on New Year's Day, the rabbi of Berditchev sang:

"The dwellers above and the dwellers below, they shake and they quake in the fear of your name; the dwellers in chasms, the dwellers in graves, they quiver and shiver for fear of your name. But the just, in the pales of paradise, break into acclaim and sing your name. That is why I, Levi Yitzhak, son of Sarah, am come before you with pleas and with prayers. What have you to do with Israel? To whom do you speak? To the children of Israel! To whom do you give commandments? To the children of Israel! Whom do you bid say the benedictions? The children of Israel! And so I ask you: What have you to do with Israel? Are there not plenty of Chaldeans, and Medes, and Persians? It must be that they are dear to you, the children of Israel—children of God they are called. Blessed art thou, O Lord our God, King of the world!"

The True King

On another New Year's Day he prefaced the liturgy of the sanctification of God in this wise: "*Fonye* [a nickname current among the Jews to designate the Russians—here used to designate the czar], says he is king." And then he proceeded to enumerate the rulers of great countries, calling each by his nickname. In the end he shouted with joy, and cried: "But I say: 'Glorified and sanctified be His great Name!'"

A Deal

In the middle of a prayer Rabbi Levi Yitzhak said:
"Lord of all the world! A time there was when you went around with that Torah of yours and were willing to sell it at a bargain, like apples that have gone bad, yet no one would buy it from you. No one would even look at you! And then we took it!

Because of this I want to propose a deal. We have many sins and misdeeds, and you an abundance of forgiveness and atonement. Let us exchange! But perhaps you will say: 'Like for like!' My answer is: Had we no sins, what would you do with your forgiveness? So you must balance the deal by giving us life, and children, and food besides!"

An Interruption

On the forenoon of the Day of Atonement, when the rabbi of Berditchev came to that place in the recital of the Temple Service where the high priest sprinkles the atoning drops of blood and has to say the words: "And thus did he count: one: one and one: one and two: one and three . . ." he was so overwhelmed with fervor that—when he had said "one" the second time—he fell on the floor and lay as one dead. In vain did those standing near seek to revive him. They lifted him from the floor, carried him to his room, and laid him on his bed. Then the hasidim, who knew very well that this was a state which had to do with the soul, and not a sickness of the body, continued in prayer. Toward evening—they had just begun to say the Closing Prayer —the rabbi rushed in, and up to the pulpit, shouting: ". . . and one!" Then he bethought himself and said the prayers in the correct sequence.

Struggle

Once, on the Day of Atonement, the rabbi of Berditchev was praying in the synagogue of Lwow. In the middle of the Additional Prayer he suddenly stopped, and the people heard him say in Polish, in a threatening voice: "I'll show you . . ."
During the evening meal the son of the rabbi of Lwow said to him of Berditchev: "I shall not take the liberty of criticizing your manner of praying. But may I ask you one thing: How could you interrupt your prayer, and with Polish words at that?"
The rabbi of Berditchev replied: "I managed to down my other enemies, but this was the only way I could get the better of the prince-demon of Poland."

The Wish

Every year on the Day of Atonement a woman came to Berditchev to pray with the congregation of Rabbi Levi Yitzhak. Once she was delayed and when she reached the House of Prayer night had already fallen. The woman was vexed and sorrowful, for she was certain the Evening Service must be over. But the rabbi had not even begun. He had waited for the woman to come —and his astonished congregation with him. When she grew aware that he had not yet recited "All Vows," she was filled with great joy and said to God: "Lord of the world, what shall I wish you in return for the good you have vouchsafed me! I wish you may have as much joy of your children as you have just now granted me!"

Then—even while she was speaking—an hour replete with the grace of God came upon the world.

How to Weigh

Once, when the Day of Atonement was over, Shemuel, the rabbi of Berditchev's favorite disciple, came into his master's room to see how he was after the long fast and the almost superhuman fervor he had put into the day's service. Although the night was well advanced, the zaddik's cup of coffee still stood before him untasted. When he saw his disciple he said: "Good that you have come, Shemuel. Now I can tell it. For you must know that today Satan preferred charges against the judgment of Heaven. 'You, the court of justice,' he said, 'tell me why this is: When a man steals a ruble from his fellow, you weigh the coin in order to measure his sin. But if a man gives his fellow a ruble out of charity, you weigh the recipient and all the persons in his house who have been benefited by the gift. Why do you not merely weigh the coin in this instance too? Or why, in the first instance, do you not put in the scales the man who has been robbed and all those who have suffered because of the robbery?' Then I came forward and explained: 'A benefactor wishes to preserve the lives of people, and so the people must be weighed. But the robber wants only the money. He does not even think of the people he is taking it from, and that is why—in this instance—the coin alone need be weighed.' That was how I silenced the plaintiff!".

The Song of "You"

The rabbi of Berditchev used to sing a song, part of which is as follows.

> Where I wander—you!
> Where I ponder—You!
> Only You, You again, always You!
> You! You! You!
> When I am gladdened—You!
> When I am saddened—You!
> Only You, You again, always You!
> You! You! You!
> Sky is You! Earth is You!
> You above! You below!
> In every trend, at every end,
> Only You, You again, always You!
> You! You! You!

Suffering and Prayer

Whenever Rabbi Levi Yitzhak came to that passage in the Haggadah of Passover which deals with the four sons, and in it read about the fourth son, about him who "knows not how to ask," he said: " 'The one who knows not how to ask,' that is myself, Levi Yitzhak of Berditchev. I do not know how to ask you, Lord of the world, and even if I did know, I could not bear to do it. How could I venture to ask you why everything happens as it does, why we are driven from one exile into another, why our foes are allowed to torment us so. But in the Haggadah, the father of him 'who knows not how to ask,' is told: 'It is for you to disclose it to him.' And the Haggadah refers to the Scriptures, in which it is written: 'And thou shalt tell thy son.' And, Lord of the world, am I not your son? I do not beg you to reveal to me the secret of your ways—I could not bear it' But show me one thing; show it to me more clearly and more deeply: show me what this, which is happening at this very moment, means to me, what it demands of me, what you, Lord of the world, are telling me by way of it. Ah, it is not why I suffer, that I wish to know, but only whether I suffer for your sake."

His Wife's Prayer

A prayer has come down to us from Pearl, the rabbi of Berditchev's wife. Whenever she kneaded and baked the loaves for the sabbath, she prayed: "Lord of the world, I beg you to help me that, when my husband Levi Yitzhak says the blessing upon these loaves on the sabbath, he may have in his mind what I have in my mind this very hour that I knead them and bake them."

Two Kinds of Praying

Once, on the eve of the sabbath, Rabbi Levi Yitzhak prayed before the congregation of a town in which he was stopping as a guest. As always, now too he drew out the prayer far beyond its usual length through the many exclamations and gestures not provided for in any liturgy. When he had finished, the rav of that town went up to him, proffered the sabbath greetings, and asked: "Why are you not more careful not to tire the congregation? Do not our sages relate of Rabbi Akiba that, whenever he prayed *with* the congregation, he did so quickly, but that when he prayed alone, he yielded himself to his transports, so that frequently he began in one corner of the room and ended up in another."

The rabbi of Berditchev replied: "How is it possible to assume that Rabbi Akiba with his countless disciples hastened his prayer in order not to tire the congregation! For surely every member of it was more than happy to listen to his master hour after hour! The meaning of this talmudic story is more likely this: When Rabbi Akiba really prayed with the congregation, that is to say, when the congregation felt at heart the same fervor as he, his prayer could well be short, for he had to pray only for himself. But when he prayed alone, that is to say, when he prayed with his congregation, but his was the only heart fervent among them, he had to draw out his prayer to lift their hearts to the level of his."

With Open Eyes

Once Rabbi Levi Yitzhak told the maggid of Koznitz, whose guest he was, that he intended going to Vilna, the center of the opponents of hasidic teachings, in order to debate with them. "I should like to ask you a question," said the maggid. "Why do you go contrary to the custom, in that you recite the Eighteen Benedictions with open eyes?"

"Dear heart," said the rabbi of Berditchev, "do you think that—when I do this—I see anything at all?"

"I know very well," the maggid replied, "that you see nothing whatsoever, but what will you say to those others when they ask you this question?"

The Hoarse Reader

In the congregation of Rabbi Levi Yitzhak there was a reader who had grown hoarse. The rabbi asked him:

"How is it that you are hoarse?"

"Because I prayed before the pulpit," answered the other.

"Quite right," said the rabbi. "If one prays before the pulpit one grows hoarse, but if one prays before the living God, then one does not grow hoarse."

The Absent Ones

Once, after he had recited the Eighteen Benedictions, the rabbi of Berditchev went up to certain persons in the House of Prayer, and greeted them, saying: "Peace be with you," several times over, as though they had just come back from a long journey. When they looked at him in surprise, he said: "Why are you so astonished? You were far away, weren't you? You in a market-place, and you on a ship with a cargo of grain, and when the sound of praying ceased, you returned, and so I greeted you."

Babbling Sounds

Rabbi Levi Yitzhak once came to an inn where many merchants were stopping on the way to market their wares. The place was far from Berditchev and so no one knew the zaddik. In the early morning the guests wanted to pray, but since there was only a single pair of phylacteries in the whole house, one after another put them on and rattled off his prayer, and handed them on to the next. When they had all prayed, the rabbi called the young men to him, saying that he wanted to ask them something. When they had come close, he looked gravely into their faces and said: "Ma—ma—ma; va—va—va."

"What do you mean?" cried the young men, but he only repeated the same meaningless syllables. Then they took him for a fool.

But now he said: "How is it you do not understand this language which you yourselves have just used in speaking to God?"

For a moment the young men were taken aback and stood silent. Then one of them said: "Have you never seen a child in the cradle, who does not yet know how to put sounds together into words? Have you not heard him make babbling sounds, such as 'ma—ma—ma; va—va—va'? All the sages and scholars in the world cannot understand him, but the moment his mother comes, she knows exactly what he means."

When the rabbi heard this answer, he began to dance for joy. And from that time on, whenever on the Days of Awe he spoke to God in his own fashion in the midst of prayer, he never failed to tell this answer to him.

The Foolish Prayer

At the close of the Day of Atonement, the rabbi of Berditchev said to one of his hasidim: "I know what you prayed for this day! On the eve, you begged God to give you the thousand rubles which you need in order to live and usually earn in the course of a year, all at once, at the beginning of the year, so that the toil and trouble of business may not distract you from learning and prayer. But in the morning you thought better of it and decided that if you had the thousand rubles all at once, you would probably launch a new and bigger business enterprise which would take up even more of your time. And so you begged to receive half the amount every half year. And before the Closing Prayer, this too seemed precarious to you, and you expressed the wish for quarterly instalments, so you might learn and pray quite undisturbed. But what makes you think that your learning and praying is needed in Heaven? Perhaps what is needed there is that you toil and rack your brains."

The End of Prayers

At the close of the seventy-second psalm are the words: "And let the whole earth be filled with His glory. Amen, and Amen. The prayers of David the son of Jesse are ended."

Concerning this Rabbi Levi Yitzhak said: "All prayers and hymns are a plea to have His glory revealed throughout the world. But if once the whole earth is, indeed, filled with it, there will be no further need to pray."

Worldly Talk

When Rabbi Levi Yitzhak came to Nikolsburg to visit Rabbi Shmelke who had taught him the way of fervor when he was young, and whom he had not seen in a long time, he went into the kitchen, covered with his prayer shawl and with double phylacteries on his forehead, and asked Rabbi Shmelke's wife —on this very first morning—what dishes were being prepared for the noonday meal. His question, though rather surprising, was answered. Then he went on to ask whether the cooks had really mastered their art, and other things of the same sort. Rabbi Shmelke's disciples, who heard of this, took him for a veritable glutton. He, however, now entered the House of Prayer and—while the congregation prayed—began to talk to an utterly insignificant man, despised by all, on quite unimportant worldly subjects, as those standing near could determine. One of the disciples could not bear to observe such behavior any longer and said roughly to the stranger: "Silence! Idle chatter is forbidden here!" But the rabbi of Berditchev paid no attention to him and continued his conversation.

At the midday meal, Rabbi Shmelke greeted him joyfully, bade him sit at his side, and ate from the same bowl as he. His disciples, who had heard of the curious manners of the visitor, marked these signs of favor and friendship with sullen surprise.

When the meal was over, one of them could no longer suppress his annoyance and asked his master why he showered honors on so empty-headed and impudent a man who had behaved in such and such a way. The zaddik replied: "In the Gemara we read: 'Rab (Abba Areka), for all the days of his life never spoke of worldly matters.' Is this praise not strange? Does it indicate that the other masters spent their time in worldly talk? Can nothing worthier be told of Rab? The meaning is this: Whatever worldly affairs he discussed with people in the course of the day, each of his words was, in reality, filled with secret significance and a secret purpose, and made itself felt in the higher world; and his spirit remained steadfast in such service all day long. That is why our sages have accorded him praise of which none other was found worthy. What others could do for only three hours, after which they sank from this level, he could do throughout the day. And the same is true of Rabbi Levi Yitzhak. What I can do for only three hours, he can do the whole day through: concentrate his spirit, so that it makes itself felt in the world of Heaven, even with talk which men consider idle."

He Who Laughed

Rabbi Moshe Leib of Sasov was deeply devoted to the zaddik of Berditchev. His disciple Abraham David, later the rabbi of Buczacz, besieged his master for permission to go to that other, whose manner of teaching he wished very much to observe at close quarters. Rabbi Moshe Leib did not want to grant his request. "In the book of Daniel," he said, "we read that 'they had ability to stand in the king's palace.' Our sages explain these words in this way: that they had learned to restrain themselves from laughing, sleeping, and other things besides. Now Rabbi Levi Yitzhak never ceases to burn with unfailing fire. Into all he does he puts his flame-like soul. And so he who ventures into his presence must be very sure he is able to contain his laughter at observing the curious gestures of the holy man when he prays and when he eats."

The disciple promised he would not give way to laughter, and so the rabbi of Sasov permitted him to go to Berditchev for the sabbath. But when, at table, he saw the convulsive movements of the zaddik, and the faces he made, he could no longer control himself and burst out laughing. Then, he fell into a frenzy; his fits of laughter recurred over and over. Finally he had to be led away from the table and—when the sabbath was over—sent back to Sasov under guard.

When Rabbi Moshe Leib saw him, he wrote to the zaddik: "I sent you a vessel which was whole, and you gave it back to me in pieces."

The sickness of Abraham David lasted thirty days. Then he was suddenly well. From that time on he gave a feast of thanks on the anniversary of that day, and on this occasion told the story of his visit to Berditchev, ending with the words of the psalm: "Give thanks unto the Lord, for He is good, for His mercy endureth forever."

Day After Day

Every evening the rabbi of Berditchev examined in his heart what he had done on that day, and repented every flaw he discovered. He said: "Levi Yitzhak will not do this again." Then he chided himself: "Levi Yitzhak said exactly the same thing yesterday!" And added: "Yesterday Levi Yitzhak did not speak the truth, but he does speak the truth today."

He used to say: "Like a woman who suffers overwhelming pain in child-birth, and swears she will never lie with her husband again, and yet forgets her oath, so on every Day of Atonement we confess our faults and promise to turn, and yet we go on sinning, and You go on forgiving us."

Eternal Beginnings

A student asked the rabbi of Berditchev: "The Talmud teaches that 'Those who are perfect in righteousness cannot stand in that place where those stand who turn to God.' According to this, one who has been stainless from youth comes after one who has transgressed against God many times, and cannot attain to his rung?"

The zaddik replied: "He who sees a new light every day, light he did not see the day before, if he wishes truly to serve, must condemn his imperfect service of yesterday, atone for it, and start afresh. The stainless one who believes he has done perfect service, and persists in it, does not accept the light, and comes after him who ever turns anew."

Envy

Walking in the street, the rabbi of Berditchev once went up to a man who held an important office and was as evil-minded as he was powerful, took hold of the hem of his coat, and said: "Sir, I envy you! When you turn to God, each of your flaws will become a ray of light, and you will shine with a great light. Sir, I envy you your flood of radiance!"

The Seder of the Ignorant Man

Once Rabbi Levi Yitzhak held the seder of the first night of Passover so devoutly, that every word and every rite glowed at the zaddik's table, with all the holiness of its secret significance. In the dawn after the celebration Rabbi Levi Yitzhak sat in his room, joyful and proud that he had performed so successful a service. But, of a sudden, he heard a voice, saying: "More pleasing to me than your seder is that of Hayyim, the water-carrier."

The rabbi summoned the people in his house and his disciples, and inquired about the man whose name he had heard. Nobody knew him. At the zaddik's bidding some of his disciples went in search of him. They had to ask around for a long time before—at the outskirts of the city, where only poor people live—they were shown the house of Hayyim, the water-carrier. They knocked at the door. A woman came out and asked what they wanted. When they told her she was amazed. "Yes," she said, "Hayyim, the water-carrier, is my husband. But he cannot go with you because he drank a lot yesterday and is sleeping it off now. If you wake him you will find that he cannot manage to lift his feet."

All they said in reply was: "It is the rabbi's orders." They went and shook him from his sleep. He only blinked at them, could not understand what they wanted him for, and attempted to turn over and go on sleeping. But they raised him from his bed, took hold of him, and between them brought him to the zaddik, all but carrying him on their shoulders. The rabbi had him put in a chair near him. When he was seated, silent and bewildered, Levi Yitzhak leaned toward him and said: "Rabbi Hayyim, dear heart, what mystic intention was in your mind when you gathered what is leavened?"

The water-carrier looked at him dully, shook his head, and replied: "Master, I just looked into every corner, and gathered it together."

The astonished zaddik continued questioning him: "And what consecration did you think upon in the burning of it?"

The man pondered, looked distressed, and said hesitatingly: "Master, I forgot to burn it. And now I remember—it is all still lying on the shelf."

When Rabbi Levi Yitzhak heard this, he grew more and more uncertain, but he continued asking. "And tell me, Rabbi Hayyim, how did you celebrate the seder?"

Then something seemed to quicken in the eyes and limbs of the man, and he replied in humble tones: "Rabbi, I shall tell you the truth. You see, I always heard that it is forbidden to drink brandy the eight days of the festival, so yesterday morning I drank enough to last me eight days. And so I got tired and fell asleep. Then my wife woke me, and it was evening, and she said to me: 'Why don't you celebrate the seder like all other Jews?' Said I: 'What do you want with me? I am an ignorant man, and my father was an ignorant man, and I don't know what to do and what not to do. But one thing I know: Our fathers and mothers were in captivity in the land of the Gypsies, and we have a God, and he led them out, and into freedom. And see: now we are again in captivity and I know, and I tell you that God will lead us to freedom too.' And then I saw before me a table, and the cloth gleamed like the sun, and on it were platters with matzot and eggs and other dishes, and bottles of red wine. I ate of the matzot and eggs and drank of the wine, and gave my wife to eat and to drink. And then I was overcome with joy, and lifted my cup to God, and said: 'See, God, I drink this cup to you! And do you lean down to us and make us free!' So we sat and drank and rejoiced before God. And then I felt tired, lay down, and fell asleep."

At the Holy Feast of the Seven Shepherds

Rabbi Levi Yitzhak often welcomed at his table an honest and untaught man whom his disciples regarded askance because they thought him incapable of understanding what the rabbi said. And what business has one who boils pitch among those who compound ointments! But because the man was good-natured and simple, he either did not notice the attitude of the rabbi's disciples, or did not let it ruffle him, so that finally they asked the zaddik's wife to show the lout the door. Since she did not want to do this without her husband's permission, she reported to him the misgivings and the request of his disciples. The rabbi replied: "When the Seven Shepherds once sit at the holy feast: Adam, Seth, Methuselah to the right, Abraham, Jacob, Moses to the left, David in the middle, and a poor untutored man, Levi Yitzhak of Berditchev, goes up to them, I believe they will even nod to that lout."

Moses and Mount Sinai

Once the rabbi of Berditchev was asked this question: "How is it that Moses, who in his great humility had implored God not to send him but another to Pharaoh, did not for a single instant hesitate to receive the Torah?"
"He had seen the tall mountains come before God," said the rabbi, "and each beg the privilege of being the one on which the revelation should come to pass. But God chose little Mount Sinai. That is why—when he saw that he too was chosen—Moses did not resist, but followed the call."

His Second Name

Rabbi Levi Yitzhak's second name was *Derbarmdiger,* "Merciful," and by this name which was, however, not his father's, he was known to the authorities and inscribed in their books. And this was how it happened. The king issued a decree that everyone must add to his name a second name, and since the Jews were slow to obey, the sheriff of Berditchev went from house to house to enforce the new law. When he crossed Rabbi Levi Yitzhak's threshold and mumbled his question by rote, the zaddik looked at him as one human being looks at another, and—ignoring the question—said: "Endeavor to imitate the quality of God. As he is merciful, so you too shall be merciful." But the sheriff only pulled out his list and noted down: "First name, Levi Yitzhak, second name Merciful."

The Phylacteries of God

In the middle of a prayer, the rabbi of Berditchev once said to God: "Lord of the world, you must forgive Israel their sins. If you do this—good. But if you do not do this, I shall tell all the world that the phylacteries you wear are invalid. For what is the verse enclosed in your phylacteries? It is a verse of David's, of your anointed: 'Who is like thy people Israel, a unique nation on earth!' But if you do not forgive Israel their sins, then they are no longer a 'unique nation on earth,' the verse contained in your phylacteries is untrue, and they are become invalid."

Another time he said: "Lord of the world, Israel are your head-phylacteries. When the phylacteries of a simple Jew fall to the ground, he picks them up carefully, cleans them, and kisses them. Lord, your phylacteries have fallen to the ground."

The Drayman

Once the rabbi of Berditchev saw a drayman arrayed for the Morning Service in prayer shawl and phylacteries. He was greasing the wheels of his wagon. "Lord of the world!" he exclaimed delightedly. "Behold this man! Behold the devoutness of your people. Even when they grease the wheels of a wagon, they still are mindful of your name!"

The Woman Who Cried

The rabbi of Berditchev told the following:

"Once, just before New Year's Day, a woman came to me and cried and cried. I asked her, 'Why are you crying? Why are you crying?' She said: 'Why shouldn't I cry? My head hurts!

222

My head hurts!' Said I to her: 'Don't cry. If you cry, your head
will only hurt more.' She answered: 'Why shouldn't I cry?
Why shouldn't I cry? I have an only son, and now this holy
and awful day is coming, and I don't know whether my son
will pass when God makes judgment.' Said I to her: 'Don't cry!
Don't cry! He will surely pass when God makes judgment, for
look, it is written: Is not Ephraim a precious son unto Me? Is
he a child of delight? For as often as I speak against him, I do
earnestly remember him still. Therefore my heart yearneth for
him. I will surely have compassion upon him, saith the Lord.' "
This incident the rabbi of Berditchev used to relate in a curious singing tone, and in the same tone the hasidim still tell
it today.

On the Ground

A man came to Rabbi Levi Yitzhak and complained: "Rabbi,
what shall I do with the lie that keeps sneaking into my heart?"
He stopped and then cried aloud: "Oh, and even what I just
said was not said truthfully! I shall never find truth!" In despair he threw himself on the ground.
"How fervently this man seeks the truth!" said the rabbi. With
a gentle hand he raised him from the ground and said: "It is
written: 'The truth will grow out of the ground.' "

The Thick Prayerbook

On one eve of the Day of Atonement, the rabbi of Berditchev
waited for a while before going to the pulpit to read the prayers and walked back and forth in the House of Prayer. In a
corner he found a man crouched on the floor and weeping.
When he questioned him, the man replied: "Up to a short time
ago I had all good things, and now I am wretched. Rabbi, I
lived in a village and no hungry man went from my door unfed.
My wife used to bring home poor wayfarers she met on the
road, and see to their needs. And then He comes along"—here
the man pointed toward the sky—"takes my wife and my house
from one day to the next. There I was with six small children,
without a wife, without a house! And I had a thick prayerbook,
and all the hymns were in it in just the right order; you didn't

have to hunt around, and that burned up along with everything else. Now you tell me, Rabbi, can I forgive Him?"

The zaddik had them look for a prayerbook like the one the man described. When it was brought, the man began to turn the pages to see if everything was in the correct sequence, and the rabbi of Berditchev waited the while. Finally he asked: "Do you forgive Him now?"

"Yes," said the man. Then the rabbi went to the pulpit and intoned the prayer "All Vows."

The Wisdom of Solomon

They asked Rabbi Levi Yitzhak of Berditchev: "With regard to that passage in the Scriptures which states that King Solomon was wiser than all other men, it has been observed: 'Even wiser than fools.' What meaning can there be in these apparently meaningless words?"

The rabbi of Berditchev explained: "One characteristic of a fool is that he considers himself wiser than anyone else, and no one can convince him that he is a fool and that what he does is folly. But Solomon's wisdom was so great that it could assume many different guises, including the guise of the fool. That was why he could hold true converse with fools, and impress their hearts until they recognized and professed the sort of people they were."

Abraham and Lot

In the course of a journey, the rabbi of Berditchev stopped in Lwow and went to the house of a rich and respected man. When he was admitted to the master of the house, he begged for a day's lodging but was silent concerning his name and calling. The rich man answered him gruffly: "I have no use for wayfarers. Why don't you go to an inn?"

"I am not a man to stay at an inn," said the rabbi. "Just give me a little space in one of your rooms and I shall not trouble you for anything else."

"Away with you!" cried the other. "If—as you say—you are not a man to stay at an inn, go to the school-teacher around the corner. He likes to welcome vagrants like yourself with honor, and to give them food and drink."

Rabbi Levi Yitzhak went to the school-teacher, was received with honor, and given food and drink. But on his way there someone had recognized him, and soon the whole town buzzed with the news that the holy rabbi of Berditchev was there and had taken lodgings in the house of the school-teacher. Hardly had he rested a little, when a great throng of people desiring to enter gathered at the door. When it was opened they flooded in to be blessed by the zaddik. Among them was the rich man. He fought his way to the rabbi and said: "May the master forgive me and honor my house with his visit! All the zaddikim who ever came to Lwow were my guests."

Rabbi Levi Yitzhak turned to those standing around him and said: "Do you know the difference between our Father Abraham, peace be with him, and Lot? Why does such a spirit of satisfaction pervade the story of how Abraham set before the angels curd and milk and tender calf? Did not Lot also bake for them and give them to eat? And why is the fact that Abraham received them in his tent regarded as so deserving an action? For Lot also asked them in and gave them shelter. Now this is the truth of the matter: In the case of Lot it is written that angels came to Sodom. But concerning Abraham, the Scriptures say: ' . . . and he lifted up his eyes and looked, and lo, three men stood over against him.' Lot saw angelic shapes, Abraham poor, dusty wayfarers in need of food and rest."

Drudgery

Rabbi Levi Yitzhak discovered that the girls who knead the dough for the unleavened bread drudged from early morning until late at night. Then he cried aloud to the congregation gathered in the House of Prayer: "Those who hate Israel accuse us of baking the unleavened bread with the blood of Christians. But no, we bake them with the blood of Jews!"

Charity

When Levi Yitzhak became rav in Berditchev, he made an agreement with the leaders of the congregation that they were not to ask him to their meetings unless they intended to discuss the introduction of a new usage or a new procedure. One day they asked him to come to a meeting. Immediately after greeting them, he asked: "What is the new procedure you wish to establish?"

They answered: "From now on we do not want the poor to beg at the threshold. We want to put up a box, and all the well-to-do people are to put money into it, each according to his means, and these funds shall be used to provide for the needy."

When the rabbi heard this, he said: "My brothers, did I not beg you not to call me away from my studies and summon me to a meeting for the sake of an old usage or an old procedure?"

The leaders were astonished and protested: "But master, the procedure under discussion today *is* new!"

"You are mistaken," he cried. "It is age-old! It is an old, old procedure that dates back to Sodom and Gomorrah. Do you remember what is told about the girl from Sodom, who gave a beggar a piece of bread? How they took her and stripped her and smeared her naked body with honey, and exposed her for bees to devour, because of the great crime she had committed! Who knows—perhaps they too had a community box into which the well-to-do dropped their alms in order not to be forced to face their poor brothers eye to eye."

In a Hurry

The Rabbi of Berditchev saw a man hurrying along the street, looking neither right nor left. "Why are you rushing so?" he asked him.

"I am after my livelihood," the man replied.

"And how do you know," continued the rabbi, "that your livelihood is running on before you, so that you have to rush after it? Perhaps it is behind you, and all you need do to encounter it is to stand still—but you are running away from it!"

What Are You Doing?

Another time the Rabbi of Berditchev saw a man in the marketplace, a man so intent upon his business that he never looked up. He stopped him and asked: "What are you doing?"

The man answered hurriedly: "I have no time to talk to you now."

But the zaddik refused to be snubbed. He repeated his question: "What are you doing?"

Impatiently the man cried: "Don't delay me. I have to attend to my business."

But the rabbi insisted. "All right," he said. "But you, yourself—what are you doing? Everything you are so worried about is in the hands of God, and all that is in yours is to fear God."

The man looked up—and for the first time he knew what the fear of God was.

The Two Generals

Rabbi Levi Yitzhak said: "Whether a man really loves God—that can be determined by the love he bears his fellow-men. I shall give you a parable.

"Once upon a time a country was suffering from the ravages of war. The general who headed the army which was sent against the foe, was vanquished. The king discharged him and put in his place another man who succeeded in driving out the invader. The first general was suspected of betraying his country. The king wondered whether there was any way to find out whether he really loved or hated him. He realized that there was one unerring sign which would discover the truth to him: if the man, about whom he was in doubt, showed friendship for his rival and expressed unalloyed joy at his success, he might be regarded as trustworthy; but if he plotted against his rival, this would prove his guilt.

"God created man to strive against the evil in his soul. Now there is many a man who does, indeed, love God, but is defeated in that bitter struggle. He can be recognized by his ability to share whole-heartedly and without reservations in the happiness of his victorious fellow-man."

Amalek

This is how Rabbi Levi Yitzhak expounded the verse in the Scriptures: "Remember what Amalek did unto thee."

Because you are a man, you first are permitted to remember what the power of evil has done to you. But when you ascend to the rung of the zaddikim, and your heart has rest from all your enemies round about, then you will "blot out the remembrance of Amalek from under Heaven," and will remember only what the power of evil has done to Heaven: how it set up a wall between God and Israel, and drove into exile the Divine Presence.

The Greatness of Pharaoh

Rabbi Levi Yitzhak said:
"I envy Pharaoh! What glorification of the Name of God did his stubbornness beget!"

Chameleons

Rabbi Levi Yitzhak said:
"It is written: '. . . and shall deal corruptly, and make a graven image, even the form of any thing . . .' This refers to the 'chameleons,' who when they go among hasidim, act like hasidim, and when they are among renegades, adapt themselves to the ways of renegades, and make for themselves the forms of all manner of things."

Perhaps

A very learned man who had heard of the rabbi of Berditchev— one of those who boasted of being enlightened—looked him up in order to debate with him as he was in the habit of doing with others, and refuting his old-fashioned proofs for the truth of his faith. When he entered the zaddik's room, he saw him walking up and down, a book in his hand, immersed in ecstatic thought. The rabbi took no notice of his visitor. After a time, however, he stopped, gave him a brief glance and said: "But perhaps it is true after all!"
In vain did the learned man try to rally his self-confidence. His knees shook, for the zaddik was terrible to behold and his simple words were terrible to hear. But now Rabbi Levi Yitzhak turned to him and calmly addressed him: "My son, the great Torah scholars with whom you debated, wasted their words on you. When you left them you only laughed at what they

had said. They could not set God and his kingdom on the table before you, and I cannot do this either. But, my son, only think! Perhaps it is true. Perhaps it is true after all!" The enlightened man made the utmost effort to reply, but the terrible "perhaps" beat on his ears again and again and broke down his resistance.

The False Messiahs

An unbeliever once expounded to the rabbi of Berditchev that even the great old masters had erred gravely, that Rabbi Akiba, for instance, had taken Bar Kokhba, the rebel, for the Messiah and honored him accordingly.

The rabbi of Berditchev replied: "There was an emperor whose only son fell ill. One physician advised them to spread an acrid salve on a piece of linen and wrap it around the bare body of the patient. Another contradicted him, saying that the boy was too weak to bear the great pain the salve would cause him. A third prescribed a sleeping potion, but the fourth feared it might prove injurious to the patient's heart. Then the fifth suggested that they give the prince a spoonful whenever he woke up and was in pain. And so it was done.

"When God saw that the soul of Israel had sickened, he wrapped it in the acrid linen of the Exile, and that the soul might bear it, he swathed it in numbing sleep. But lest this destroy it, he wakes it from time to time with the hope in a false Messiah, and then lulls it to rest again until the night is past and the true Messiah appears. And for the sake of this, even the eyes of sages are sometimes blinded."

In the Market-Place

The rabbi of Berditchev was once in a big market-place where he saw a welter of men, each possessed with the greed of making profits. He climbed on the roof of a house and called down in a loud voice: "You people, you are forgetting to fear God."

Once and Now

The rabbi of Berditchev said: "What I see before me is a topsy-turvy world. Once the whole truth was in the alleys and market-places of Israel; there everyone told the truth. But when they came to the House of Prayer, they managed to tell lies. Now it is just the other way round. In the streets and in the squares they utter falsehoods, but when they enter the House of Prayer, they confess the truth. For once it was thus in Israel: Truth and faithfulness were the lamps lighting their steps, and when they went to the market-place and into the world of trade, with their souls they proved the words: Your 'yes' be true and your 'no' be true, and all their trading was done in good faith. But when they came to the House of Prayer they beat their breasts and said: 'We have trespassed! We have dealt treacherously! We have robbed!' And all this was a lie because they had kept faith before God and Man. Today the reverse takes place: in trading they lie and cheat; in their prayer they profess the truth."

The Holy of Holies

Rabbi Levi Yitzhak said: "We are forbidden to think evil thoughts, for the mind of man is the Holy of Holies. In it is the Ark with the tablets of the law, and if he permits evil thoughts to arise within him, he is setting an idol up in the Temple. But when, in the midst of praying, the zaddik is seized with great fervor, when he kindles with flame and lifts his hands, it is as once, when—in the Holy of Holies—the cherubim pointed upward their wings."

The Wicked Plot

"We must not mortify our flesh!" That is what the rabbi of Berditchev used to say. "It is nothing but the tempting of the Evil Urge which wants to weaken our spirit, in order to keep us from serving God rightly.

"Once two strong men were wrestling with each other and neither could prevail over his opponent. Then one of them had an idea. 'I must manage to lessen the power of his mind,' he said to himself. 'With that I shall have conquered his body.' That is just what the Evil Urge wants to do when it tempts us to mortify our flesh."

230

True Sorrow and True Joy

When he was asked which was the right way, that of sorrow or that of joy, the rabbi of Berditchev said:

"There are two kinds of sorrow and two kinds of joy. When a man broods over the misfortunes that have come upon him, when he cowers in a corner and despairs of help—that is a bad kind of sorrow, concerning which it is said: 'The Divine Presence does not dwell in a place of dejection.' The other kind is the honest grief of a man who knows what he lacks. The same is true of joy. He who is devoid of inner substance and, in the midst of his empty pleasures, does not feel it, nor tries to fill his lack, is a fool. But he who is truly joyful is like a man whose house has burned down, who feels his need deep in his soul and begins to build anew. Over every stone that is laid, his heart rejoices."

The Dance

When his son had died, Rabbi Levi Yitzhak danced as he followed the bier. Some of his hasidim could not refrain from expressing their astonishment. "A pure soul," said he, "was given to me. A pure soul I render back."

Discipledom

When Rabbi Kalman, the author of the well-known book "Light and Sun," was five years old, he hid under the prayer shawl of the rabbi of Berditchev, as children like to do, and looked up into his veiled face. Then burning strength entered his heart, suffused it, and took possession of him.

After many years Rabbi Elimelekh took some of his noblest disciples to the rabbi of Berditchev. Among them was young Kalman. Rabbi Levi Yitzhak looked at him and recognized him. "That one is mine!" he said.

Knowing

The rabbi of Berditchev and Aaron, his disciple, were on a journey. They stopped in Lizhensk and were the guests of Rabbi Elimelekh. When the rabbi of Berditchev left, his disciple remained behind, settled down in the "Klaus," the House of Study and Prayer of Rabbi Elimelekh, and began to study there without having told him anything about it. In the evening the zaddik went there and noticed him. "Why did you not leave with your rabbi?" he asked.

Aaron replied: "I know my rabbi, and I stayed here because I want to learn to know you too."

Rabbi Elimelekh went close up to him and took him by the coat. "You think you know your rabbi!" he exclaimed. "Why, you don't even know his coat!"

Rabbi Elimelekh's Answer

During the period when, in many places, the enemies of hasidic teachings attacked Rabbi Levi Yitzhak because of his manner of conducting the service, and did him all possible harm, some understanding people wrote to the great Rabbi Elimelekh and asked him how it was that these persons dared to do such things. He answered: "Why does this surprise you? This sort of thing has always gone on in Israel. Alas for our souls! If this were not so, no nation in the whole world could subjugate us!"

The First Page

They asked Rabbi Levi Yitzhak: "Why is the first page number missing in all the tractates of the Babylonian Talmud? Why does each begin with the second?"

He replied: "However much a man may learn, he should always remember that he has not even gotten to the first page."

Hidden Teachings

Rabbi Levi Yitzhak said: "It is written in Isaiah: 'For instruction shall go forth from me.' How shall we interpret this? For we believe with perfect faith that the Torah, which Moses received on Mount Sinai, cannot be changed, and that none other will be given. It is unalterable and we are forbidden to question even one of its letters. But, in reality, not only the black letters but the white gaps in between, are symbols of the teaching, only that we are not able to read those gaps. In time to come God will reveal the white hiddenness of the Torah."

232

On the last New Year's festival in the life of Rabbi Levi Yitzhak, they tried in vain to blow the ram's horn. No one could wring from it a single note. Finally the zaddik himself put it to his lips, but he too did not succeed. It was clear that Satan was involved in this matter. Rabbi Levi Yitzhak put down the horn, laid it aside and cried: "Lord of the world! In your Torah it is written that we Jews are to blow the ram's horn the day on which you created the world. Look down upon us and you will see that all of us have come with our wives and children to do your command. But if we are denied this, if we are no longer your beloved people, well—then let Ivan blow the ram's horn for you!"

All wept and in the depths of their hearts they turned to God. After a time the rabbi put the ram's horn to his lips again, and now it emitted a flawlessly pure sound. After the prayer Rabbi Levi Yitzhak turned to his congregation and said: "I vanquished him, but it will cost me my life. Here I am, a sin-offering for Israel."

He died a few weeks later.

A Period Extended

At the close of the Day of Atonement, as Rabbi Levi Yitzhak came out of the House of Prayer, he said to the people thronging around him: "I tell you that today the time of my life is up and I should be leaving the world this very hour. But I was disturbed and troubled that I would not be able to fulfil the two precious commands, to dwell in the holiday booth and to say the blessing of the citron, that are coming and will be with us in four days. And so I prayed that my time might be extended until after the Feast of Tabernacles, and God heard me." And so it was: on the day after the Rejoicing in the Law the rabbi of Berditchev fell ill, and on the day after that, he died.

The Gates of Prayer

They tell that the hour Rabbi Levi Yitzhak died, a zaddik teaching in a distant city suddenly interrupted his discourse in which he was trying to fuse the power of the doctrine with that of worship, and said to his disciples: "I cannot go on. Everything went dark before my eyes. The gates of prayer are closing. Something must have happened to the great worshipper, to Rabbi Levi Yitzhak."

The Friend

In Rabbi Levi Yitzhak's time, a holy man lived in the city of Berditchev. They called him the rabbi of Morchov because he had grown up in Morchov, in the Ukraine. There was friendship between these two, and in their relation to each other, reproof was open and love hidden. When the zaddik died, the rabbi of Morchov came to walk behind his bier. When they had carried the body out of the house, he went close up to it, leaned down, and whispered something in the ear of the dead. Only the last words were audible: "As it is written: 'Seven weeks you shall count.'" When seven weeks had passed, he himself died.

From That Time On

Rabbi Levi Yitzhak was dead, and from that time on there was no rav in Berditchev. The congregation could find no one to fill the place he had left empty.

ZUSYA OF HANIPOL

The Blessings

Rabbi Zusya used to say: "My mother Mirl, peace be with her, did not pray from the book, because she could not read. All she knew was how to say the blessings. But wherever she said the blessing in the morning, in that place the radiance of the Divine Presence rested the livelong day."

The Parable of the Wood-Cutter

In his youth, Zusya joined the congregation of the Great Maggid, Rabbi Baer of Mezritch. But he did not stay with the other disciples. He roamed through the woods, lay down in hidden places, and sang his praises to God, until the people quoted Solomon's words when they spoke of him: "With her love be thou ravished always." His younger brother Elimelekh, who was still a boy and did not as yet belong to the congregation, sat over his books. He wondered at Zusya and once asked him: "Brother, why do you act so, that everyone in the House of Study says it is strange?" Zusya answered him with a smile: "My brother, I shall tell you a story." And this is the story.

"A poor wood-cutter had a great longing to see the king face to face. So he left his village and walked for many days until he came to the city where the king lived. After trying for a long time, he succeeded in getting employment in the king's palace. He was to tend the stoves. And now he put all the zeal and good sense he was capable of into his work. He went to the forest himself, fetched the best wood, fragrant with resin, split it into even logs, and—at just the right hour—stacked these deftly in the various fire-places. The king enjoyed the good, living warmth. It was better than what he had had, and he asked how this came about. When they told him about the wood-cutter and his work, he sent him a message that he could nave a wish. The poor man begged that he might be allowed to see the king every once in a while. His wish was granted. They made a window in a narrow passage which led to the woodshed and this window faced the king's living-room, so the wood-cutter could look through and satisfy his longing.

"Now once, when the prince was seated at his father's board, he said something which displeased him and was punished by a year's banishment from the king's apartments. For a time he lived in bitter loneliness. Then he began to wander mournfully through the corridors of the palace. When he came to the little window they had made for the wood-cutter, he was seized with still greater longing to see his father again and begged the man to let him look through. They got to talking together.

"My brother," said Zusya to Elimelekh, when he had reached this point in his story, "this is what the wood-cutter told the prince when they were talking to each other. 'You are at home in the rooms of the lord and eat at his table. All you need do is to govern your speech wisely. But I have neither wisdom nor learning, and so I must perform my lowly service that I may sometimes see the lord's face.'"

The Word

This was told by Rabbi Israel of Rizhyn.

"All the pupils of my ancestors, the Great Maggid, transmitted the teachings in his name—all except Rabbi Zusya. And the reason for this was that Rabbi Zusya hardly ever heard his teacher's sermon out to the end. For at the very start, when the maggid recited the verse from the Scriptures which he was going to expound, and began with the words of the Scriptures: 'And God said,' or 'and God spoke,' Rabbi Zusya was overcome with ecstasy, and screamed and gesticulated so wildly that he disturbed the peace of the round table and had to be taken out. And then he stood in the hall or in the woodshed, beat his hands against the walls, and cried aloud: 'And God said!' He did not quiet down until my ancestor had finished expounding the Scriptures. That is why he was not familiar with the sermons of the maggid. But the truth, I tell you—

I tell you, the truth is this: If a man speaks in the spirit of truth and listens in the spirit of truth, one word is enough, for with one word can the world be uplifted, and with one word can the world be redeemed."

Only the Good

Once when young Zusya was in the house of his teacher, Rabbi Baer, a man came before the Great Maggid and begged him to advise and assist him in an enterprise. Zusya saw that this man was full of sin and untouched by any breath of repentance, he grew angry, and spoke to him harshly, saying: "How can a man like yourself, a man who has committed this crime and that, have the boldness to stand before a holy countenance without shame, and without the longing to atone?" The man left in silence, but Zusya regretted what he had said and did not know what to do. Then his teacher pronounced a blessing over him, that from this moment on, he might see only the good in people, even if a person sinned before his very eyes.

But because Zusya's gift of vision could not be taken from him through words spoken by man, it came to pass that from this time on he felt the sins of the people he met, as his own, and blamed himself for them.

Whenever the rabbi of Rizhyn told this about Rabbi Zusya, he was likely to add: "And if all of us were like him, evil would long since have been destroyed, and death overcome, and per fection achieved."

Suffering

When Rabbi Shmelke and his brother visited the maggid of Mezritch, they asked him about the following. "Our sages said certain words which leave us no peace because we do not understand them. They are that men should praise and thank God for suffering just as much as for well-being, and receive it with the same joy. Will you tell us how we are to understand this, rabbi?"

The maggid replied: "Go to the House of Study. There you will find Zusya smoking his pipe. He will give you the explanation." They went to the House of Study and put their question to Rabbi Zusya. He laughed. "You certainly have come to the right man! Better go to someone else rather than to me, for I have never experienced suffering." But the two knew that, from the day he was born to this day, Rabbi Zusya's life had been a web of need and anguish. Then they knew what it was: to accept suffering with love.

The Garments of Mercy

They asked Rabbi Zusya: "We pray, 'And bestow good mercy upon us,' and 'Who bestowest good mercy . . .' Is not every mercy good?"

He explained: "Of course every mercy is good. But the truth of the matter is that all God does is mercy. Only that the world cannot bear the naked fill of his mercy, and so he has sheathed it in garments. That is why we beg him that the garment too may be good."

The Recipient

A man who lived in the same town as Rabbi Zusya saw that he was very poor. So each day he put twenty pennies into the little bag in which Zusya kept his phylacteries, so that he and his family might buy the necessaries of life. From that time on, the man grew richer and richer. The more he had, the more he gave Zusya, and the more he gave Zusya, the more he had.

But once he recalled that Zusya was the disciple of a great maggid, and it occurred to him that if what he gave the disciple was so lavishly rewarded, he might become even more prosperous if he made presents to the master himself. So he traveled to Mezritch and induced Rabbi Baer to accept a substantial gift from him. From this time on, his means shrank until he had lost all the profits he had made during the more fortunate period. He took his trouble to Rabbi Zusya, told him the whole story, and asked him what his present predicament was due to. For had not the rabbi himself told him that his master was immeasurably greater than he?

Zusya replied: "Look! As long as you gave and did not bother to whom, whether to Zusya or another, God gave to you and

238

did not bother to whom. But when you began to seek out especially noble and distinguished recipients, God did exactly the same."

The Offering

They said to Rabbi Zusya: "It is written: 'Speak unto the children of Israel, that they take for Me an offering.' Should it not rather be: 'that they *make* for Me an offering'?"
Rabbi Zusya replied: "It is not enough for him who gives to the needy, to do this in the spirit of holiness. The needy must also take in the spirit of holiness. It is not enough to give in the name of God. What is given, must also be taken in the name of God. That is why it is written: 'that they take for Me an offering.' "

On the Road

For three years Zusya and Elimelekh journeyed through the land, for they wanted to share the lot of the Divine Presence in exile, and convert to it erring mankind. Once they spent the night at an inn where a wedding was being celebrated. The guests were rough and tough fellows to begin with, and had drunk far more than was good for them. They were just trying to think up some new fun for themselves when the poor travelers arrived—in the nick of time for their purpose. They had hardly lain down in a corner, Rabbi Elimelekh against the wall, and Rabbi Zusya beside him, when those fellows came, grabbed Zusya, who was closest to hand, beat him, and tormented him. After a time, they let him slide to the floor and began to dance. Elimelekh was annoyed that they had let him lie on his sack undisturbed. He envied his brother the blows he had received. So he said: "Dear brother, now let me lie in your place, and you sleep in my corner." And they changed places. When the fellows had finished dancing, they wanted to go on with the fun they had had, and laid hands on Rabbi Elimelekh. But one of them cried: "This isn't according to law and order! Let the other one have his share of our gifts of honor!" With that they dragged Zusya out of his corner, gave him a second drubbing, and shouted: "You too shall carry away a souvenir of the wedding!"

Then Zusya laughed and said to Elimelekh: "You see, dear brother. If blows are appointed to a man, they will always find him out, no matter where he puts himself."

The Horses

In the course of their long wanderings, the two brothers, Rabbi Zusya and Rabbi Elimelekh, often came to the city of Ludmir. There they always slept in the house of a poor, devout man. Years later, when their reputation had spread all over the country, they came to Ludmir again, not on foot as before, but in a carriage. The wealthiest man in that little town, who had never wanted to have anything to do with them, came to meet them, the moment he heard they had arrived, and begged them to lodge in his house. But they said: "Nothing has changed in us to make you respect us more than before. What is new is just the horses and the carriage. Take them for your guests, but let us stop with our old host, as usual."

The Fruits of Wandering

When Rabbi Noah of Kobryn, the grandson of Rabbi Moshe of Kobryn, was in Sadagora, he heard someone say, "You will find hasidim up to the point the brothers Rabbi Zusya and Rabbi Elimelekh reached in their long wanderings; beyond that you will not find hasidim."

The Sabbath Feeling

Week after week, from the coming of the Sabbath to the going, and especially when they ate the sabbath meal among the hasidim, and spoke words of teaching, Rabbi Elimelekh and Rabbi Zusya were overcome by a feeling of holiness. Once, when they were together, Rabbi Elimelekh said to Rabbi Zusya: "Brother, I am sometimes afraid that my feeling of holiness on the sabbath may not be a true feeling, and that—in that case—my service may not be the right service."

"Brother," said Zusya, "I too am sometimes afraid of that very thing."

"What shall we do about it?" asked Elimelekh.

Zusya replied: "Let each of us, on a week-day, prepare a meal

240

which is exactly like the sabbath meal. And let us sit with the
hasidim and say words of teaching. Then, if we have that
feeling of holiness, we shall know that our way is not the
true way. But if we do not have it, this will prove that our way
is right."

And they did accordingly. They prepared a sabbath meal on a
week-day, put on sabbath clothes and the fur caps they wore
on the sabbath, ate with the hasidim, and spoke words of
teaching. And the feeling of holiness overcame them just as on
the sabbath. When they were alone together, Rabbi Elimelekh
asked: "Brother, what shall we do?"

"Let us go to the rabbi of Mezritch," said Rabbi Zusya. They
went to Mezritch and told their teacher what was weighing
upon them.

The maggid said: "If you put on sabbath clothes and sabbath
caps, it is quite right that you had a feeling of sabbath holiness. Because sabbath clothes and sabbath caps have the power
of drawing the light of sabbath holiness down to earth. So you
need have no fears."

Zusya and the Sinner

Once Rabbi Zusya came to an inn, and on the forehead of the
innkeeper he saw long years of sin. For a while he neither
spoke nor moved. But when he was alone in the room which
had been assigned to him, the shudder of vicarious experience
overcame him in the midst of singing psalms and he cried
aloud: "Zusya, Zusya, you wicked man! What have you done!
There is no lie that failed to tempt you, and no crime you
have not committed. Zusya, foolish, erring man, what will be
the end of this?" Then he enumerated the sins of the innkeeper,
giving the time and place of each, as his own, and sobbed.
The innkeeper had quietly followed this strange man. He
stood at the door and heard him. First he was seized with dull
dismay, but then penitence and grace were lit within him, and
he woke to God.

Joint Penance

This was told by a reader in the House of Prayer.
When I heard that Rabbi Zusya helped people to turn to God,

241

I decided to go to him. When I arrived in Hanipol, I immediately went to his house, put down my stick and knapsack, and asked for him. The rabbi's wife told me to go to the House of Study. I could see the rabbi from the threshold. He was wearing his prayer shawl, had just taken off his phylacteries, and was reciting the psalm: "Answer me when I call!" While he said these words, he wept more bitterly than I had ever heard or seen anyone weep. And then, on the floor, I saw a man who was moaning quietly to himself. Suddenly he screamed: "I am a great sinner!" It took me quite a while to understand what was going on, and later I learned the whole story.

The man was an assistant in the House of Study of the town he lived in. He had been urged to go to Rabbi Zusya to be told what to do as a penance. But when he stood in front of the rabbi, he refused to do penance. Then—but the rabbi himself told me what happened then. It was when I discussed my own affairs with him and mentioned what I had seen.

"What did Zusya do then?" he said to me. "I climbed down all the rungs until I was with him, and bound the root of my soul to the root of his. Then he had no choice but to do penance along with me." And it was a very great and very terrible penance. But when the man stopped screaming and moaning, I saw the rabbi go up to him. He bent down, took him by the curls at his temples, and gently turned his head around. Finally he lifted him with both hands and set him on his feet. "Thine iniquity is taken away," he said, "and thy sin expiated."

"But I myself"—so the man who told me the story added—"later became the reader in Rabbi Zusya's House of Prayer."

The Bold-faced and the Shame-faced

Our sages say: "The bold-faced go to hell, the shame-faced to paradise." Rabbi Zusya, God's fool, expounded these words as follows. "Whoever is bold in his holiness, may descend to hell in order to raise what is base. He may roam about in alleys and market-places and need not fear evil. But he who

is shame-faced, who lacks boldness, must keep to the heights
of paradise, to studying and praying. He must beware of coming in contact with evil."

Zaddik and Hasidim

On one of the days of heart-searching, the days between New
Year and the Day of Atonement, Rabbi Zusya sat in his chair,
and his hasidim stood around him from morning until evening.
He had lifted his eyes and his heart to Heaven, and loosed
himself from all bodily bonds. While looking at him, one of
his hasidim was overcome with the desire to turn to God, and
the tears streamed over his face. And just as a burning coal
kindles those beside it, so man by man was lit with the flame
of turning. Then the zaddik looked around and fixed them with
his gaze. Again he lifted his eyes and said to God: "Lord of
the world, this is, indeed, the right time for the turning. But
you know that I have not the strength to do penance—so
accept as penance my love and my shame."

Humility

Rabbi Zusya and his brother Rabbi Elimelekh were once dis-
cussing the subject of humility. Elimelekh said: "If a man
contemplates the greatness of the Creator, he will arrive at
true humility."
But Zusya said: "No! A man must begin by being truly
humble. Only then will he recognize the greatness of his
Creator."
They asked their teacher, the maggid, who was right. He decided it in this way. "These and those are the words of the
living God. But the inner grace is his who begins with himself, and not with the Creator."

Of Adam

Zusya once asked his brother, wise Rabbi Elimelekh: "Dear
brother, in the Scriptures we read that the souls of all men
were comprised in Adam. So we too must have been present,
when he ate the apple. I do not understand how I could have
let him eat it! And how could you have let him eat it?"

Elimelekh replied: "We had to just as all had to. For had he not eaten, the poison of the snake would have remained within him in all eternity. He would always have thought: 'All I need do is eat of this tree and I shall be as God—all I need do is eat of this tree, and I shall be as God.' "

"Get Thee Out of Thy Country"

Rabbi Zusya taught:

God said to Abraham: "Get thee out of thy country, and from thy kindred, and from thy father's house, unto the land that I will show thee." God says to man: "First, get you out of your country, that means the dimness you have inflicted on yourself. Then out of your birth-place, that means, out of the dimness your mother inflicted on you. After that, out of the house of your father, that means, out of the dimness your father inflicted on you. Only then will you be able to go to the land that I will show you."

"And Israel Saw"

They asked Rabbi Zusya: "It is written: 'And Israel saw Egypt dead upon the sea-shore.' Why are the Egyptians referred to in the singular and not in the plural? And further on it is written: 'And Israel saw the great hand.' Had they not seen it up to then?"

He expounded: "As long as the prince demon of Egypt was alive and ruled, he saw to it that a curtain separated Israel from their Father in Heaven, so that they could not see his splendor. But when the prince demon of Egypt—and this is the reason for the singular—lay dead on the sea-shore, the curtain tore asunder, and with their open eyes they saw His great hand."

Zusya and His Wife

Zusya's wife was a shrew. She kept nagging him to give her a divorce and his heart was weighed down by her words. One night he called her name and said to her: "Look!" And he showed her that his pillow was wet with tears. Then he went on: "In the Gemara it is written that if a man puts his first

244

wife away, the altar itself will shed tears for him. My pillow is wet with these tears. And now—what do you want? Do you still want a letter of divorce?" From this moment on, she grew quiet. And when she was really quiet, she grew happy. And when she was happy, she grew good.

Zusya and the Birds

Once Rabbi Zusya traveled cross-country collecting money to ransom prisoners. He came to an inn at a time when the innkeeper was not at home. He went through the rooms, according to custom, and in one saw a large cage with all kinds of birds. And Zusya saw that the caged creatures wanted to fly through the spaces of the world and be free birds again. He burned with pity for them and said to himself: "Here you are, Zusya, walking your feet off to ransom prisoners. But what greater ransoming of prisoners can there be than to free these birds from their prison?" Then he opened the cage, and the birds flew out into freedom.

When the innkeeper returned and saw the empty cage, he was very angry, and asked the people in the house who had done this to him. They answered: "A man is loitering about here and he looks like a fool. No one but he can have done this thing." The innkeeper shouted at Zusya: "You fool! How could you have the impudence to rob me of my birds and make worthless the good money I paid for them?" Zusya replied: "You have often read and repeated these words in the psalms: 'His tender mercies are over all His works.'" Then the innkeeper beat him until his hand grew tired and finally threw him out of the house. And Zusya went his way serenely.

His Days

Every morning at rising, before he spoke a word to God or to men, it was Rabbi Zusya's custom to call out: "Good morning to all of Israel!"

During the day, he wrote everything he did down on a slip of paper. Before going to bed at night, he fetched it, read it, and wept until the writing was blurred with his tears.

The Blessing

Whenever Zusya met a Jewish boy, he blessed him with the words: "Be healthy and strong as a goy."

The Song

Once, on the eve of the Day of Atonement, Rabbi Zusya heard a cantor in the House of Prayer, chanting the words: "And it is forgiven," in strange and beautiful tones. Then he called to God: "Lord of the world! Had Israel not sinned, how could such a song have been intoned before you?"

He Who Answers Amen

Concerning the words of our sages: "He who answers 'amen' shall not raise his voice above his who says the blessing," Rabbi Zusya said: "The soul says the blessing; the body answers 'amen.' The body shall not dare to speak more fervently than the soul has spoken."

Zusya's Devotions

Zusya was once a guest in the house of the rabbi of Neskhizh. Shortly after midnight, the host heard sounds coming from his guest's room, so he went to the door and listened. Zusya was running back and forth in the room, saying: "Lord of the world, I love you! But what is there for me to do? I can't do anything." And then he started running back and forth again, repeating the same thing, until suddenly he bethought himself and cried: "Why, I know how to whistle, so I shall whistle something for you." But when he began to whistle, the rabbi of Neskhizh grew frightened.

The Fear of God

Once Zusya prayed to God: "Lord, I love you so much, but I do not fear you enough! Lord, I love you so much, but I do not fear you enough! Let me stand in awe of you like your angels, who are penetrated by your awe-inspiring name." And God heard his prayer, and his name penetrated the hidden heart of Zusya as it does those of the angels. But Zusya crawled under the bed like a little dog, and animal fear shook him until he howled: "Lord, let me love you like Zusya again!" And God heard him this time also.

The Creation of Angels

Once Rabbi Zusya was pondering over that passage in the Talmud which deals with hospitality. There it is written: "Those of Israel, holy are they. Many a one wants to, and has not. Many a one has, and does not want to." He could not understand why both, the hospitable man who has not, and the miser, should be called holy. And because he could not understand, he wept. Then the meaning was revealed to him. Everybody knows that an angel springs from each good deed. But angels have a soul and a body, just as we do, only that their body consists of fire and wind. Now, who wants to and has not, can create only the soul of the angel. Who has, and does not want to, and invites a guest only because he is ashamed not to, can create only the body of the angel. But we know that in Israel everyone vouches for everyone else. And so their works fuse as though they were those of a single being. In the same way, the soul and the body of the angel which has been created are fused together. The miser, to be sure, remains just as unholy as he was. But if the created soul finds a body with which it can clothe itself, the fusion of the two creations manifests the holiness of Israel.

The Accuser

This is Rabbi Zusya's comment on the passage in the Sayings of the Fathers: "He who commits one transgression has gotten himself one accuser." "Every sin begets an accusing angel. But I have never seen a complete angel spring from the sin of a devout man of Israel. Sometimes he lacks a head; sometimes his body is crippled. For when a man of Israel believes in God, believes in him even while he is sinning, his heart aches, and what he does, he does not do with all his will, and so the angel never emerges complete."

247

Above Them

A hasid asked Rabbi Zusya: "Concerning Abraham receiving the three angels, it is written: 'And he took curd and milk and the calf which he had dressed, and set it before them; and he stood above them, under the tree, and they did eat.' It is not strange that here the man stood 'above' the angels?"

Rabbi Zusya expounded: "When a man eats in a state of consecration, he redeems the holy sparks which are imprisoned in food. But the angels are not aware of this service unless the man has told them of it. That is why it is written of Abraham that he 'stood above them.' He let the consecration of the meal descend on them."

The Wheel

Rabbi Israel of Rizhyn had been falsely accused and put in prison. There he said:

"Heaven once revealed to Rabbi Zusya that he was to go to a village not far from Hanipol and guide a tax collector on the true way. He went there immediately and found the man selling vodka to the peasants. He tried to make him stop and say a prayer, but the collector became more and more impatient. When Rabbi Zusya continued to exhort him in spite of his rejection, and even laid an urgent hand on his arm, he took hold of the intruder, shoved him out into the court, and shut the door on him. It was very cold and the rabbi shivered all over. Then he caught sight of an old wagon wheel lying on the ground and put it against his body. And instantly it became a wheel of the Chariot of Heaven and gave out delicious warmth. That was how the tax collector found him. When he saw the blissful smile on Rabbi Zusya's lips, he experienced the truth about life in one small second, and already, with faltering feet and full of amazement at himself, he stood on the true way."

At the Crossroads

On one of his wanderings, Rabbi Zusya came to a crossroads and did not know which of the two roads to take. Then he lifted his eyes and saw the Divine Presence leading the way.

Rabbi Nathan Adler of Frankfort related:

"It is not for nothing that they say the Poles have no *savoir vivre*. No matter when I lift my soul to Heaven, Rabbi Zusya is always there ahead of me. Once I fasted for a long time, in order to reach the gates of Heaven while they are still closed. I stood before the gates, and when they were opened, I was the very first to enter. And whom do you suppose I saw inside? Rabbi Zusya! How he got in, I don't know; but he was certainly there. He had not had the grace to wait until he was admitted. It is not for nothing that they say the Poles have no *savoir vivre*."

Zusya, and Fire and Earth

Zusya once put his hand into the fire. When the flames scorched him and he drew it back, he was surprised and said: "Dear me, how crude is Zusya's body, that it fears fire!"

Another time he said to the earth: "Earth, Earth, you are better than I, and yet I trample on you with my feet. But soon I shall lie under you and be subject to you."

Fire and Cloud

It is told:

On a certain Feast of Tabernacles, before the world had become aware of Zusya, he lived in the booth of the rav of Ostrog. When evening came, the rav lay down on his soft couch heaped high with pillows and blankets, while Zusya slept on the ground in the manner of poor sabbath guests. In the course of the night he said to himself: "Ah, Zishe feels cold; he cannot sleep in the booth." That very instant a fire descended from Heaven and warmed the booth so well that the rav of Ostrog had to throw off feather-beds and blankets. "Now it is warm enough," said Zusya. Immediately the Prince of Fire departed, and the rav of Ostrog had to pull up one cover after another. This recurred a number of times: heat alternated with cold and when morning came the rav of Ostrog no longer addressed his guest as "Zishe," but "Reb Zishe."

When the Feast of Tabernacles was over, Zusya wanted to

continue his journey, but his sore feet would not carry him, and he sighed: "O Lord of the world, Zishe cannot walk!" Then a cloud floated down and said: "Get in."

"Rabbi!" shouted the rav of Ostrog. "I'll rent a carriage for you, but send that cloud away!" From that time on, he no longer called him "Reb Zishe," but "Rebbe Reb Zishe," and ever since then, that was the name he went by in the entire country.

Terror

It is told:

It was after maneuvers, and the victorious army returned via Hanipol. There they made themselves at home in the inn, drank everything in sight, and did not pay a red penny. They wanted to go on drinking, but since there was nothing left, they smashed all the glasses and utensils. Then they demanded more liquor, and because there was none, they beat up the innkeeper and his helpers. The terrified man finally got a message through to Rabbi Zusya. Zusya came at once, stopped outside the window, looked in at the soldiers, and—three times in succession—said the words of the prayer: "Uvekhen ten pahdekha . . . Lord, our God, lay your terror on all of your creatures." At that, all the soldiers rushed out of the door and the windows in mad haste, left their guns and knapsacks behind, and ran down the street without paying any attention to their commanding officer, who came toward them at the outskirts of the town. Not until he called to them in an angry voice, did they stop. They told him: "An old Jew came and yelled: 'Pahdakh!' Then we were scared to death—we don't know how or why— and even now, we are still afraid." The commander led them back to the inn where they had to pay for the damage they had done and give compensation for the beatings, before he let them march on.

The Shepherd's Song

Rabbi Zusya once passed a meadow where a swine-herd in the midst of his flock was playing a song on a willow-flute. He came close and listened until he had learned it and could take it away with him. In this way the song of David, the shepherd boy, was freed from its long captivity.

Sickness

Rabbi Zusya grew to be very old. He spent the last seven years of his life on a sick-bed, for—so it is written of him—he had taken suffering upon himself in order to shrive Israel.

One day he received as visitors the "Seer" of Lublin and Rabbi Hirsh Leib of Olik. The latter said to the Seer: "Why can you not do what Rabbi Yohanan did for his sick friends: give him your hand so that he may rise?"

The rabbi of Lublin burst into tears. Then the rabbi of Olik asked him: "Why do you weep? Do you think he is sick because such is his destiny? He has taken suffering upon himself of his own free will, and is taking it, and if he wanted to rise, he would not need the hand of a stranger to do so."

The Query of Queries

Before his death, Rabbi Zusya said "In the coming world, they will not ask me: 'Why were you not Moses?' They will ask me: 'Why were you not Zusya?'"

The Tombstone

On Rabbi Zusya's tombstone are the words: "One who served God with love, who rejoiced in suffering, who wrested many from their sins."

The Fire

A certain rav in Hanipol, one of our own day, wrote down the following:

At night, when not a soul was in the graveyard, the lantern above Rabbi Zusya's grave fell to the ground. Rabbi Zusya's "tent" lies between that of the Great Maggid and another zaddik. It was a very old rule that no one should visit these graves without having been in the bath of purification, and without taking off his shoes. Only one watchman was allowed to go there without observing these rules, to tend the everlasting light three times a day. The everlasting light burned in three lamps set into one lantern. It burned over a wooden shrine erected above the graves. The shrine was covered with boards, and in it were hundreds of pleas on slips of paper, each brought by another visitor. On the earth lay twigs, and these too had been laid down on the graves by visitors, for such was the custom. Now, when the lantern fell and fire broke out, all the papers in the shrine were burned, and all the withered sprays on the ground, but the flames did not harm the wood of the shrine itself—though it was very dry.

The Secret of Sleep

Rabbi Zusya's younger son said:
"The zaddikim who, in order to serve, keep going from sanctuary to sanctuary, and from world to world, must cast their life from them, time and again, so that they may receive a new spirit, that over and over, a new revelation may float above them. This is the secret of sleep."

ELIMELEKH OF LIZHENSK

His Watch

When Rabbi Elimelekh said the Prayer of Sanctification on the sabbath, he occasionally took out his watch and looked at it. For in that hour, his soul threatened to dissolve in bliss, and so he looked at his watch in order to steady himself in Time and the world.

When the Sabbath Began

When the sabbath began, Rabbi Elimelekh could not endure the voices proclaiming it. He had to stop up his ears to keep the holy thunder of the sabbath from deafening him.

Good Works

Rabbi Elimelekh once set out for home from a city he had visited and all the hasidim accompanied him for a long stretch of the way. When his carriage drove through the gate, he got out, told the coachman to drive on, and walked behind the carriage in the midst of the throng. The astonished hasidim asked him why he had done this. He answered: "When I saw the great devotion with which you were performing the good work of accompanying me, I could not bear to be excluded from it!"

Answers

Rabbi Elimelekh once said: "I am certain to have a share in the coming world. When I stand in the court of justice above, and they ask me: 'Have you studied all you should?' I shall answer, 'No.' Then they will ask: 'Have you prayed all you should?' And again I shall answer, 'No.' And they will put a third question to me: 'Have you done all the good you should?' And this time too, I shall have to give the same answer. Then they will pronounce the verdict: 'You told the truth. For the sake of truth, you deserve a share in the coming world.'"

The First Light

Rabbi Elimelekh said: "Before the soul enters the air of this world, it is conducted through all worlds. Last of all, it is shown the first light which once—when the world was created—illumined all things, and which God removed when mankind grew corrupt. Why is the soul shown this light? So that, from this hour on, it may yearn to attain it, and approach it rung by rung, in its life on earth. And those who reach it, the zaddikim—into them the light enters, and out of them it shines into the world again. That is the reason why it was hidden."

On Sinai

Rabbi Elimelekh said: "Not only that I remember how all the souls of Israel stood by the burning mountain of Sinai, I even remember what souls stood next to me."

God Sings

The psalm reads: "For singing to our God is good."
Rabbi Elimelekh expounded this: "It is good if man can bring about that God sings within him."

The Servants

A very old woman who, in her youth, had been a servant in Rabbi Elimelekh's house, was often asked to tell some story or other about the zaddik. But whenever they urged her, she said: "I don't know anything. There's only one thing I remember. During the week there were always cross words in the kitchen, for servants are apt to quarrel. But on the eve of the sabbath, something came over us: we embraced, and one said to the other: 'Dear heart, forgive me whatever wrong I have done you during this week!' "

The First Sin

Rabbi Hayyim of Zans told: "My holy master, Rabbi Elimelekh, used to say that, if a man wants to turn to God, he must go back of each sin, back to the one which gave rise to it, and so on to the first sin; and even for this, he has to do penance.

He himself did penance for treading on his mother's breasts with his feet, when he was a babe in arms."

The Penitent

For six years and then for another six years, Rabbi David of Lelov had done great penance: he had fasted from one sabbath to the next, and subjected himself to all manner of rigid discipline. But even when the second six years were up, he felt that he had not reached perfection and did not know how to attain what he still lacked. Since he had heard of Rabbi Elimelekh, the healer of souls, he journeyed to him to ask his help. On the evening of the sabbath, he came before the zaddik with many others. The master shook hands with everyone except Rabbi David, but from him he turned and did not give him a glance. The rabbi of Lelov was appalled and left. But then he thought it over and decided that the master must have taken him for someone else. So he approached him in the evening, after the prayer, and held out his hand. But he was treated just as before. He wept all night and in the morning resolved not to enter the zaddik's House of Prayer again, but to leave for home at the end of the sabbath. And yet—when the hour of the holy third meal had come, the meal at which Rabbi Elimelekh spoke words of teaching, he could not restrain himself and crept up to the window. There he heard the rabbi say:

"Sometimes people come to me who fast and torment themselves, and many a one does penance for six years and then for another six—twelve whole years! And after that, they consider themselves worthy of the holy spirit, and come and ask me to draw it down to them: I am to supply the little they still lack. But the truth of the matter is that all their discipline and all their pains are less than a drop in the sea, and what's more: all that service of theirs does not rise to God, but to the idol of their pride. Such people must turn to God by turning utterly from all they have been doing, and begin to serve from the bottom up and with a truthful heart."

When Rabbi David heard these words, the spirit moved him with such force, that he almost lost consciousness. Trembling and sobbing, he stood at the window. When the Havdalah was concluded, he went to the door with faltering breath, opened it in great fear, and waited on the threshold. Rabbi Elimelekh rose from his chair, ran up to his motionless visitor, embraced him and said: "Blessed be he that comes!" Then he drew him toward the table and seated him at his side. But now Eleazar, the zaddik's son, could no longer restrain his amazement. "Father," he said, "why, that is the man you turned away twice because you could not endure the mere sight of him!"

"No, indeed!" Rabbi Elimelekh answered. "That was an entirely different person! Don't you see that this is our dear Rabbi David!"

The Impure Fire

On his journey to Rabbi Elimelekh whom — after the death of the Great Maggid—he had chosen for his second teacher, young Jacob Yitzak, later the rabbi of Lublin, came to a little town, and in the House of Prayer heard the rav of that place reciting the Morning Prayer with deep fervor. He stayed with him over the sabbath and noticed the same fervor in all he said and did. When he came to know him a little better, he asked him whether he had ever served a zaddik. The answer was "no." This surprised Jacob Yitzhak, for the *way* cannot be learned out of a book, or from hearsay, but can only be communicated from person to person. He asked the devout rav to go to his teacher with him, and he agreed. But when they crossed Rabbi Elimelekh's threshold, he did not come forward to meet his disciple with his customary affectionate greeting, but turned to the window and paid no attention to his visitors. Jacob Yitzhak realized that the rejection was directed to his companion, took the violently excited rav to an inn and returned alone. Rabbi Elimelekh advanced toward him, greeted him fondly, and then said: "What struck you, my friend, to bring with you a man in whose face I can see the tainted image of God?" Jacob Yitzhak listened to these words in dismay, but did not venture to reply or to ask a question. But Rabbi Elimelekh understood what was going on within him and continued: "You know that there is one place lit only by the planet Venus, where good and evil are blended. Sometimes a man begins to serve God and ulterior motives and pride enter into his service. Then, unless he makes a very great effort to change, he comes to live in that dim place and does not even know it. He is even able to exert great fervor, for close by is the place of the impure fire. From there he fetches his blaze and kindles his service with it, and does not know from where he has taken the flame."

Jacob Yitzhak told the stranger the words of Rabbi Elimelekh and the rav recognized the truth in them. In that very hour, he turned to God, ran weeping to the master, who instantly gave him his help, and with this help, he found the way.

Satan's Threat

It is told:

Satan came to Rabbi Elimelekh and said: "I simply won't stand for it any longer that you persecute me with your hasidim! Don't imagine you can get the best of me! I shall make all the world hasidim and then you will no longer have power."

Some time after this, Rabbi Elimelekh went into the House of Study with a cane to drive out some of the hasidim. No one knows why he did not do it. I suppose he did not venture to single out the messengers of Satan.

Elijah

Rabbi Elimelekh told about a man to whom the prophet Elijah had appeared. Someone expressed surprise that this could be, since even Master Ibn Ezra, who had a spirit belonging to a far loftier sphere, had — according to his own words — been denied such a vision. "What you say, is true," said the zaddik. "And yet it is as I have said. You know that after Elijah was transfigured, he became the Angel of the Covenant, and is present at the circumcision of every Jewish boy. But how can this be, since circumcision always takes place in the hour after prayer, and many circumcisions occur in the same hour in all parts of the world? I shall tell you how! Elijah moved all the people of Israel with the spirit of turning, so that they fell on their faces and cried out the name of the true God, and because of this he was given the whole soul of Israel. And so, wherever a boy is brought to the covenant, a part of Elijah's soul is present and enters the boy — a big part or a little part, according to the kind of child and the root of its being. And if the growing boy develops his Elijah-soul to the full, then he has a vision of the Elijah-soul contained within him. Thus the man of whom I was speaking made manifest through his good works the small part of the prophet which was within him. But Ibn Ezra did not have the strength to perfect the great part he had been given."

A Transaction

It is told:

The emperor in Vienna issued an edict which was bound to make thoroughly miserable the already oppressed Jews in Galicia. At that time, an earnest and studious man by the name of Feivel lived in Rabbi Elimelekh's House of Study. One night he rose, entered the zaddik's room, and said to him: "Master, I have a suit against God." And even as he spoke he was horrified at his own words.

But Rabbi Elimelekh answered him: "Very well, but the court is not in session by night."

The next day, two zaddikim came to Lizhensk, Israel of Koznitz and Jacob Yitzhak of Lublin, and stayed in Rabbi Elimelekh's house. After the midday meal, the rabbi had the man who had spoken to him called and said: "Now tell us about your law-suit."

"I have not the strength to do it now," Feivel said falteringly.

"Then I give you the strength," said Rabbi Elimelekh.

And Feivel began to speak. "Why are we held in bondage in this empire? Does not God say in the Torah: 'For unto Me the children of Israel are servants.' And even though he has sent us to alien lands, still, wherever we are, he must leave us full freedom to serve him."

To this Rabbi Elimelekh replied: "We know God's reply, for it also is written in the passage of reproof through Moses and the prophets. But now, both the plaintiff and the defendant shall leave the court-room, as the rule prescribes, so that the

judges may not be influenced by them. So go out, Rabbi Feivel.
You, Lord of the world, we cannot send out, because your
glory fills the earth, and without your presence, not one of us
could live for even a moment. But we herewith inform you
that we shall not let ourselves be influenced by you either."
Then the three sat in judgment, silently and with closed eyes.
After an hour, they called in Feivel and gave him the verdict:
that he was in the right. In the same hour, the edict in Vienna
was cancelled.

Upsetting the Bowl
It is told:
Once Rabbi Elimelekh was eating the sabbath meal with his
disciples. The servant set the soup bowl down before him. Rabbi
Elimelekh raised it and upset it, so that the soup poured over
the table. All at once young Mendel, later the rabbi of Rymanov, cried out: "Rabbi, what are you doing? They will put
us all in jail!" The other disciples smiled at these foolish
words. They would have laughed out loud, had not the presence
of their teacher restrained them. He, however, did not smile.
He nodded to young Mendel and said: "Do not be afraid, my
son!"
Some time after this, it became known that on that day an
edict directed against the Jews of the whole country had been
presented to the emperor for his signature. Time after time
he took up his pen, but something always happened to interrupt
him. Finally he signed the paper. Then he reached for the
sand-container but took the inkwell instead and upset it on
the document. Hereupon he tore it up and forbade them to
put the edict before him again.

The Miraculous Meal
They tell:
On New Year's Day, it was usual for fifteen hasidim to come
to Rabbi Elimelekh, and his wife gave them to eat and to drink.
But she could not serve them very generous portions, because
at that time she did not have much money to spend for the
household.
Once—quite late in the day—no less than forty men came

instead of the expected fifteen. "Will you have enough for them to eat?" asked Rabbi Elimelekh.

"You know how we are fixed!" she replied.

Before the Afternoon Prayer he asked her again: "Couldn't we divide what food we have among the forty, for they have—after all—come 'under the shadow of my roof'!"

"We have hardly enough for fifteen," said his wife.

When he said the Evening Prayer, the rabbi prayed fervently to God who provides for all creatures. After the prayer, he announced: "Now let everyone come and eat!" When the forty had eaten all they wanted, the bowls and platters were still full.

The Wine of Life

It is told:

Once, on the second evening of the Feast of Weeks, the hasidim were seated around Rabbi Elimelekh's table and rejoicing in the feast. The rabbi looked around and nodded to each in turn, for he rejoiced in their joy. And he said smilingly: "See, we have everything here to make us joyful. Is there anything still lacking?"

Then a headstrong foolish young man cried out: "All we still lack is to drink of the wine of life, like the devout in paradise." The zaddik said to him: "Take the pole on your shoulders. Fasten two pails to it, and go to the gates of the cemetery. When you get there, set down the pails, turn your back on them, and say: 'Elimelekh has sent me to fetch wine.' Then turn around, lift the full pails, fasten them to the pole, and bring them here to us. But be careful not to talk to anyone—no matter who should speak to you."

The young man shuddered, but did as he was bidden. He fetched the wine at the gate of the cemetery, shuddered, and brought it back with him. All about him the moonless night vibrated with the sound of voices, begging him for a drop: old voices and young voices, and they all sighed and moaned. He hastened on in silence and behind him he heard the dragging of countless ghostly steps. He was almost on Elimelekh's threshhold, when they approached him from the other side. "Now you can't do anything to me!" he shouted. The pole broke in two. The pails fell and cracked, and he felt something strike him on both cheeks. He tottered through the half-open door. Outside all was silent as death. Inside the zaddik spoke: "Fool, sit down at our table."

The Fish Vendor

They say that Rabbi Elimelekh did not celebrate with all due rites the post-sabbath meal, which is called "King David's Feast," and that for this the king was angry with him.

They also tell this:

One Friday afternoon, a man in peasant's dress, who was carrying a basket of fish on his back, came to Rabbi Elimelekh and offered to sell him his wares. He spoke the dialect of that region. The zaddik sent the vendor to his wife, but she told him to go away because she had finished preparing the food for the sabbath several hours ago. The man refused to be denied and again went to the rabbi. He sent word to his wife to buy a little something from him, but she persisted in her rejection. For the third time, the man entered the zaddik's room, fetched his fish out of the basket, threw them on the floor where they wriggled around, and grumbled: "It would be a good idea for you to use them for the King David's Feast." Then Rabbi Elimelekh raised his eyebrows. They were very big and he was in the habit of raising them whenever he wanted to look at anyone closely. He was silent for a while and then said:

"I no longer have the strength to celebrate your meal with all due rites, but I shall command my children to do so."

Gruel

During the last two years of his life, Rabbi Elimelekh ate and drank only very little, and even that little he took only because his family urged him to. Once, when his son Eleazar begged him with tears to eat at least enough to keep him alive, he said with a smile on his lips: "Oh, what coarse food you set before me! Now, if I could only get a plate of gruel, the kind my brother Zusya and I were served in the little red inn on the Dniester, in the days of our wanderings!"

Some time after Rabbi Elimelekh's death, his son set out on a journey to the little red inn on the Dniester. When he arrived there, he asked for a night's lodging and inquired what there was for supper. "We are poor people," said the innkeeper's wife. "We give the peasants vodka in exchange for flour and dried peas and beans. Most of this my husband takes to market and barters for more vodka, and the rest we eat. So I can offer you nothing but gruel for supper."

"Prepare it for me right away," said Rabbi Eleazar. By the time he had said the Evening Prayer, the soup was on the table. He ate one plate of it, and then another, and asked for a third helping. "Tell me what it was you put into the soup to make it so tasty?"

"Believe me, sir," she said. "I put nothing into it at all." But when he pressed her, she finally said: "Well, if it tastes so good to you, paradise itself is responsible for it." And now she told: "It is very long ago, but once two pious men stopped here. You could see that they were true zaddikim. And because I had nothing to serve them except gruel, I prayed to God while I was cooking it: 'Lord of the world, I have nothing else in the house, and you have everything. So have mercy upon your tired and hungry servants and put some herbs from paradise into their soup!' And when the gruel was put on the table, the two of them emptied the whole big bowl, and I refilled it and they emptied it a second time, and one of them said to me: 'Daughter, your soup tastes of paradise.' And just now I prayed again."

The True Wonder

They asked Rabbi Elimelekh: "In the Scriptures we read that Pharaoh said to Moses and Aaron: 'Show a wonder for you.' How are we to understand this? It would have been more logical for him to say: 'Show a wonder to me.'

Rabbi Elimelekh explained: "Magicians know what they want to accomplish and how to accomplish it. It is not a wonder for them but only for the beholders. But those who work something because God gives them power to do it know of no whence and no how, and the wonder which rises out of

262

their doing, overwhelms them themselves. And this is what Pharaoh meant: 'Do not pretend to me! Get you a wonder from the true world, so that it may thus testify for you.' "

The Hidden Zaddikim

Rabbi Gabriel, a disciple of Rabbi Elimelekh's, once went to visit his master in a carriage he had rented from a man of uncouth bearing who—to his annoyance—insisted on telling him coarse and improper jokes during the entire drive. When they came to the zaddik's house, Elimelekh ran toward the coachman, greeted him with great happiness, and scarcely noticed Rabbi Gabriel. On the way back, the disciple wanted to perform services for the man who had been treated with such respect, but was rejected with a curt phrase.

A few months later, Rabbi Gabriel went to the city and there saw the coachman talking to a mason. He followed the two men to their inn, unobserved, and heard one say to the other: "At Melekh's, you still hear a bit of truth—but nowhere else." And the other repeated: "At Melekh's you hear a bit of truth!" Then they happened to see the rabbi in a corner and shouted at him: "Get out! What are you doing among common folks!" And there was nothing for it; he had to go.

After Rabbi Elimelekh's death, Gabriel was driving through a wood, when the carriage of his friend, Rabbi Uri, came toward him. They dismounted and walked a way together. Then Gabriel told his friend what he had once heard the coachman and the mason say to each other. The two leaned against trees, and wept, and lamented: "A bit of truth was in the world, and now that too has been taken from us!"

The Artery

Rabbi Moshe Efraim, the Baal Shem's grandson, was against the Polish hasidim because he had heard that they mortified their flesh too severely, and destroyed the image of God in themselves instead of making perfect every part of their body, and merging it with the soul into one holy vessel for the service of the Lord. When—after the death of Rabbi Elimelekh—his disciple, Rabbi Mendel of Rymanov, came to Moshe Efraim, to ask him about a successor, as his dying master had bidden him, he was recognized as a Pole and given a rather curt and cool reception. This made him feel so sad that a change came over his face. Rabbi Moshe Efraim watched him attentively: his brow, which had paled, and his wide-open eyes were not those of a base man. He asked him kindly: "Have you studied with a zaddik?"

"I served my teacher, Rabbi Elimelekh," said Mendel.

Then Rabbi Efraim looked at him even more attentively and asked: "And what seemed most wonderful to you about that wonderful man?" But while he was putting this question he thought: "Now this hasid with his luminous face will reveal his true colors and tell me some miracle tale."

Rabbi Mendel replied: "Day by day, when my master was sunk in the contemplation of the awfulness of God, his arteries grew as stiff as hard ropes. And the artery behind the ear, which stirs at nothing in the world, and does not tremble until the hour of death—day after day I saw that artery throb with a strong pulse."

Rabbi Moshe Efraim was silent. Then he said: "I did not know that." Twice he repeated: "I did not know that." And he received Rabbi Mendel like a son.

SHNEUR ZALMAN OF LADI ("THE RAV")

No Returning

In the years immediately after his marriage, Zalman boarded
with his parents-in-law, according to the custom. But his aloofness, his manner of praying, and all the ways in which he
performed his service to God were strange to them and—while
they admired his learning—they thought him a fool. Their
daughter rejected their demands to ask for a letter of divorce
from her husband, and so they had to content themselves with
making life difficult for him. They refused him candles, so
that he had to study at the window by the light of the moon,
and in winter nights, when he often stayed up until dawn,
they let him suffer cold. This went on until—at the age of
twenty—he set out for the Great Maggid in Mezritch.

Later, when the fame of Rabbi Zalman began to spread, his
mother-in-law regretted the hardships which she and her husband—who had died in the meantime—had imposed on the
zaddik, and begged him to live in her house again. She would
see to it, she said, that he lacked nothing, and would also take
care of his hasidim. Rabbi Zalman refused her invitation, and
when the woman did not cease pressing him, he said: "Look!
Who can be better off than the child in his mother's womb?
He need not worry about his food and his drink. A light burns
upon his head, and all day he learns the entire Torah. But
when the child is born, an angel comes and strikes him on the
mouth, and he forgets all he has learned. And yet—even if he
were able to return, he would not want to. Why do you suppose? Because he has reached his full measure."

Permission

Zalman talked it over with his brother, and they decided to
go to study with the holy maggid of Mezritch. Then he asked
his wife to consent to this and she did. But she made him

promise to return after a year and a half. She had saved up thirty rubles. These she gave him and he bought a horse and carriage. His brother, however, had not asked his wife's consent. When they came to the city of Orsha, the horse fell down and died. "That is because you set out without permission," Zalman said to his brother. "And what has happened means that you must not take this course. So you go home, and I shall continue on my way, and whatever I attain, I will share with you." Then they parted, and Zalman proceeded on foot.

The Gaze of the Master

The room of the Great Maggid adjoined that in which his disciples slept. Sometimes he went to them at night, a light in his hand, and looked into their sleeping faces. Once he bent down to the low bench by the stove on which young Zalman lay under a threadbare, three-cornered cover. He looked at him for a long time and then said to himself: "Miracle of miracles that so great a God lives in so frail a dwelling."

Upward

Rabbi Shneur Zalman told: "Before I went to Mezritch, my service was based on reflection, and from this arose my love and my fear of God. In Mezritch I mounted to the rung where awareness is, in itself, love and fear.

"When I first heard the holy maggid say: 'God's attribute of mercy is our love of God; God's attribute of rigor is our fear of God,' I regarded this as an interpretation. But then I saw that it is so: The mercy of God is the love of God; the rigor of God is the fear of God."

The Language of Birds

On his second journey to Mezritch, young Zalman visited Rabbi Pinhas of Koretz. Rabbi Pinhas wanted to teach him the language of birds and the language of plants, but the younger man refused. "There is only *one* thing men need understand," he said.

In his old age, Rabbi Shneur Zalman was once driving through the country with his grandson. Birds were hopping about and twittering everywhere. The rabbi put his head out of the carriage for a while. "How fast they chatter," he said to the child. "They have their own alphabet. All you need do is listen and grasp well, and you will understand their language."

Concerning Ardent Zeal

After the maggid died, Shneur Zalman decided to leave the town of Mezritch for good. When he parted from the maggid's son, from Rabbi Abraham, the Angel, who had instructed him in secret wisdom, his teacher said he would accompany him and got into the carriage. When they were out of the city-gate, Rabbi Abraham called to the coachman: "Urge on your horses and let them run until they forget they are horses." Zalman took the words to heart. "It will take me a while to learn this way of serving, properly," he said, and remained in Mezritch for another year.

At the Lower End

After the death of his teacher, the Great Maggid, Shneur Zalman used to go to Rabbi Menahem of Vitebsk, and was regarded as his disciple, even though his years of studying were actually over. On the sabbath and on feast-days, all the hasidim ate at their rabbi's table. Shneur Zalman always sat at the lower end. On New Year's Eve the rabbi of Vitebsk saw that his place was empty. He went to the House of Study, where he found Zalman standing and praying, listened for a time, unobserved, and went back into the room. "Do not disturb him," he said. "He is delighting in God, and God in him."

To God

Once Zalman interrupted his prayers and said: "I do not want your paradise. I do not want your coming world. I want You, and You only."

Extricated from Time

Rabbi Shneur Zalman told his hasidim:
"I was walking in the street toward evening and happened to see something improper. I was deeply troubled that I had not

guarded my eyes, placed myself with my face to a wall and
cried my heart out. When I turned around I saw that it was
dark and the time for the Afternoon Prayer had passed. Then
I took counsel with myself. I extricated myself from Time and
said the Prayer."

Fear

When hasidim began to come to him, and he happened to look
out of the window and saw a throng approaching, he was terrified and cried: "What do they want of me? Why do they come
to me? What do they see in me?"
Then his wife said to him: "Be calm. They are not coming to
you for your sake. They only want you to tell them about the
holy maggid, because you have lived in his shadow."
"Then all is well," he said and his heart grew quiet. "I shall
tell them, yes, I shall tell them." But when he once began to
talk, he could no longer keep back the teachings.

Where Are You?

Rabbi Shneur Zalman, the rav of Northern White Russia, was
put in jail in Petersburg, because the mitnagdim had denounced
his principles and his way of living to the government. He
was awaiting trial when the chief of the gendarmes entered his
cell. The majestic and quiet face of the rav, who was so deep
in meditation that he did not at first notice his visitor, suggested
to the chief, who was a thoughtful person, what manner of
man he had before him. He began to converse with his prisoner
and brought up a number of questions which had occurred to
him in reading the Scriptures. Finally he asked: "How are we
to understand that God, the all-knowing, said to Adam: 'Where
art thou?'"
"Do you believe," answered the rav, "that the Scriptures are
eternal and that every era, every generation, and every man is
included in them?"
"I believe this," said the other.
"Well then," said the zaddik, "in every era, God calls to
every man: 'Where are you in your world? So many years
and days of those allotted to you have passed, and how far

have you gotten in your world?' God says something like this: 'You have lived forty-six years. How far along are you?'"
When the chief of the gendarmes heard his age mentioned, he pulled himself together, laid his hand on the rav's shoulder, and cried: "Bravo!" But his heart trembled.

Question and Answer

The rav asked a disciple who had just entered his room: "Moshe, what do we mean when we say 'God'?" The disciple was silent. The rav asked him a second and third time. Then he said: "Why are you silent?"
"Because I do not know."
"Do you think I know?" said the rav. "But I must say it, for it is so, and therefore I must say it: He is definitely there, and except for him nothing is definitely there—and this is He."

What He Prayed With

The rav once asked his son: "What do you pray with?" The son understood the meaning of the question, namely on what he based his prayer. He answered: "With the verse: 'Every stature shall prostrate itself before thee.'" Then he asked his father: "And with what do you pray?" He said: "With the floor and the bench."

Out of One Bowl

Among the disciples of the maggid of Mezritch was one whose name has been forgotten. No one knows it any more. But once in the maggid's House of Study he was regarded as the foremost among his companions, and all who wanted to have the words of their master repeated and explained, turned to him. Then came the time when the disciples began to talk, and said a worm was gnawing at him. After that he disappeared and rumor had it that he had taken to drinking. He roamed through the countryside with a staff and knapsack and drank silently in some inn until he was drunk; then one wise saying after another came from his lips. Years later he came to the town of Lozhni where Rabbi Shneur Zalman was still living at that

time, and entered the House of Study at an hour when the rav
was teaching there. No one noticed him in the crowd, and he
listened for a while. Then he mumbled to himself: "We all ate
out of one bowl, but it is he who has all the food," and left the
house. When the rav heard of it, he realized who his visitor
was and had them look for him everywhere, for he wanted
to persuade him to give up his wandering and stay. But the
rover was nowhere to be found.

Reflection

One of the mitnagdim once visited the rav and asked him all
sorts of questions. Finally he wished to know why the zaddik
had a servant at his door who did not admit visitors to him
at all times. The rav put his head in his hands. After a time,
he looked up and said: "The head and the trunk form one
body, and yet the head must be covered in a different manner
and guarded more carefully." The mitnaged was satisfied with
this answer and left. But the zaddik's son was not satisfied.
"You did not have to put your head in your hands and reflect
in order to give the answer you did," he said.
Rabbi Zalman said: "When Korah said to Moses: 'All the
congregation are holy, every one of them, and the Lord is
among them; wherefore then lift ye up yourselves above the
assembly of the Lord,' Moses heard and fell on his face. Only
after that, did he answer Korah. But why? He could have said
what he had to say, right then and there! But Moses reflected:
Perhaps these words are sent from above, and Korah is only
a messenger. In that case, how could I reply to him! And so
he fell on his face and reflected on whether he really sought
to lift himself above the rest. And when he had reflected and
come to the conclusion that no vestige of such a desire was
within him—and according to God's own words Moses was
very humble, more humble than all other men—he knew that
Korah had not been sent to him, and he answered his question."

Concerning the Messiah

A man once asked the rav in jest: "Will the Messiah be a
hasid or a mitnaged?" He answered: "I think a mitnaged, for

if he were a hasid, the mitnagdim would not believe in him; but the hasidim will believe in him, no matter what he is."

The Dark-Tempered and the Light-Tempered

A wealthy man who was devoted to his studies and known for his stinginess, once asked the rav of Ladi: "How are we to interpret the passage in the Talmud, in which we are told that Rabbi Haninah ben Teradion who publicly instructed his disciples in the teachings in an era of rabid persecution, and to the very day he died as a martyr, doubted that he was appointed to life in the coming world? And that, when he expressed his doubt to a friend, he was asked in return, whether he had done a single good work? And that he received a reassuring answer only when he claimed to have distributed his money among the poor. How are we to interpret this?"

"There are two kinds of men," said the rav, "those with black gall and those with light. The dark-tempered sit over the books of the teachings and are of a miserly disposition. The light-tempered love company and are generous. Rabbi Haninah was dark-tempered, devoted to his studies, and withdrawn. His merit did not lie in living for the teachings, but in governing his nature, and giving freely of what he possessed. But once he had done this, and he had learned to live with his fellow-men, his studying was no longer a necessity, but a virtue."

Seeing

On a day shortly before his death, the rav asked his grandson: "Do you see anything?" The boy looked at him in astonishment. Then the rav said: "All I can still see is the divine nothingness which gives life to the world."

The Apparition

One night, the wife of Rabbi Mendel of Lubavitch, the rav's grandson, was awakened by a loud noise coming from her husband's room which was next to hers. She ran to him and saw Rabbi Mendel lying on the floor by his bed. In reply to her questions, he told her that his grandfather had been to see him. She tried to calm him, but he said: "When a soul from the world above and a soul from this world want to be together, the one must put on a garment, and the other must take one off."

Once he said to his close friends: "In the Palestinian Talmud we read that he who says a word in the name of him who originated it, must—in his mind's eye—conjure the author up before him. This is only a fancy, but he who sings a melody another devised—that other is really with him while he sings." And he sang the familiar wordless tune the rav had sung and hummed time and again, the tune: "The Fervor of the Rav."

SHELOMO OF KARLIN

The Meeting

The cities of Pinsk and Karlin lie close to each other, the one
on the north, the other on the south bank of a river. When
Rabbi Shelomo was a poor young man who taught little children in Karlin, Rabbi Levi Yitzhak, later the rabbi of Berditchev, was the rav of Pinsk. One day he told his servant to go
to Karlin, and look for a man by the name of Shelomo, son
of Yuta. He was to ask him to come to Pinsk. The servant
inquired around for a long time. Finally, at the edge of the
town, in a ramshackle little house, he found the melammed
Shelomo and gave him his message. "I shall get there in time,"
said Rabbi Shelomo.

When he crossed Rabbi Levi Yitzhak's threshold a few hours
later, the rav rose and said, "Blessed be he that comes," and
drew up a chair for his guest himself. For an hour they sat
opposite each other, with glowing faces, with intense eyes—in
silence. Then they rose and laughed aloud. "What can they be
laughing about!" thought the servant who had been listening
at the door. And Rabbi Shelomo made his farewells.

But the hasidim said that through the meeting of these two,
the exile, which had been threatening the Jews of that region,
had been averted, and that this was the cause of their joyful
laughter.

He Who Returned

It is told:

Rabbi Aaron of Karlin died young, and Rabbi Shelomo, whose
fellow disciple he had been in the house of the Great Maggid
and who had followed his elder friend as his teacher, refused
to take his place. Then Rabbi Aaron appeared to him in a
dream and promised that if he took on himself the yoke of
leadership, he would be granted the power of beholding all
the wanderings of souls. This promise beguiled him in his

273

dream, and he agreed to assume the succession. The next morning, he was able to see the destinies of the souls of all men. That very day, they brought him a note of request together with a sum of money. The sender was a rich man who lay dying. At the same time, the woman who supervised a home for the poor, came to ask him to pray for a pauper under her care, who had been in labor for days, and still had not borne her child. Rabbi Shelomo saw that the child could not come into the world until the rich man died, for his soul was to pass into the baby. And the news of the death and the birth did, indeed, come, one on the heels of the other. When the rabbi was told a little later that there was not enough fire-wood in the home, and that the young mother and her infant son were freezing, he took some of the money he had received from the rich man, and told them to buy wood with it. For he told himself: this child is really the rich man himself, and so it is his own money. Shortly after, he also gave what remained of the sum for the care of the boy.

Presently the woman left with other beggars and went from town to town. When the boy was six years old, they happened to come to Karlin again and learned that the Bar Mitzvah [confirmation] of the rich man's youngest son was to be celebrated soon. According to the custom, the poor were invited to attend the feast, and mother and son went with the others. But the boy could not be persuaded to sit at the pauper's table. In a loud voice and with arrogant gestures, he demanded a place at the head of the guest-table. Rabbi Shelomo, who noticed this, urged them to give in to the child, so that he might not cause a disturbance. "He is the master of the house, after all," he thought to himself. "And he is asking no more than his due." When the meal was served, the same thing occurred: the boy insisted that he be served with the choicest food, and again the zaddik let him have his way. When the mother was asked whether her son always behaved in this way, she said she had never observed anything of the kind in him. At the end of the feast, when Rabbi Shelomo had already gone home, they distributed money among the poor. When the boy's turn came, he cried: "How dare you offer me coppers! Get gold out of the chest!" Then the sons of the rich man threw him out bodily.

When Rabbi Shelomo discovered how they had treated their returned father, he begged Heaven to take from him his miraculous power.

Refusal

It is told:

Those in Heaven wanted to reveal to Rabbi Shelomo of Karlin the language of birds, the language of trees, and the language of the serving angels. But he refused to learn them, before finding out of what importance each of these languages was for the service of God. Not until after he had been told this, did he consent to learn them, and then he served God with them also.

The Stages

When Rabbi Shelomo of Karlin was traveling through Russia, he kept enumerating the various stages, and said: " 'These are the stages of the children of Israel, by which they went forth out of the land of Egypt.' " When they asked him what he meant by this, he said: "The sacred Book of Splendor interprets God's words, 'Let us make man,' in the following way: that from every world, from the highest to the lowest, God took some part, and from all these parts made man. It was to the worlds, that God said 'Let us.' And that is the meaning of the stages man passes through in his life: he must go from rung to rung until, through him, everything is united in the highest world. And that is why it is written: 'And these are their stages at their goings forth.' The stages of man shall take him to where he has come from."

The Venture of Prayer

Someone asked Rabbi Shelomo of Karlin to promise to visit him the next day. "How can you ask me to make such a promise?" said the zaddik. "This evening I must pray and recite 'Hear, O Israel.' While I say these words, my soul goes out to the utmost rim of life. Then comes the darkness of sleep.

And when it is day, the great Morning Prayer is apacing through all worlds, and finally, when I fall on my face, my soul leans over the rim of life. Perhaps I shall not die this time either, but how can I now promise to do something at a time after the prayer?"

The Piece of Sugar

It is told:

When Rabbi Shelomo drank tea or coffee, it was his custom to take a piece of sugar and hold it in his hand the entire time he was drinking. Once his son asked him: "Father, why do you do that? If you need sugar, put it in your mouth, but if you do not need it, why hold it in your hand!"

When he had emptied his cup, the rabbi gave the piece of sugar he had been holding to his son and said: "Taste it." The son put it in his mouth and was very much astonished, for there was no sweetness at all left in it.

Later, when the son told this story, he said: "A man, in whom everything is unified, can taste with his hand as if with his tongue."

With the Sword at His Throat

Rabbi Shelomo was on a journey in the company of one of his disciples. On the way, they stopped at an inn and sat down at a table. Then the rabbi gave orders to warm mead for him, for he liked his mead warm. In the meantime, soldiers arrived, and when they saw Jews sitting at the table, they told them to get up in loud, angry tones. "Is the mead warm yet?" the rabbi asked the man who served drinks. At that the soldiers struck the table with their fists and shouted: "Off with you, or else . . . !" The rabbi only said: "Isn't it warm yet?" The leader of the soldiers drew his sword from the scabbard and put the blade to the maggid's throat. "Because, you know, it mustn't get really hot!" said Rabbi Shelomo. Then the soldiers left the inn.

Without Ecstasy

Rabbi Shelomo of Karlin said: "When he, who has done all the commandments of the Torah, but has not felt the blaze of holy ecstasy in so doing, comes to that other world, they open the gates of paradise for him. But because he has not felt the blaze of ecstasy in this world, he does not feel the ecstasy of paradise. Now, if he is a fool, and complains, and grumbles: 'And they make so much to-do about paradise!' he is instantly thrown out. But if he is wise, he leaves of his own accord, and goes to the zaddik, and he teaches the poor soul how to feel ecstasy."

A Little Light

"When can one see a little light?" asked Rabbi Shelomo and answered his own question: "If one keeps oneself quite lowly, as it is written: 'If I make my bed in the nether world, behold, Thou art there! '"

Climbing Down

Rabbi Shelomo said: "If you want to raise a man from mud and filth, do not think it is enough to keep standing on top and reaching down to him a helping hand. You must go all the way down yourself, down into mud and filth. Then take hold of him with strong hands and pull him and yourself out into the light."

To Open

Rabbi Shelomo of Karlin said to someone: "I have no key to open you." And the man cried out: "Then pry me open with a nail!" From this time on, the rabbi always said words of warm praise about him.

The Cure

A grandson of Rabbi Shelomo told:
To a zaddik came a man whose soul had become enmeshed in a tangle of oppressive impulses, which defy writing down. "I cannot help you," said the zaddik. "You must go to Rabbi Shelomo of Karlin."
So he came to my grandfather, and arrived just at the hour he was lighting the Hanukkah candles and reciting psalms the

while, for this was his way. The man stopped and listened. My grandfather went on speaking without looking around, but when he came to the words: "And hath delivered us from our oppressors," he turned to his guest, patted him on the shoulder, and asked: "Do you believe that God can wrest us from all oppression?" "I believe," said the man. From that hour on, all his disturbing impulses left him.

The Disciple Speaks

Rabbi Asher of Stolyn said about his teacher, Rabbi Shelomo: "Whenever he prays, the rabbi stands with one foot over here, and the other over there, and it is the foot over there, on which he rests. And everything only in spirit, as it is written: 'And Thy footsteps were not known.' "

Once he entered Rabbi Shelomo's room and said to him: "Rabbi, your footsteps are not known."

"What makes you follow me all the time?" the rabbi retorted. "Come, and I shall tell you when you may, and when you may not."

But the disciple reflected: "Once he has told me, I shall not be able to transgress. So I'd rather not hear it."

Showing and Concealing

Rabbi Asher of Stolyn, a disciple of Rabbi Shelomo's, said concerning the hasidim of his time: "They are peasants of clay and cossacks of straw! When they come to the rabbi, they show him what is good, and what is bad they conceal from him. Now, when I came to my sweet, holy, darling rabbi (and while he said this, he kissed his finger-tips), I concealed the good from him, but I showed him what was bad. For it is written that the priest shall look on the plague."

Into the Inn

Rabbi Shelomo asked his disciple Rabbi Asher: "When did you come to prayer?"

"At just the right time for the inn named, Exult, O ye righteous!" was his reply.

"Well done," said the zaddik. "If you drive, you drive, and if you stop, you look around to see if anything is wrong. For if you stop midway, it is easy to fall behind."

Origin

This is what Rabbi Uri told about his teacher Rabbi Shelomo. "I had been with him a long time, and still he had not asked me my mother's name, as it is the custom to do. Once I mustered my courage and asked him about this. He answered: 'Ox, lion, eagle, man,' and nothing further. I did not dare beg him to expound his words. Only after many years did I come to understand that the great zaddikim, the healers of souls, want to know in which of the four carriers of the throne-chariot of God the soul had its origin, and not in what earthly womb it received its body."

Beyond Music

One day, musicians played for Rabbi Uri of Strelisk, known as "The Seraph." Later he said to his hasidim: "They say that music unites the three principles: life, intellect, and soul. But the musicians of today base their playing only on the principle of life." After a while he continued: "Of all the halls of Heaven, the hall of music is the lowest and the smallest, but he who wants to approach God, has only to enter this hall. My teacher, Rabbi Shelomo of Karlin, had no need of this."

Abel and Cain

Rabbi Uri said: "My teacher, Rabbi Shelomo of Karlin, had the soul of Abel. Now, there are people within whom the good traits of Cain's soul have their habitation, and these are very great."

Leftovers

Rabbi Shelomo and his disciple Rabbi Mordecai of Lechovitz once traveled cross-country. It was toward the end of the period in which the blessing of the New Moon can be spoken, and since the shining sickle had broken from the clouds which had been veiling it, they appeared for the sacred rite. But the coachman anticipated them. The moment he saw the moon, he wiped his hands on the rim of the wheel and mumbled the benediction. Rabbi Mordecai laughed, but his teacher reproved him.

"A king," so he told him, "once gave order to collect all the leftovers of the meal eaten in his army, and store them in a certain place. No one knew the reason for this command. But presently the country was at war, the king's army was surrounded by the enemy and cut off from outside provisions. Then the king fed his army on the leftovers which the enemy laughingly let pass. The army kept up its strength and was victorious."

Out of Travail

Once, at the close of the Day of Atonement, when Rabbi Shelomo was in a gay mood, he said he would tell everyone what he had asked of Heaven on these holy days, and what answer was intended for his request. To the first of his disciples who wanted to be told, he said: "What you asked of God was that he should give you your livelihood at the proper time and without travail, so that you might not be hindered in serving him. And the answer was that what God really wants of you is not study or prayer, but the sighs of your heart, which is breaking because the travail of gaining a livelihood hinders you in the service of God."

What Was Learned

Rabbi Shelomo said to his disciples: "After death, when a man reaches the world of truth, they ask him: 'Who was your teacher?' And when he has told them the name of his teacher, they ask: 'What did you learn from him?' This is what is meant by the words we read in Midrash: 'At some future time, each one will stand and say what he has learned.'"

One of the disciples cried: "I have already prepared what I shall say in your name. It is: 'May God give us a pure heart and pure thinking, and from our thinking, may purity spread through all of our being, so that in us the word may be ful-field: 'Before they call, I will answer.' "

The Dowry

Rabbi Shelomo of Karlin could not bear to have money in his purse or laid away in the table-drawer. It weighed on his heart until he had given it to someone who was in need.

On a certain day, he betrothed his son to the daughter of Rabbi Barukh of Mezbizh, the grandson of the Baal Shem Tov. Rabbi Barukh was fervent, devout, and wise, but at the same time, concerned with receiving his due. When the date given in the engagement-contract for the payment of the dowry had elapsed, and the money had not been paid, he wrote to Rabbi Shelomo that he would return the contract and annul the engagement. The Rabbi of Karlin asked him to set another date, and sent two of his followers to travel through the country and collect the amount of the dowry among the hasidim. But when the sum was in Rabbi Shelomo's hands, and poor people stood in the court of his house, he could not endure the thought that out there were the needy, while money was here in his possession. He went into the court and distributed everything he had. Again Rabbi Barukh sent him a stern letter. The rabbi of Karlin replied that they should go ahead with preparations for the wedding, that he himself would bring the dowry. Again he sent two men to collect the necessary amount, and again they brought it back with them. But this time they were cautious and did not give it to the rabbi until he was seated in the carriage beside his son.

The route took them to a city in which Rabbi Nahum of Tchernobil was imprisoned as the result of a denunciation, such as the opponents of hasidim frequently indulged in. The rabbi of Karlin succeeded in getting the permission of the authorities to see his friend for a short time. When they stood face to face, Rabbi Shelomo at once saw that Rabbi Nahum had taken sorrow upon himself for the sake of Israel, and Rabbi Nahum at once saw what was going on in him. "How do you know?" he asked. "For I begged God that neither angel nor seraph might know."

"An angel or a seraph does not know," said the rabbi of Karlin. "But Shelomo, son of Yuta, knows. But I promise you that when my turn comes, no creature shall know." Now, this was the day just before the rabbi of Tchernobil was to leave the jail. When the rabbi of Karlin had taken leave of him, he went to the official in charge of the prison, gave him the four hundred rubles which constituted the dowry, and thus had his friend released a day sooner. Then he drove on to the wedding with his son.

There are various versions of what happened after this. According to one of them, Rabbi Barukh never mentioned the dowry during the seven days of the celebration. When the rabbi of Karlin was ready to leave for home, his son said to him: "You are going home, and I am staying behind with my father-in-law. What shall I do if he asks me for the dowry?" "Should he ever worry you about it," Rabbi Shelomo replied, "stand somewhere or other, with your face to the wall, and say: 'Father, father, my father-in-law is worrying me about the dowry.' Then he will stop asking you for it."

Some time passed and nothing happened until one Friday evening when Rabbi Barukh recited the Song of Songs and his son-in-law stood opposite him. When Rabbi Barukh came to the words "a bundle of myrrh," he paused and lightly touched his left hand with his right as if he were counting a bundle of bills. Then he continued with the Song of Songs. But his son-in-law could not bear to remain. He rushed into his room, turned his face to the wall, and said: " 'Father, father, my father-in-law is worrying me about the dowry.' " From that moment on, he was left in peace.

The Worst

Rabbi Shelomo asked: "What is the worst thing the Evil Urge can achieve?" And he answered: "To make man forget that he is the son of a king."

How God Loves

Rabbi Shelomo said: "If only I could love the greatest zaddik as much as God loves the greatest ne'er-do-well!"

When Rabbi Shelomo of Karlin was in the little town of
Dobromysl, near Lozhny, where his former companion, Rabbi
Shneur Zalman, was living at that time, and stopped in the
House of Study, Rabbi Zalman said on a Friday, to some
hasidim who had come to him: "Now I am not the rabbi. The
holy zaddik, our master Rabbi Shelomo, is within my district,
so now he is the rabbi. You must go to Dobromysl and stay
with him over the sabbath." They did so and ate the three
sabbath meals at the table of the rabbi of Karlin. And though
he spoke no word of teaching, as their own teacher did on these
occasions, their spirit beheld the holy light, and it was incom-
parably more radiant than ever before. At the third sabbath
meal, Rabbi Shelomo preceded the saying of grace by the
brief psalm which begins with: "His foundation is in the holy
mountains," and ends: "All my springs are in thee," which he
translated: "All my springing is in thee." And instantly the
springs of their spirit gushed forth. The spirit possessed them
so utterly that until long after the sabbath they did not know
the difference between day and night. When they returned to
Rabbi Zalman and told him what had happened to them, he
said: "Yes, who can compare to the holy Rabbi Shelomo! He
knows how to translate? We cannot translate. Who can compare to the holy Rabbi Shelomo! For he is a hand's-breadth
above the world!"

Armilus

Rabbi Shelomo used to say: "If only the Messiah, the son of
David would come! At a pinch, I myself can be the Messiah,
son of Joseph, who precedes him and is killed. What is there
to fear for me, and whom shall I fear! Shall I fear the crooked
cossack?" The people thought he was calling Death a crooked
cossack, and were very much surprised at this.

* * * * *

Again and again, the community of Ludmir asked him to come
to them, for many of his friends lived there. He always refused.
But when envoys from Ludmir came to him once more — it
was on Lag ba-Omer, on the thirty-third day of the days of the
counting of Omer, between the feasts of Passover and the Revel-

ation — he asked them smilingly: "And what do you do in Ludmir on Lag ba-Omer?"

"Well," said the envoys, "just what is usually done. All the boys, big and the little, go out into the fields with their bows and shoot."

The rabbi laughed and said: "Well, if that's the way it is, if you shoot, that makes all the difference! Then I will come to you."

* * * * *

When the rabbi was already living in Ludmir, the Russians put down a revolt of the Poles in that region, and pursued the defeated rebels right into the town. The Russian commander gave his men permission to loot at will for two hours. It was the day before the Feast of the Revelation which, in that year, fell on a sabbath. The Jews were gathered in the House of Prayer. Rabbi Shelomo was praying, and in such ecstasy that he heard and saw nothing that went on around him. Just then a tall cossack came limping along, went up to the window, looked in, and pointed his gun. In a ringing voice, the rabbi was saying the words, "for thine, O Lord, is the kingdom," when his little grandson, who was standing beside him, timidly tugged at his coat, and he awoke from his ecstasy. But the bullet had already struck him in the side. "Why did you fetch me down?" he asked. When they brought him to his house and laid him down, he had them open the Book of Splendor at a certain passage and prop it up in front of him while they bound up his wound. It stayed there, open before his eyes until the following Wednesday, when he died.

Now, it is said that the name of that limping cossack was Armilus. And that is the name of the fiend who, according to the old tradition, is to kill the Messiah son of Joseph.

The Rope That Gave

A few days before he died of his wound, Rabbi Shelomo wrote to his disciple Mordecai of Lechovitz: "Come, so that I may consecrate you to leadership." Mordecai at once set out on his journey. On the way, he suddenly felt as if a rope which was carrying him safely across an abyss gave, as if he were falling through shoreless space. "I have been severed from my teacher," he screamed, and after that, did not utter another word. His companions took him to the old rabbi of Neskhizh, known as a wonder-worker throughout the land, and asked him to heal Rabbi Mordecai who was quite out of his mind. "Tell him," said the rabbi of Neskhizh, "that his teacher is dead. Then he will recover." They conveyed this news to him very cautiously, for they feared he might do harm to himself. But the moment he grasped their message, his face regained its composure, in a firm voice he pronounced the benediction which is said at the news of death, and cried: "He was my teacher, and he shall remain my teacher."

Out of Mercy

Rabbi Asher of Stolyn told:
My teacher, Rabbi Shelomo, used to say: "I have to prepare what I shall have to do in hell," for he was certain that no better end was in store for him. Now, when his soul ascended after death, and the serving angels received him joyfully, to guide him to the highest paradise, he refused to go with them. "They are making fun of me," he said. "This cannot be the world of truth." At last the Divine Presence herself said to him: "Come, my son! Out of mercy, I shall give you of my treasure." Then he gave in and was content.

"I Am Prayer"

It is told:
A complaint was once lodged in the tribunal of Heaven. It was that most Jews prayed without fixing their souls on prayer. And because this was so, a king was allowed to arise on earth, who wanted to prohibit the Jews in his realm from praying together in a congregation. But some angels objected and would not permit this to happen. Finally they decided to ask the souls of the zaddikim who dwell in the upper world, and they gave their consent to the prohibition. But when they came to Rabbi Shelomo of Karlin, he shook the world with the storm of his prayer, and said: "I am prayer. I take it on myself to pray in lieu of all Israel." And the prohibition did not go through.

ISRAEL OF KOZNITZ

The Story of the Cape

A woman came to Rabbi Israel, the maggid of Koznitz, and told him, with many tears, that she had been married a dozen years and still had not borne a son. "What are you willing to do about it?" he asked her. She did not know what to say. "My mother," so the maggid told her, "was aging and still had no child. Then she heard that the holy Baal Shem was stopping over in Apt in the course of a journey. She hurried to his inn and begged him to pray she might bear a son. 'What are you willing to do about it?' he asked. 'My husband is a poor book-binder,' she replied, 'but I do have one fine thing that I shall give to the rabbi.' She went home as fast as she could and fetched her good cape, her 'Katinka,' which was carefully stowed away in a chest. But when she returned to the inn with it, she heard that the Baal Shem had already left for Mezbizh. She immediately set out after him and since she had no money to ride, she walked from town to town with her 'Katinka' until she came to Mezbizh. The Baal Shem took the cape and hung it on the wall. 'It is well,' he said. My mother walked all the way back, from town to town, until she reached Apt. A year later, I was born."

"I, too," cried the woman, "will bring you a good cape of mine so that I may get a son."

"That won't work," said the maggid. "You heard the story. My mother had no story to go by."

Studying

When Israel was seven years old, he studied in the Talmud School by day, but in the evening he went to the House of Study and studied on his own. The first night of Hanukkah, his father did not permit him to go to the House of Study, for he suspected him of wanting to play a certain game, popular at this season, with the other boys. But since he had neither a book nor a candle at home, he promised his father to stay in the House of Study only as long at it took a three-penny candle to burn down. Now, either other candles were burning in the room, or the angels, who rejoiced in the studying of the boy, kept the three-penny candle miraculously alight — at any rate, the boy remained in the House of Study long after he was supposed to. When he finally came home, his father beat him until the blood came.

"And did you not tell your father that you were studying all that time?" they asked the maggid when he told the story many years after.

"I might have told him, of course," he answered. "And my father would have believed me, for he knew that I never lied, but is it right to use the greatness of the Torah to save one's own skin?"

Knowledge

They say that, in his youth, Rabbi Israel studied eight hundred books of the Kabbalah. But the first time he saw the maggid of Mezritch face to face, he instantly knew that he knew nothing at all.

His Torah

The maggid of Koznitz said: "Our sages very properly emphasize that in the first psalm, the Torah is called 'the law of the Lord,' and later 'his Torah.' For if a man learns the Torah for its own sake, then it is given to him, and it is his, and he may clothe all his holy thoughts in the holy Torah."

The Sheepskin Coat

It is told:

When he was young, Rabbi Israel was poor and in need. Once he went to visit Rabbi Yitzhak, later the rav of Berditchev, who was then still living in Zelechov, a nearby town. Later the zaddik saw him out. First they stood on the threshold of the house and kept on talking. And they conversed so earnestly, that they walked on and on together. It was bitterly cold, and

Rabbi Levi Yitzhak had not taken his coat. "Lend me your sheepskin for a while," he said to his disciple and friend, and he gladly gave it to him. Freezing in his thin clothing, he walked beside the zaddik and they never stopped talking. This went on for some time. "Now it is enough, Israel," the rabbi finally said. "Now you shall be warm too." From that hour on, Israel's destiny altered.

Sickness and Strength

Rabbi Israel was in poor health from childhood on. He was as lean as a stick and the doctors were surprised that he stayed alive. For the most part, he lay on his bed wrapped in rabbit-skins. When he rose, he put on slippers lined with bear's fur, because he could not stand shoes on his feet. They carried him to the House of Prayer in a litter. But the moment he had said on the threshold: "How full of awe is this place," he was transformed. On Mondays and Thursdays, the days on which the Scriptures are read, he walked in prayer shawl and phylacteries, the scroll of the Torah in his arms, so lightly and quickly through the two rows of waiting people, that the servants who accompanied him carrying the candles could hardly keep up with him. With dancing motion, he leaned toward the holy Ark into which he put the scroll, walked with dancing step to the desk on which the candelabrum stood, and set the candles in it. Then, in his ordinary low voice, he said the first words of the prayer, but from one word to the next his voice gained in power, until he swept upward with it every heart. After prayer, when the servants carried him home in his litter, he was pale as one dying, but his pallor was luminous. That was why they said that his body shone like a thousand souls.

Once, when he had been asked to attend a circumcision, and was about to get into the carriage, some people came forward to help him in. "Fools," he said, "why should I need your strength? It is written: 'But they that wait for the Lord shall change their strength'; I shall change my strength for the strength of God; He has strength to spare." And he jumped into the carriage.

The Coat

Whatever the rabbi of Koznitz said sounded as if he were praying, only weaker and in a lower voice.

He liked to hum to himself proverbs and sayings current among the Polish peasants. After a Purim feast, which he had presided over in great happiness, he said: "How right, what the people say:

> 'Doff your coat, dear soul, and prance
> Merrily at feast and dance.'

But how curious a coat is the body!"

Sometimes he even spoke to God in Polish. When he was alone, they would hear him say: "*Moj kochanku*," which means: "My darling."

A Prayer

The rabbi of Koznitz said to God: "Lord of the world, I beg of you to redeem Israel. And if you do not want to do that, then redeem the goyim."

Another Prayer

Once the maggid of Koznitz said: "Lord, I stand before you like a messenger boy, and wait for you to tell me where to go."

Testimony

This is what Rabbi Moshe of Koznitz, son of the maggid, writes in his book, the "Well of Moses."

"My father and teacher said to me: 'Believe me, my son, the alien thoughts which seized on me from time to time came only while I was praying, and with the help of God I brought them all home to their source and their root, to where their tent stood in the beginning of time."

Dead and Living Prayers

Once Rabbi Israel heard the "Cursed be . . . " passage in the Scriptures read in the House of Prayer, and cried out at the words: "And thy carcasses shall be food unto all fowls of the air." Later, at the meal, he said: "The prayers which are said without fear and without love, are called the 'carcasses.' But He, who hears the praying of every mouth, has mercy upon His creatures. From above He pours awakening into the heart of man, so that one single time he can pray with his soul as he should, and then his prayer grows great and destroys the prayers which are carcasses, and mounts like a bird to the flood-gates of Heaven."

Music

The maggid of Koznitz said:
" 'Make sweet melody,' is what Isaiah said to Tyre, the 'harlot long forgotten.' Make sweet your way and you shall be given melody."

Every Day

The maggid of Koznitz said:
"Every day, man shall go forth out of Egypt, out of distress."

For His Sick Son

When his beloved little son fell ill, and the doctors had given up hope, the maggid of Koznitz sat up all night and could think of nothing but his great grief. But when the time for the Morning Prayer had come, he said: "It is written: 'And she cast the child under one of the shrubs.' The shrubs, the shrubs, the great shrub of prayer! So that one word of the prayer might be said with rejoicing!"

When Rabbi Levi Yitzhak, who at that time was still living in the neighboring town of Zelechov, heard of it, he went to the bath and dipped under with the holy intent of changing the maggid's trend of thought so that he might pray for the recovery of his son. And he succeeded. While the maggid was praying, the trend of his thoughts was changed, and with great fervor he implored God to let his child recover.

At that time — so the hasidim say — not only little Moshe, the maggid's son, but all the sick children, far and wide, recovered.

Each year, the maggid of Koznitz visited his father's grave in the city of Apt. On one such occasion, the heads of the community came to him to ask him to preach in the great House of Prayer on the sabbath, as he had done the year before. "Is there any reason to believe," he said, "that I accomplished anything with my last year's sermon?" The men left in dismay, and the entire community was stricken with grief. A crowd collected in front of the maggid's inn. All stood silent with bowed heads. But then a man, a craftsman, came forward, went into the maggid's room, and said to him: "You claim that you did not accomplish anything with the sermon you preached last year. You did accomplish something as far as I am concerned. For at that time I heard from your lips the words that every son of Israel must do as it says in the Scriptures: 'I have set the Lord always before me.' Ever since then I see the name of the Lord before me, like black fire on white fire."

"If that is the case," said the maggid, "I shall go and preach a sermon."

Self-Mortification

To the maggid of Koznitz came a man who — in order to mortify himself — wore nothing but a sack on his bare body, and fasted from one sabbath to the next. The maggid said to him: "Do you think the Evil Urge is keeping away from you? It is tricking you into that sack. He who pretends to fast from sabbath to sabbath but secretly eats a little something every day, is spiritually better off than you, for he is only deceiving others, while you are deceiving yourself."

Rejection

A woman came to the maggid of Koznitz and told him, weeping bitterly all the while, that her husband had turned from her, and said she was ugly. "And perhaps you are really ugly?" said Rabbi Israel.

"Rabbi," cried the woman, "did I not seem beautiful and dear to him when we stood under the wedding canopy? Why have I now grown black?"

Then a tremor went through the rabbi, and it was only with difficulty that he could bring himself to comfort the woman, saying he would pray that God might turn her husband's heart back to her. When she had gone, he said to God: "Think of this woman, Lord of the world, and think of Israel. When the people of Israel said at Sinai: 'All that the Lord hath spoken will we do,' and you chose them and wedded them to yourself, were they not beautiful and dear? Why have they now grown black?"

Rich People's Food

A rich man once came to the maggid of Koznitz.
"What are you in the habit of eating?" the maggid asked.
"I am modest in my demands," the rich man replied. "Bread and salt, and a drink of water are all I need."
"What are you thinking of!" the rabbi reproved him. "You must eat roast meat and drink mead, like all rich people." And he did not let the man go until he had promised to do as he said.
Later the hasidim asked him the reason for this odd request.
"Not until he eats meat," said the maggid, "will he realize that the poor man needs bread. As long as he himself eats bread, he will think the poor man can live on stones."

In Order

It is told:
A villager and his wife came to the maggid of Koznitz and begged him to pray that they might have a son, for they were childless. "Give me fifty-two gulden," said the maggid, "for this is the numerical value of the word *ben*, son."
"We should be glad to give you ten gulden," said the man, but the maggid refused to accept them. Then the man went to the market-place and staggered back under a sack of copper coins. He spread them out on the table. There were twenty gulden. "Look, what a lot of money!" he cried. But the maggid would not come down with his demand. At that the villager grew angry, gathered up his money, and said to his wife: "Come on, let's go. God will help us without the maggid's prayer."
"You have already been granted his help," said the rabbi. And he was right.

292

It is told:

When Prince Adam Czartoryski, the friend and counsellor of
Czar Alexander, had been married for many years and still
had no children, he went to the maggid of Koznitz and asked
him to pray for him, and because of his prayer the princess
bore a son. At the baptism, the father told of the maggid's
intercession with God. His brother who, with his young son,
was among the guests, made fun of what he called the prince's
superstition. "Let us go to your wonder-worker together," he
said, "and I shall show you that he can't tell the difference
between left and right."

Together they journeyed to Koznitz, which was close to where
they lived. "I beg of you," Adam's brother said to the maggid,
"to pray for my sick son."

The maggid bowed his head in silence. "Will you do this for
me?" the other urged.

The maggid raised his head. "Go," he said, and Adam saw that
he only managed to speak with a great effort. "Go quickly, and
perhaps you will still see him alive."

"Well, what did I tell you?" Adam's brother said laughingly
as they got into their carriage. Adam was silent during the ride.
When they drove into the court of his house, they found the
boy dead.

The Pudding

Once a simple man of the people came to the maggid of Koznitz
with his wife and said that he wished to divorce her. "Why
do you want to do that?" asked the maggid.

"I work very hard all week," said the man, "and on the sabbath I want to have some pleasure. Now at the sabbath meal,
my wife first serves the fish, and then the onions and the heavy
main dish, and by the time she puts the pudding on the table,
I have eaten all I want and have no appetite for it. All week I
work for this pudding and when it comes I cannot even taste of
it, and all my labor was for nothing! Time after time, I have
asked my wife to put the pudding on the table right after the
benediction over the wine, but no! She says that the way she
does it, is according to the custom."

The maggid turned to the woman. "From now on," he said, "make two puddings. Serve the one right after the benediction over the wine and the other after the main dish, as before." Both husband and wife agreed to this, and went away well pleased.

On the same day, the maggid said to his wife: "From now on, make two puddings on Friday. Serve one right after the benediction over the wine, and the other after the main dish, as you have been doing." From that time on, this was the custom in the maggid's house, and continued to be the custom among his children and his children's children: One pudding was served immediately after the blessing over the wine, and this was called the Peace-at-Home Pudding.

Adam's Share

It is told that once, when the maggid of Koznitz was praying, Adam, the first man, came to him, and said: "You have atoned for your share in my sin — now won't you atone for my share in it too?"

The Cantonist at the Seder

It is told:

In the Russia of those days, it was common to draft Jewish boys into the army, in which they were forced to serve to their sixtieth year. They were known as "cantonists."

On the eve of Passover, a man whose uniform identified him as a cantonist arrived in Koznitz and asked to be admitted to the holy maggid. When he stood in his presence, he begged to be allowed to participate in the Seder, and the maggid gave his permission.

When, in the course of the rites of the Seder, they came to the words: "The Ceremony of the Passover has been celebrated in due order," the guest asked whether he might sing, and his request was granted. After the closing words of the song: ". . . peduyim lezion berina," which means, "Redeemed unto Zion with joy," he cried out in Russian: "Podjom!" that is, "Let's go!" The maggid rose and said in a voice filled with jubilation: "We are ready to go to Zion." But the guest had vanished.

A grandson of the maggid of Koznitz told:

"Once a man who was possessed came to the holy maggid — may his memory protect us! — and asked to be redeemed. The maggid called on the spirit to confess his sins. The spirit said: 'When the prophet Zechariah predicted destruction to the people, I was the first to run forward from the throng and strike him in the face. Only then did the others shower blows upon him until they struck him dead. Ever since that time, I am forced to wander from soul to soul and can find no rest.' But when the holy maggid began his work of redemption by rubbing the fringes one against the other, the spirit burst into insolent laughter and cried: 'In my day it was the tailors and the shoemakers who knew how to do this sort of thing.' 'And if you were so clever,' said the maggid, 'why did you strike the prophet dead?' Then the spirit replied: 'It is a law that he who keeps his prophecy to himself incurs the death penalty. On the other hand, it is said that if the prophet does not utter his prophecy, it becomes invalid. So it would have been better if Zechariah had kept his prophecy to himself and thus sacrificed himself for the community. That is why we killed him.' The holy maggid said: 'To tell this — that is the reason why you came here,' and completed the work of redemption."

That is how the grandson of the maggid of Koznitz told the story. But it is also told that when the maggid heard the words of the spirit, he could not complete his work, and that the man who was possessed had to go to Rabbi Issachar Baer of Radoshitz, the wonder-worker, who in his youth had been a disciple of the maggid's, and that he performed the work of redemption.

His Sister's Spirit

It is told:

The maggid of Koznitz had a sister who died young. But in the upper world, they gave her permission to remain in her brother's house.

The maggid always saw to it that clothing was made for poor orphans. When dealers brought him the material for this, he said: "I shall ask my sister whether this stuff is durable and a good buy," and she always gave him correct information.

She watched everything the servants did, and when one or another of them stole a loaf of bread or a piece of meat, she instantly reported the theft to her brother. He detested this tale-bearing, but he could not break her of it. Once his temper grew short and he said to her: "Wouldn't you like to take a little rest?" From that time on, she was gone.

The Soul of the Cymbalist

It is told:

Once, on a midnight, a voice drifted into the room of the maggid of Koznitz and moaned: "Holy man of Israel, have pity on a pour soul which, for ten years, has been wandering from eddy to eddy."

"Who are you?" asked the maggid. "And what did you do while you were on earth?"

"I was a musician," said the voice. "I played the cymbal and I sinned like all wandering musicians."

"And who sent you to me?"

Then the voice groaned: "Why, I played at your wedding, rabbi, and you gave me praise and wanted to hear more, and so I played one piece after another and you were well pleased."

"Do you still remember the tune you played when they conducted me under the wedding-baldachin?" The voice hummed the tune. "Well then, you shall be redeemed on the coming sabbath," said the maggid.

On the Friday evening after that, when the maggid stood in front of the reader's desk, he sang the song: "Come, my friend, to meet the bride," in a tune no one knew, and not even the choir could join in.

The World of Melody

The "Yehudi," the zaddik of Pzhysha, once saw with the eyes of his mind that the maggid of Koznitz, who had fallen ill, was now in danger of dying. Immediately he told two of his faithful men who were excellent singers and players, to go to Koznitz and gladden Rabbi Israel's heart with music. The two set out at once, reached the maggid's house on Friday, and were told to welcome in the sabbath with their singing and playing. When the sounds entered the room where Rabbi Israel lay, he listened intently and his face brightened. Gradually, his breath grew even, his forehead cool, and his hands stopped twitching and lay quietly on the coverlet. When the music ended he looked up as though he had just awakened and said: "The Yehudi saw that I had passed through all the worlds. The only world in which I was not, was the world of melody. So he sent two messengers to lead me back through that world."

The Melody of Angels

Rumor had it that the melody the maggid of Koznitz left behind was one he had heard from the lips of angels who sang it in honor of God. But one of his disciples said this was not so, that the angels had heard it from his lips. In later years, when a son of that disciple told the story, he added: "They were the angels who were born from the deeds of the holy maggid."

With One Look

One sabbath, at the third meal, young Zevi Elimelekh heard his teacher, Rabbi Mendel of Rymanov, say: "He who lives in the era of the maggid of Koznitz, and has not looked upon his face, will not be found worthy to look upon the face of the Messiah, when he comes."

The moment the light was put on the table, Zevi Elimelekh took leave of the rabbi, fetched his stick, slung his knapsack over his shoulder and walked day and night with scarcely any respite, for who knows if the Messiah will not come this very week? When he reached Koznitz, he went straight to the maggid's House of Study, without even stopping to leave his stick and knapsack at an inn, for who knows if the Messiah will not come this very hour? They showed him into a little room where many people were standing around the maggid's bed. Zevi Elimelekh leaned against the wall, rested one hand on his stick, the other on a man in front of him, hoisted himself up, and looked into the maggid's face. "With one look," he said to himself, "one can gain the coming world."

Extension

In his old age, Rabbi Israel said: "There are those zaddikim who—as soon as they have accomplished the task appointed to them for their life on earth—are called to depart. And there are those zaddikim who—the moment they have accomplished the task appointed to them for their life on earth—are given another task, and they live until that too is accomplished. That is the way it was with me."

Pebbles

In the year of Napoleon's Russian campaign, the rabbi of Apt visited the maggid of Koznitz on the Feast of the Revelation. He found him lying on his sick-bed as usual, but saw that his face was quickened with a strange expression of decision. "How are you?" asked the visitor.

"I am a soldier now," said the maggid. "The five pebbles young David picked up for his sling, to fight Goliath the Philistine—those five pebbles I have right here in my bed!"

In the night before the first holiday, two hours after midnight, the maggid went to the desk in the House of Prayer, stood there until morning, said the Morning Prayer, read the Scriptures, recited the liturgy for the feast, and finished his prayer three hours after twelve o'clock noon.

Before the End

When the maggid of Koznitz, who was sick unto death, prayed in front of the Ark, the month before he died, on the eve of the Day of Atonement, he paused before saying the words: "The Lord said: 'I have pardoned,'" and said to God: "Lord of the world, you alone know how great your power is, and you alone know how great is the weakness of my body. And this too you know: that all through this month, day after day, I have prayed in front of the Ark, not for my own sake, but for the sake of this, your people of Israel. And so I ask you: If it grew easy for me to take the yoke of your people upon myself and to perform the service with my wretched body, how can it be difficullt for you, who are all-powerful, to say three words?" Then he bade them sing a song of joy, and called out in a strong voice: "The Lord said: 'I have pardoned '"

JACOB YITZHAK OF LUBLIN ("THE SEER")

His Old Teacher

Rabbi Jacob Yitzhak once journeyed to a distant city in the company of some of his friends and disciples. It was Friday afternoon and they must have been quite close to their destination when they came to a crossroads. The coachman asked which road he was to take. The rabbi did not know and so he said: "Give the horses their head and let them go where they want." After a time they saw the houses of a town. Soon, however, they discovered that it was not the one they were bound for. "Well, after that, better not call me rabbi any more," said the Seer of Lublin.

"But how are we going to get food and shelter for the sabbath," his disciples asked, "if we are not allowed to say who you are?" Now the reason for this question was this: the zaddik never kept overnight even the smallest coins of the gifts of money he had received during the day, but gave everything to the poor.

"Let us go to the House of Prayer," he said. "There some burgher or other will take each of us home with him as his sabbath guest." And that was what happened, only that the rabbi himself took so long over his prayers that the House of Prayer was all but empty when he had done. Looking up, he saw that one man alone, a man of eighty or thereabouts, was still there. This old man asked the stranger: "Where are you going for the consecration of the sabbath?"

"I don't know," said the zaddik.

"Just go to the inn," said the old man, "and when the day of rest is over, I'll take up a collection to settle your bill."

"I cannot keep the sabbath at the inn," said Rabbi Jacob Yitzhak, "because there they do not say the blessing over the lights."

The old man hesitated. Then he said: "In my house I have only a little bread and wine for my wife and myself."

"I am not a big eater," the rabbi of Lublin assured him, and they went off together.

First the old man said the blessing over the wine, and then the rabbi. After the blessing over the bread, the old man asked: "Where do you come from?"

"From Lublin."

"And do you know *him?*"

"I am always in his company."

Then the old man begged his guest in a voice that trembled: "Tell me something about him!"

"Why are you so eager to know?"

"When I was young," said the old man, "I was an assistant at the school and he was one of the children assigned to my care. He did not seem especially gifted. But then I heard that he became a very great man. Since that time I fast one day every week, that I may be found worthy to see him. For I am too poor to ride to Lublin and too weak to walk there."

"Do you remember anything at all about him?" the rabbi inquired.

"Day after day," said the old man, "I had to look for him when the time to study the prayer-book had come, and I never found him. After a fairly long time he came of his own accord, and then I smacked him. Once I watched where he was going and followed. There he sat on an ant-hill in the woods and cried aloud: 'Hear, O Israel, the Lord our God, the Lord is one.' After that I never smacked him any more."

Now Rabbi Jacob Yitzhak knew why his horses had taken him to this town. "I am he," he said. When the old man heard this, he fainted and it took a long time to revive him.

At the end of the sabbath, the zaddik left the city with his disciples, and the old man accompanied him until he grew tired and had to turn back. He reached home, lay down, and died. While this was happening, the rabbi and his companions were having the post-sabbath meal at a village inn. When they had finished eating, he rose, and said: "Now let us return to the city and bury my old teacher."

In the course of his long wanderings, Rabbi Zusya came to the town where the father of the boy Jacob Yitzhak lived. In the House of Study he went back of the stove to pray—for this was his way—and covered his whole head with the prayer shawl. Suddenly he half turned, looked out from it, and without letting his glance rest on anything else, looked the boy Jacob Yitzhak straight in the eyes. Then he turned back to the stove and went on praying. The boy was seized with an irresistible impulse to cry. A well of tears opened up within him and he wept for an hour. Not until his tears ceased to fall, did Zusya go up to him. Then he said: "Your soul has been wakened. Now go to my teacher, the maggid of Mezritch, and study with him, so that your mind may also be roused from its sleep."

In the House of Study

A zaddik told:

"When I lived in Nikolsburg, as a disciple of Rabbi Shmelke, one of my companions was a young man by the name of Jacob Yitzhak. Years later he became the rabbi of Lublin. He and I had both been married for two years. In the House of Study he sat in an inconspicuous place. He never asked questions like the rest. He never looked at any of us, but only at the rabbi. When he was not looking at him, he kept his eyes on the ground. But his face was transfigured with a golden radiance from within, and I saw that the rabbi was very fond of him."

Holy Joy

When Jacob Yitzhak was in Rabbi Shmelke's House of Study, he seemed like an angel remote from all matters of earth, so much so that Rabbi Shmelke, who himself had a tendency to aloofness, found his disciple's attitude excessive. He sent him to Hanipol with a note to Rabbi Zusya which contained only these words: "Make our Itzikel a little lighter of heart!" And Rabbi Zusya, who had once wakened Jacob Yitzhak the boy to holy tears, now succeeded in waking holy joy within him.

Near the city of Lizhensk, where Rabbi Elimelekh taught, there is a hill. It is wooded on all sides except one, but there it is steep and stony, and the rocky peak is called Rabbi Melekh's Table to this very day. Young Jacob Yitzhak was in the habit of going to this place to meditate on how true humility and the annihilation of self can be reached. One day he was in such despair that it seemed to him all he could do was to offer up his own life. He went to the very brink of the rock and wanted to throw himself down. But a comrade of his, young Zalke from Grodzisk, had followed him unobserved. Now he ran toward him, caught him by the belt, and did not stop comforting and encouraging him until he had talked his soul out of its grim purpose.

When Jacob Yitzhak's teacher died, and he was made the rabbi of Lublin, Rabbi Zalke came to visit him. As he entered the room, the zaddik took both his hands in his and said: "Rabbi Zalke, my life, I truly love you. That is because on my soul's first excursion on earth you were my father. But when I recall what you did to me in Lizhensk, I cannot wholly love you."

His Gaze

The hasidim tell:

When the soul of the Seer of Lublin was created, it was endowed with the power of gazing from one end of the world to the other. But when it saw the great mass of evil, it knew that it could not bear this burden and begged to be relieved of its gift. Then its power was limited to seeing everything within a radius of four miles.

In his youth, he kept his eyes closed for seven years, save during the hours of praying and learning, so that he might not see anything unseemly. This made his eyes weak and nearsighted.

When he looked at anyone's forehead, or at his note of request, he saw to the root of his soul and beyond it to the first man. He saw whether that soul came from Abel or from Cain, saw how often, in its wanderings, it had assumed bodily shape, what had been destroyed or bettered in each incarnation, in what sin it had become entangled, and to what vitrue it had ascended.

Once, when he was visiting Rabbi Mordecai of Neskhizh, they spoke of this power. The rabbi of Lublin said: "The fact that I see in each what he has done, lessens my love for Israel. And so I beg you to do something to have this power taken from me."

The rabbi of Neskhizh replied: "The words in the Gemara hold for whatever Heaven decrees: 'Our God gives, but he does not take back.' "

Going Blind

It is told:

In Lublin the Afternoon Prayer was delayed even on the sabbath. Before this prayer, the rabbi sat alone in his room every sabbath, and no one was permitted to enter it. Once a hasid hid there to find out what happened on these occasions. All he saw at first was that the rabbi seated himself at the table and opened a book. But then a vast light began to shine in the narrow room, and when he saw it the hasid became unconscious. He came to himself when the rabbi left the room, and he too went out as soon as he fully regained consciousness. In the entrance, he saw nothing, but he heard them saying the Evening Prayer and realized with horror that the candles must be lit and that he, notwithstanding, was surrounded by utter darkness. He was terrified, implored the rabbi to help him, and was sent to another city, to a man who was known to perform miraculous cures. He asked the hasid about the circumstances of his going blind, and he told him. "There is no cure for you," said the man. "You have seen the original light, the light on the days of creation, which empowered the first people on earth to see from one end of the world to the other, which was hidden after their sinning, and is only revealed to zaddikim in the Torah. Whoever beholds it unlawfully—his eyes will be darkened forever."

Landscape

When Rabbi Jacob Yitzhak was a guest in the house of Rabbi Barukh, the Baal Shem's grandson, that proud and secretive man who had once said of himself that he would be the supervisor of all zaddikim, took him with him in his carriage when he drove to the ritual bath on the day before the sabbath. On the way, Rabbi Barukh gave himself up to the creative strength with which he gazed at his surroundings, and the landscape changed in tune with his thoughts. When they got out of the carriage, he asked: "What does the Seer see?" Rabbi Yitzhak replied: "The fields of the Holy Land."

When they crossed the hill between the road and the stream, Barukh asked: "What does the Seer smell?" He replied: "The air of the mountain of the Temple."

When they dipped into the stream, the grandson of the Baal Shem Tov asked: "What does the Seer feel?" And Rabbi Jacob Yitzhak answered: "The healing stream of paradise."

What Ten Hasidim Can Accomplish

A young man stole away from his wife and parents-in-law to spend the sabbath in Lublin. But hardly had he greeted the rabbi, when Jacob Yitzhak—who had looked at him closely— told him to return to his own town immediately so that he might reach home before the beginning of the holiday. The young man begged and begged, but could not induce the rabbi to change his dictum, and so he went his way deeply disturbed. He spent the night at an inn and while he lay there, unable to sleep, a group of hasidim, on the road to the rabbi of Lublin, entered the room. They heard the man moaning on his bench, asked him about himself, and discovered what had happened. Then they got some brandy, kept filling their glasses and his, drank to one another, and to him, and cried: "To life! To life!" One after another took him by the hand and then they said to him: "You are not going home! You are coming to Lublin with us and shall spend the sabbath there, and don't you worry about anything!" They drank until morning. Then they all prayed together, drank to one another and the young man once more, and went merrily toward Lublin, taking him between them.

The moment they arrived there, they went to the zaddik and greeted him. The zaddik looked at the young man and was silent for a time. Finally he asked: "Where have you been? What has happened?" When he had heard everything, the zaddik said: "It was decreed that you should die on this sabbath, and your fate has been averted. The truth of it is that no zaddik can bring about what ten hasidim can accomplish."

The Bed

It was a known fact that frequently the Seer of Lublin could not sleep in a strange bed on occasions when he was a guest in someone's house. And so, when Rabbi Yossel of Ostila heard that the zaddik was coming to his town on his next journey, he immediately gave a devout and able carpenter the order to make a bed of the very best wood and to put into it his most painstaking labor. The carpenter went to the ritual bath, concentrated his mind on his work, and was more successful than ever before. When Jacob Yitzhak had accepted Rabbi Yossel's earnest invitation to stay at his house, his host conducted him to his room, where the bed shone out in all its newness, piled with smooth pillows and soft blankets. But with pained surprise, Rabbi Yossel later heard the zaddik toss about on his bed with many sighs and realized that he could not sleep. For a while he was utterly nonplussed. Finally he offered his guest his own bed. The Seer of Lublin lay down in it, closed his eyes with immediate and evident comfort, and fell asleep. Later Rabbi Yossel mustered his courage and asked what he had found wrong with the bed a God-fearing man had made for him with the most zealous care. The zaddik said: "The man is good and his work is good, but he did it in the nine days before the anniversary of the destruction of the Temple. Since he is devout, he mourned for the Temple unceasingly, and now his sorrow clings to the bed, and exudes from it."

Lighting the Pipe

A zaddik told:
"In my youth I once attended a wedding to which the rabbi of Lublin had also been invited. Among the guests were more than two hundred zaddikim, as for the hasidim—you could

306

not even have counted them! They had rented a house with a great hall for the rabbi of Lublin, but he spent most of the time alone in a little room. Once a great number of hasidim had gathered in the hall and I was with them. Then the rabbi entered, seated himself at a small table and sat there for a time in silence. Then he rose, looked around, and—over the heads of the others pointed at me, standing up against the wall. "That young man over there," he said, "shall light my pipe for me." I made my way through the crowd, took the pipe from his hands, went to the kitchen, fetched a glowing coal, lit the pipe, brought it back into the hall, and handed it to him. At that moment I felt my senses taking leave of me. The next instant the rabbi began to speak and said a few words to me, and at once my senses returned. It was then that I received from him the gift of stripping myself of all that is bodily. Since then, I can do this whenever I want to."

Purification of Souls

Rabbi Naftali of Ropshitz said:
"I testify to this concerning my teacher, Rabbi Itzikel of Lublin: Whenever a new hasid came to him, he instantly took his soul out of him, cleansed it of all stain and rust, and put it back into him, restored to the state it had been in the hour he was born."

The "Casting off of Sins"

Once Rabbi Naftali had missed going to the river with his master, the rabbi of Lublin, for the Casting off of Sins. When the Seer was on the way home with his people, they met Naftali running toward the river. "Why are you running?" one of them asked him. "You see that the rabbi is on the way home, so what difference does it make now, whether you get to the river a little sooner or later?"
Naftali replied: "I am hurrying to gather up some of the sins the rabbi cast into the water, so that I may store them in the treasure-room of my heart."

Lighter

The rabbi of Lublin once said: "How strange! People come to me weighed down with melancholy, and when they leave, their spirit is lighter, although I myself [and here he was going to say: "am melancholy," but he paused and then continued:] am dark and do not shine."

The Little Sanctuary

One of the disciples of the rabbi of Lublin told this: "My master, the rabbi of Lublin, had not only the great disciples whom all the world knows, but also four hundred, who went by the name of 'village people' and had—every one of them!—the gift of the holy spirit."

They asked him: "If such a holy community existed, and the holy Seer was their king, why did they not join in one great attempt to bring about salvation?"

He replied: "Great things were undertaken."

They interposed: "But why didn't the whole community work together?"

He said: "When we were with our holy Seer, we were in a little sanctuary. We lacked nothing, and we did not feel the sadness of exile, nor the darkness that lies over all. Had we felt it, we should have shaken worlds, we should have split the Heavens to bring salvation closer."

The Obstacle

Once Rabbi Jacob Yitzhak confidently expected salvation to come that very year. When the year was over, he said to his disciple the Yehudi: "The rank and file of people either have turned completely to God, or can, at any rate, do so. They present no obstacle. It is the superior people who constitute a hindrance. They cannot attain humility, and therefore they cannot achieve the turning."

Payment

On one Friday evening, before the consecration of the sabbath, the rabbi had retired to his room and locked the door. Suddenly it opened, and he came out. The house was full of his great disciples in the white satin robes the great zaddikim used to wear in those days. The rabbi addressed them: "It is written: 'and repayeth them that hate Him to their face, to destroy them.' This is what it means: He pays his haters for the good works they do in this world in spite of themselves, in order to destroy them in the world which is to come. And so I ask you: given that the wrong-doer is greedy for gold, well then, he will receive his fill of gold; and given the wrong-doer is greedy for honors, well then, he shall have his fill of honors. But now suppose the wrong-doer is not out for honors, and not for gold, but for spiritual rungs, or that he is out to be a rabbi — what then? Well then, he who is out for spiritual rungs, will mount them, and he who is out to be a rabbi, will become one — in order to be destroyed in the coming world."

The Bright Light

A number of hasidim came to Lublin. Before they set out to go to the rabbi, their coachman begged them to take a slip of paper with his name on it, along with other slips of this kind, so that the rabbi might wish him well, and they did as he asked. When the Seer of Lublin read the slip, he cried: "How brightly the name of this man shines out!" The hasidim were astonished and asserted that he was a simple and ignorant man, and that in all the time they had known him, they had not detected any special virtues in him. "At this moment," insisted the rabbi, "his soul is shining out at me like pure light."

When the hasidim went to look for their coachman, they did not find him at the inn, and so they walked from street to street. Presently they met a gay procession coming toward them: first, musicians with cymbals and drums, and behind them a crowd of dancing, skipping, clapping people. In the very middle, gayer and shouting more lustily than all the rest, came the coachman. In answer to their questions, he said: "When you had gone I wanted to amuse myself a bit. So I strolled through the town and suddenly heard music and sounds of merriment from one of the houses. I went in and saw that they were celebrating the wedding of two orphans. So I cele-

brated along with them, drank, and sang, and had a good time.
But after a while there was confusion and quarreling, for it
seemed the bride did not have the money to give the groom
a prayer shawl according to the custom and what was expected
of her. They were just getting ready to tear up the marriage
contract! Then my heart beat to bursting. I could not stand
seeing the girl humiliated, pulled out my purse, and what do
you think? There was just enough in it to pay for the prayer
shawl! That is why I am so happy."

The Transition

A rich and powerful man by the name of Shalom, who was
generally called Count Shalom, fell dangerously ill. His son
at once set out for the rabbi of Lublin, to ask him to pray for
mercy. But when, after his long journey, he stood before the
zaddik and gave him the slip of paper with his request, Rabbi
Jacob Yitzhak said: "Help is no longer possible. He has already passed from the sphere of ruling into that of learning."
When the man reached home, he discovered that his father had
died that very hour, but that, in the same hour, his wife had
borne him a son. He was named Shalom after his grandfather,
and grew up to be a master of the teachings.

The Lengthy Lawsuit

The rabbi of Lublin once said to Rabbi Heshel of Komarno,
who was a disciple of his: "Why do you never look up the rav
of the city? You would do well to go to him from time to
time."
Rabbi Heshel was surprised to hear these words, for the rav,
who had been nicknamed the "Iron Head," was a declared
enemy of the hasidic way. Still, he obeyed his teacher, and
began to pray in the rav's house every afternoon. The rav
received him most cordially. One day, a lawsuit was presented
after prayer. When the parties involved had been sent out of
the room, and the discussion was under way, one of the judges
took the part of the plaintiff, the other that of the defendant,
so that the Iron Head was to tip the scales. Rabbi Heshel was

310

present and had followed the argument with the closest attention. It was entirely clear to him that the plaintiff was right, but he saw to his distress that the rav inclined to the other side. He did not know what to do, and yet he could not sit in silence and suffer injustice done. Finally he happened to remember a gloss to the passage in the Talmud which presented his own interpretation of the matter as the right one. He fetched the volume of the Gemara, wènt up to the rav, and asked him to expound the gloss. The Iron Head seemed irritated and refused him on the grounds that this was not the proper time for giving an interpretation. But Heshel repeated his request so insistently that the rav took the book from his hand, and glanced at the page in question. He changed color, told Heshel he would expound the comment to him the next day, and dismissed him.

The following day, when Rabbi Heshel inquired about the result of the session, he was told that the plaintiff had won the case. That same evening, the rabbi of Lublin said to him: "Now you don't have to go to the rav any more." When his disciple looked at him in astonishment, he added: "Those two, the plaintiff and the defendant, had been on earth ninety-nine times, and over and over justice was perverted and both their souls continued to be unredeemed. So I had to send you to help them."

The Rabbi of Lublin and the Iron Head

Rabbi Azriel Hurwitz, rav of the city of Lublin, who was also known by the name of Iron Head, kept plaguing Rabbi Jacob Yitzhak with constant objections and reproaches. Once he said to him: "You, yourself, know and admit that you are no zaddik. Then why do you guide others to your way, and gather a community around you?"

Rabbi Jacob Yitzhak replied: "What can I do about it? They come to me of their own free will, rejoice in my teaching, and desire to hear it."

Then the other said: "Tell all of them, this coming sabbath, that you are not one of the great, and they will turn from you." The zaddik agreed. On the next sabbath, he begged his assembled listeners not to give him rank and honors that were not his due. As he spoke, their hearts were set aflame with humility, and from that moment on, they followed him even more fervently than before.

When he told the Iron Head of his efforts and their result, the rav reflected, and then said: "That is the way you hasidim are: you love the humble and eschew the haughty. Tell them that you are one of the elect and they will turn from you."

Rabbi Jacob Yitzhak replied: "I am not a zaddik, but neither am I a liar, and how can I say what is not true!"

On another occasion, Rabbi Azriel Hurwitz asked the Seer: "How is it that so many flock about you? I am much more learned than you, yet they do not throng to me."

The zaddik answered: "I too am astonished that so many should come to one as insignificant as myself, to hear God's word, instead of looking for it to you whose learning moves mountains. Perhaps this is the reason: they come to me because I am astonished that they come, and they do not come to you, because you are astonished that they do not come."

The Rabbi of Lublin and a Preacher

A famous traveling maggid was once preaching in a city, when word came that the rabbi of Lublin had arrived. And immediately all the maggid's audience left to greet the zaddik. The preacher found himself quite alone. He waited for a little while and then he too saw the Seer's table heaped with the "ransom-money" which petitioners and other visitors had brought him. The maggid asked: "How is this possible! I have been preaching here for days and have gotten nothing, while all this came your way in a single hour!"

Rabbi Yitzhak replied: "It is probably because each wakens in the hearts of men what he cherishes in his own heart: I, the hatred of money, and you the love of it."

Truth

A disciple asked the rabbi of Lublin: "Rabbi, you taught us that if a man knows his own worth and casts honest accounts with his soul, then this saying of the people can be applied to him: 'To cast accounts is paying half the bill.' How are we to understand this?"

"When merchandise is shipped across the border," said the rabbi, "the king's seal is put upon it, and thus it is certified. So when a man knows his worth and casts honest accounts with his soul, then truth, the seal of God, is set on him and he is certified."

The Way

Rabbi Baer of Radoshitz once said to his teacher, the rabbi of Lublin: "Show me one general way to the service of God."
The zaddik replied: "It is impossible to tell men what way they should take. For one way to serve God is through the teachings, another through prayer, another through fasting, and still another through eating. Everyone should carefully observe what way his heart draws him to, and then choose this way with all his strength."

In Many Ways

Some time after Rabbi Shalom, the son of Rabbi Abraham, the Angel, had died, two of his disciples came to Lublin to study with the Seer. They found him out in the open, saying the blessing of the New Moon. Now, because he did this a little differently in some details from what their teacher had accustomed them to, they did not promise themselves much from Lublin and decided to leave the town the very next day. When they entered the rabbi's house, shortly after, he spoke words of greetings to them and immediately added: "A God whom one could serve only in one set way — what kind of God would that be!" They bowed before him and became his disciples.

The Reluctant Hand

They asked the rabbi of Lublin: "Why does it say: "And Abraham stretched forth his hand,' and right after that, 'and took the knife . . . ' Is not the first part superfluous?"
He replied: "Abraham had consecrated all his strength and all his limbs, that they might do nothing against the will of God. Now when God commanded him to offer up his son, he

313

understood this to mean that he was to slay him. But since all his strength and all his limbs were consecrated, that they might do nothing against the will of God, Abraham's hands refused to obey Abraham, and take the knife, since this was not God's true will. Abraham had to overwhelm his hand with the power of his fervor, and send it out like a messenger who must do the errand of his sender. Only then could he take the knife."

True Justice

The words in the Scriptures: "Justice, justice shalt thou follow," were interpreted in the following way by the rabbi of Lublin:

"When a man believes that he is wholly just and need not strive further, then justice does not recognize him. You must follow and follow justice and never stand still, and in your own eyes, you must always be like a new-born child that has not yet achieved anything at all — for that is true justice."

The Second Mother

They asked the Rabbi of Lublin: "Why is it that in the holy Book of Splendor, the turning to God which corresponds to the emanation 'understanding,' is called 'Mother'?"

He explained: "When a man confesses and repents, when his heart accepts Understanding and is converted to it, he becomes like a new-born child, and his own turning to God is his mother."

Dialogue

The rabbi of Lublin was asked by one of his disciples: "Our sages say that God speaks to the community of Israel, as it is written: 'Return unto me, and I will return unto you,' but Israel replies, as it is written: 'Turn thou us unto Thee . . . and we shall be turned.' What does this mean? What God said to them is so, for we know that the awakening from below, brings about that from above."

The rabbi replied: "Our sages say: 'A woman only enters upon a union with him who has made her a vessel, for in the first mating, her husband made of her a vessel, to awaken her

314

womanhood.' And so Israel says to God: 'Make us your vessel once more, that our turning may waken again and again.' And that is why further on in the answer which Israel gave to the Lord, we read: 'Renew our days as of old.' By 'of old' the time before the creation of the world is meant, when nothing existed except the awakening from above."

Sin and Despondency

A hasid complained to the rabbi of Lublin that he was tormented with evil desire and had become despondent over it. The rabbi said to him: "Guard yourself from despondency above all, for it is worse and more harmful than sin. When the Evil Urge wakens desires in man, he is not concerned with plunging him into sin, but with plunging him into despondency by way of his sinning."

The Wicked and the Righteous

The rabbi of Lublin said: "I love the wicked man who knows he is wicked more than the righteous man who knows he is righteous. But concerning the wicked who consider themselves righteous, it is said: 'They do not turn even on the threshold of Hell.' For they think they are being sent to Hell to redeem the souls of others."

The Merry Sinner

In Lublin lived a great sinner. Whenever he wanted to talk to the rabbi, he readily consented and conversed with him as if with a man of integrity and one who was a close friend. Many of the hasidim were annoyed at this, and one said to the other: "Is it possible that our rabbi, who has only to look once into a man's face to know his life from first to last, to know the very origin of his soul, does not see that this fellow is a sinner? And if he does see it, that he considers him worthy to speak to and associate with?" Finally they summoned up courage to go to the rabbi himself with their question. He answered them: "I know all about him as well as you. But you know how I love gayety and hate dejection. And this man is so great a sinner! Others repent the moment they have sinned,

315

are sorry for a moment, and then return to their folly. But he knows no regrets and no doldrums, and lives in his happiness as in a tower. And it is the radiance of his happiness that overwhelms my heart."

Patchwork

A hasid of the rabbi of Lublin once fasted from one sabbath to the next. On Friday afternoon he began to suffer such cruel thirst that he thought he would die. He saw a well, went up to it, and prepared to drink. But instantly he realized that because of the one brief hour he had still to endure, he was about to destroy the work of the entire week. He did not drink and went away from the well. Then he was touched by a feeling of pride for having passed this difficult test. When he became aware of it, he said to himself: "Better I go and drink than let my heart fall prey to pride." He went back to the well, but just as he was going to bend down to draw water, he noticed that his thirst had disappeared. When the sabbath had begun, he entered his teacher's house. "Patchwork!" the rabbi called to him, as he crossed the threshold.

Alien Thoughts

A man came to ask the rabbi of Lublin to help him against alien thoughts which intruded on him while he prayed. The rabbi indicated what he was to do, but the man went on asking him questions and would not stop. Finally the rabbi said: "I don't know why you keep complaining to me of alien thoughts. To him who has holy thoughts, an impure thought comes at times, and such a thought is called 'alien.' But you — you have just your own usual thoughts. To whom do you want to ascribe them?"

Service

Rabbi Jacob Yitzhak was in the habit of taking poor wayfarers into his house and waiting on them himself. Once he had served such a man with food, filled his glass, and stood beside his chair ready to fetch him whatever he needed. After the meal, he took away the empty plates and platters and carried them into the kitchen. Then his guest asked him: "Master, will you tell me something? I know that you, in serving me, have fulfilled the command of God, who wishes the beggar to be honored as his envoy. But why have you taken the trouble to carry out the empty dishes?"

The rabbi replied: "Is not the carrying out of the spoon and the coal-pan from the Holy of Holies part of the service of the high priest, on the Day of Atonement!"

In the Hut

A disciple of the rabbi of Lublin told:

Once I celebrated the Feast of Tabernacles in Lublin. Before the paeans of praise, the rabbi went into the hut to say the blessing over the "Four Plants." For almost an hour I observed his violent movements which seemed impelled by overwhelming fear. All the people who watched thought that this was the essential part of the ceremony; a feeling of great fear passed over into them, and they too moved and trembled. But I sat on a bench and did not take the subsidiary for the essential, but waited until all the restlessness and anxiety was past. Then I rose to see better when the rabbi came to the blessing. And I saw how he — on the highest rung of the spirit — said the blessing motionlessly, and I heard the heavenly blessing. Thus, long ago, Moses did not heed the clap of thunder and the smoking mountain, where the people stood and shuddered, but approached the motionless cloud out of which God spoke to him.

His Clothes

Rabbi Bunam said: "The rabbi of Lublin had better hasidim than I, but I knew him better than all the rest. For once I entered his room when he was not at home, and then I heard a whispering: his clothes were telling one another of his greatness."

The Harpist

In the very act of praying, the rabbi of Lublin would occasionally take a pinch of snuff. A most diligent worshipper noticed this and said to him: "It is not proper to interrupt the prayer." "A great king," answered the rabbi of Lublin, "was once walking through his chief city and heard a ragged old street singer singing a song and playing the harp. The music pleased him. He took the man into his palace and listened to him day after day. Now the minstrel had not wanted to part with his old harp and so he often had to stop and tune it in the middle of playing. Once a courtier snapped at the old man: 'You really might see to the tuning of your instrument beforehand!' The harpist answered: 'In his orchestras and choirs, our king has lots of people better than I. But if they do not satisfy him and he has picked out me and my harp, it is apparently his wish to endure its peculiarities and mine.'"

Thanking for Evil

A hasid asked the Seer of Lublin: "To the words in the Mishnah: 'Man should thank God for evil and praise him,' the Gemara adds: 'with joy and a tranquil heart.' How can that be?"
The zaddik could hear that the question sprang from a troubled heart. "You do not understand the Gemara," he said. "And I do not understand even the Mishnah. For is there really any evil in the world?"

The Wedding Gift

It was at the wedding of his granddaughter Hinda. At the very moment the gifts were presented, Rabbi Jacob Yitzhak put his head in his hands, and seemed to fall asleep. The master of ceremonies called out again and again: "Wedding gifts from the family of the bride," and waited for the rabbi, but he did not move. All fell silent and waited for him to wake up. When half an hour had passed, his son whispered in his ear: "Father, they are calling for wedding gifts from the bride's family." The old man started up from his meditations and replied: "Then I give myself. After thirteen years, the gift will be brought."
After thirteen years, when Hinda bore a son, he was called Jacob Yitzhak after his grandfather. When he grew up he resembled him in every feature, his right eye, for instance, was a little bigger than his left, just like that of the rabbi of Lublin.

NOTES · GLOSSARY · GENEALOGY
SELECTED BIBLIOGRAPHY

NOTES

Many zaddikim to whom passing reference is made in these tales are
dealt with in individual chapters, or in the Introduction.

[35] *When all souls were gathered in Adam's soul:* according to the
Kabbalah, the souls of all men were included in the soul of Adam;
from there they set out on their wanderings.

[35] *The sixty:* Cant. 3:8.

[42] *The flame of the sword:* see Gen. 3:24.

[48] *Community of the great hasidim: see* Introduction.

[50] *Rabbi Jacob Joseph of Polnoye: see* "The Story Teller," p. 56, and
"The Visit," p. 100.

[51] *Ahijah the prophet:* according to legend, the biblical prophet Ahijah (I Kings 11-14) came to the Baal Shem and instructed him in the
teachings. *See also* "Across the Dniester," p. 74.

[55] *Rabbi David Leikes: see* "Fire Against Fire," p. 174.

[55] *Rabbi Motel of Tchernobil:* Rabbi Motel (Mordecai) was the son
of Rabbi Nahum of Tchernobil. *See* "From the Circle of the Baal Shem
Tov," pp. 172 ff.; "The Passage of Reproof," p. 60; "He Will Be," p. 85.

[59] *Rabbi Leib, son of Sarah: see* "If," p. 86; "From the Circle of the
Baal Shem Tov," p. 169; "To Say Torah and to Be Torah," p. 107. It is
told that on his wanderings he met with influential lords, among them
the emperor in Vienna, who were unfriendly to Jews. In a miraculous
way he is said to have caused them to change their opinion.

[59] *The hidden zaddik:* there are in each generation thirty-six "hidden"
zaddikim who, secretly, in the disguise of peasants, artisans, or porters,
do their good deeds. These deeds constitute the true foundation of the
created world. Rabbi Leib, son of Sarah, is not numbered among them
since he was known to be a zaddik.

[60] *The Passage of Reproof:* Deut. 28: 15-68.

[64] *Rabbi Wolf Kitzes: see* "False Hospitality," p. 72, and "The Miraculous Bath," p. 77.

[67] *The Light of the Seven Days:* the great zaddik is compared to the
original light of Creation, which he has absorbed.

[74] *Rabbi Nahman of Bratzlav: see* my books *The Tales of Rabbi
Nahman* (in German) , and *A People and Its Land* (in Hebrew) , pp.
91 ff.

[74] *Unification:* sacred ceremonies designed to bring about the unification of the separated divine principles.

[75] *He who spoke to the oil:* this saying is based on a similar story in
the Babylonian Talmud (Taanit 25a) .

[75] *Rabbi Nahman of Horodenka: see* "Of the Baal Shem's Death," p. 83.

[77] *Rabbi Zevi: see* "A Halt Is Called," p. 78.

[77] *The Bath of Israel Is the Lord:* this is Rabbi Akiba's interpretation of Jer. 17:13 (Mishnah Yoma VIII. 9).

[77] *The Erev Rav:* Exod. 12:38; *see also* Neh. 13:3.

[80] *Pastuch:* shepherd (Polish).

[84] *The prince of the river: see* Glossary, *s.v.*, Prince of the Torah.

[94] *And as the bridegroom:* Isa. 62:5.

[103] *The traditional saying:* according to the Babylonian Talmud, a Heavenly Voice spoke this phrase before deciding in favor of the lenient School of Hillel as against the more rigorous School of Shammai (Erubin 13b).

[103] *But from thence:* Deut. 4:29.

[107] *And I will set:* Lev. 26.11.

[119] *The bear is in the woods:* play on the name "Dov Baer" the maggid of Mezritch; "Dov" in the Hebrew language and "Baer" in German and Yiddish mean a bear. The saying seems to imply that the strong "Baer" is to be considered the leader and that "a sage" should stand by his side as an adviser.

[121] *The words:* ascribed to Rabbi Meir, a great teacher during the early talmudic period.

[125] *He is thy psalm:* a possible interpretation of the words "He is thy glory" (Deut. 10:21). The Hebrew term means both "glory" and "psalm."

[127] *Despise not:* Sayings of the Fathers, IV,3.

[128] *The Lord is King:* Ps. 93:1.

[128] *My eyes are ever:* Ps. 25:15.

[129] *God's words:* Isa. 57:15.

[131] *The prayer:* conclusion of the Grace after meals.

[131] *Because of an idle quarrel:* a talmudic tradition (Gittin 55b) holds that a petty quarrel between two Jewish families caused one to denounce the other to the Romans, an event which set off the Roman war against Judaea, and led to the destruction of the Temple.

[141] *The secret counsel:* Ps. 25:14.

[144] *The words in praise of Moses:* Num. 12:3.

[146] *Rabbi Mendel:* a disciple of the Baal Shem Tov, one of the first hasidim to transfer his residence to Palestine.

[146] *From all my teachers:* Ps. 119:99. The correct translation is: "More than all my teachers," but the text also permits this interpretation.

[147] *But ye that cleave:* Deut. 4:4.

[147] *If ye walk in My statutes:* Lev. 26:3.

[149] *I stood:* Deut. 5:5.

[149] *I am my beloved's:* Cant. 7:11.

[149] *Ye shall be holy:* Lev. 19:2.

[151] *My mouth shall speak:* Ps. 145:21.

[153] *Who shall ascend:* Ps. 24:3.

[154] *Means the homecoming: shavat,* to stop, the root of the word *shabbat* (Sabbath) , is here combined with the root *shuv,* to return.

[155] *One generation passeth away:* Eccl. 1:4.

[165] *And in your new moons:* Num. 28:11.

[165] *A seeing eye and a hearing ear:* the complete passage (Sayings of the Fathers, II, 1) is as follows: "Know what is above you: a seeing eye, and a hearing ear, and all your deeds are written in a book."

[168] *Happy is the people:* Ps. 144:15.

[168] *Book:* the first comprehensive presentation of the Baal Shem's teachings, written in the form of a commentary on the Bible (1780) .

[175] *To make it fall off:* that is, pride leads to faithlessness to the divine law. (An uncovered head is considered a violation of religious respect.)

[180] *It is true:* the following is a quotation from the Babylonian Talmud (Baba Batra 158) .

[187] *Serve the Lord:* Ps. 2:11.

[191] *The prayer:* the Grace after meals.

[191] *Three are concerned:* according to the Talmud (Niddah 31) , a child's bones, brains, and sinews derive from the father; skin, flesh, and hair from the mother; spirit, soul, senses, and speech from God.

[198] *. . . a ladder set up:* Gen. 28:12.

[199] *Moses' prayer:* Num. 14:19.

[202] *Rabbi Israel of Rizhyn:* grandson of Rabbi Abraham, the Angel.

[203] *Unto thee:* Deut. 4:35.

[210] *Life, and children, and food:* according to the Talmud (Moed Katan 28a) , these three are gifts of heaven which are granted independently of man's merit.

[221] *At the Holy Feast:* in the world to come.

[221] *The tall mountains:* a well-known midrashic legend.

[222] *Endeavor to imitate:* a talmudic saying (Shabbat 133) .

[223] *Is not Ephraim:* Jer. 31:19.

[223] *The truth will grow:* Ps. 85:12.

[226] *What is told:* a talmudic legend (Sanhedrin 109) .

[227] *Remember what Amalek:* Deut. 25:17.

[230] *The words:* in the Babylonian Talmud (Baba Metzia 49) .

[230] *We have trespassed . . .:* the confession of sins, recited on the Day of Atonement.

[231] *The Divine Presence:* in the Talmud (Shabbat 30b) .

[233] *Here I am, a sin offering:* similar exclamations are reported in the Talmud. The meaning is: May Israel's punishment come upon me.

[235] *With her love:* Prov. 5:12.

[239] *Speak unto:* Exod. 25:2.

[242] *Thine infinity:* see Isa. 6:7.

[251] *Rabbi Hirsh Leib of Olik:* disciple of Rabbi Yehiel Mikhal of Zlotchov; (died 1811) .

[254] *For singing:* Ps. 147:1.

[258] *For unto me:* Lev. 25:55.

[277] *If I make:* Ps. 139:8.

[278] *Rabbi Asher of Stolyn:* son of Rabbi Aaron of Karlin; *see* the chapter about him.

[278] *And Thy footsteps:* Ps. 77:20.

[279] *As it is the custom to do:* telling his mother's name, which is a part of his "true" name, is an essential part of the procedure in which a hasid opens his heart to a zaddik.

[288] *How full of awe is this place:* see Gen. 28:17.

[288] *On Mondays and Thursdays:* in addition to being read on the Sabbath, a portion of the Torah is read on these days "so that no three days should go by without Torah."

[288] *But they that wait:* Isa. 40:31.

[290] *Out of distress:* a play on words (*mitzraim*—Egypt, *metzarim*—straits, distress).

[290] *And she cast:* Gen. 21:15.

[290] *The great shrub of prayer:* a play on words (the word *siah* can mean either shrub or speech, word).

[291] *I have set:* Ps. 16:8.

[295] *Fringes:* see Glossary, *s.v.*, Tallit.

[309] *And repayeth them:* Deut. 7:10.

[314] *Justice, justice:* Deut. 16:20.

[314] *Return unto me:* Zech. 1:3.

[314] *Turn Thou us:* Lam. 5:21.

[315] *They do not turn:* in the Babylonian Talmud (Erubin 19).

[318] *He was called:* The custom of naming a boy after his grandfather goes back to a primitive belief, according to which a man is reborn in his grandson.

GLOSSARY

ABAYYI AND RABA: leading talmudic teachers in Babylonia in the first half of the fourth century.

ABRAHAM IBN EZRA of Toledo: outstanding Bible exegete, Hebrew grammarian, religious philosopher, and poet (died 1167).

ADDITIONAL SERVICE: see MUSAF.

ADLER, NATHAN: rabbi of Frankfurt-am-Main, important talmudic scholar and kabbalist (died 1800).

AFTERNOON PRAYER: see MINHAH.

AKIBA: leading Palestinian teacher of the second century C.E.

ALL VOWS: see KOL NIDRE.

AMORA, pl., AMORAIM (speaker, interpreter): masters of the second talmudic epoch (about 200 to 500 C.E.), in which the Gemara originated.

ARI: Abbreviation of Ashkenazi Rabbi Isaak (Luria), the outoutstanding representative of the later Kabbalah (1534-1572). See G. Scholem, *Major Trends in Jewish Mysticism*, Seventh Lecture.

ARIEL: poetic name for Jerusalem (Isa. 29:1). Its probable meaning is "hearth of God," the place from which the sacrifice ascended.

ATTRIBUTES: of God, realized by men in their thoughts and actions. Each one of the three patriarchs symbolically represents one of the divine attributes.

AZAZEL: see Leviticus, chap. 16. In biblical times, a mysterious desert creature, to whom, on the Day of Atonement (*see* YOM KIPPUR), a goat was sent "bearing the iniquities" of

Israel. In post-biblical times this name was understood as applying to one of the fallen angels.

BADHAN (merry maker) : master of ceremonies at a wedding; at the end of the festive meal he announces the presents, lifting them up one by one and praising, mostly in a humorous manner, the giver and the gift.

BAR KOKHBA ("Son of Stars") : Simeon bar Koziba, the leader of the great rebellion against Emperor Hadrian (132-135 C.E.).

BAR MITZVAH ("son of commandment") : a boy who, upon the completion of his thirteenth year, accepts the responsibility of fulfilling the religious law. Also, the celebration of this event.

BATH: *see* IMMERSION.

BELT AND STAFF: the signs of leadership. By transmitting his staff, the rabbi confers the authority to act in his name.

BLESSED BE HE THAT COMES: greeting given to a guest upon his arrival, who answers: Blessed be the present.

BLESSING OF THE NEW MOON: outdoor benediction service on the appearance of the new moon, which determines the start of the month according to the Hebrew calendar.

BOOK OF CREATION (*Sefer Yetzirah*) : the basic work in the mystical interpretation of the numbers and letters of the alphabet. It is uncertain whether it was composed in talmudic or post-talmudic times.

BOOK OF LAWS: *see* SHULHAN ARUKH.

BOOK OF SPLENDOR: the book *Zohar*, the chief work of the earlier Kabbalah (end of 13th century). *See* G. Scholem, *Major Trends in Jewish Mysticism*, Fifth and Sixth Lectures.

BOOTHS: *see* SUKKOT.

BREAKING OF THE VESSELS: *see* SPARKS.

BURNING OF THE LEAVEN: during Passover there must be no leavened food in the house. On the evening preceding the holiday the house is thoroughly cleaned and remnants of leavened food are gathered up and burned in a fire kindled especially for the occasion.

CASTING OFF OF SINS: *see* TASHLIKH.

CHARIOT OF GOD: the vision of Ezekiel was interpreted to be the mystery of divine revelation, one of the two fundamental principles of Kabbalah. (The other principle was the mystery of creation.)

CITRON: *see* ETROG.

COURT OF LAW: the rabbinical court of law, consisting of a head (*av bet din*, father of the court of law), and two judges (*dayanim*).

DAY OF ATONEMENT: *see* YOM KIPPUR.

DIASPORA (*Gola*): the dispersion of Israel among the nations.

DIVINE NOTHINGNESS: the Habad school (*see* Introduction), which developed the teachings of the Great Maggid, held that the Divine is without limitation and opposed to all "something," which is limited. The divine is the "nothing" that subsumes all limitation and finiteness.

"DUTIES OF THE HEART" (*Hovot ha-Levavot*): an important popular work of Jewish religious philosophy and ethics, written in Arabic by Bahya ibn Pakuda in the last quarter of the eleventh century.

EIGHTEEN BENEDICTIONS: one of the oldest parts of liturgy, occurring in the regular prayer service. The worshipper, standing, recites it to himself and, according to custom, with his eyes closed. No profane word must interrupt it. After silent recitation by the worshippers it is repeated aloud by the reader.

ELIJAH: after his ascent to heaven, the prophet Elijah, according to legend, continued to help and instruct the world of man in his function as a messenger of God. Especially, he appears at every feast of circumcision and at every Seder celebration. To behold him and to receive instruction from him are considered an initiation in the mysteries of the Torah.

ELIJAH SONG: in praise of the prophet; in it Elijah is addressed as the good helper.

ELUL: the month preceding the "Days of Awe" and the days of heavenly judgment. It is devoted to inner preparation and self-examination.

ESCORT OF THE SABBATH: the meal taken after the departure of the Sabbath. This meal is understood as bidding farewell to the Queen Sabbath. It "escorts" her away. It is also called "the feast of King David." According to the legend, David was told by God that he would die on a Sabbath; he therefore feasted after every Sabbath in celebration of his continued living.

ETROG: "the fruit of goodly trees" (Lev. 23:40), *citrus medica*, upon which, together with the bouquet of palm branch, myrtle, and willow branch, the Sukkot benediction is spoken.

EVIL URGE: the inclination to evil, which is opposed to "the inclination to good." It is not considered as evil *per se*, but as a power abused by men. It is rather the "passion" in which all human action originates. Man is called upon to serve God "with both inclinations," directing his passion towards the good and holy.

FEAST OF WEEKS: *see* SHAVUOT.

FEAST OF KING DAVID: *see* ESCORT OF THE SABBATH.

FEAST OF REVELATION: *see* SHAVUOT.

FIFTY GATES OF REASON: according to talmudic legend, forty-nine of the fifty gates were disclosed to Moses.

FRANK, JACOB: the last and most dubious of the "false Messiahs"; originator of a radical Sabbatian (*see* SABBATAI

Zevi) movement in Poland, and later active in Offenbach, Germany. He and his disciples publicly embraced Christianity (died 1791).

Fringes: *see* Tallit.

Gaon ("excellence") Of Vilna: Rabbi Elijah of Vilna, a renowned rabbinical scholar, leader of a movement against hasidism (died 1797).

Gemara: "completion" of the teaching; the most extensive portion of the Talmud, an explanation and discussion of the Mishnah, the earlier part of the Talmud. There is a distinction between the Gemara of the Babylonian Talmud and of the Palestinian Talmud.

Gog: *see* Wars Of Gog.

Good Jew: a popular designation of the zaddik.

Goy (*pl.*, goyim): "nation" (in the physical sense); gentile.

Haggadah ("narrative"): the collection of sayings, scriptural interpretations, and hymns pertaining to the exodus from Egypt, as recited in the home service on Passover night (*see* Seder).

Hallel ("praise"): a group of psalms recited in the prayer service at certain festivals.

Haninah ben Teradion: one of the "ten martyrs" executed by the Romans after the rebellion of Bar Kokhba. They refused to obey the ban on the study of the law.

Hanukkah ("dedication"): an eight-day holiday beginning on the twenty-fifth day of *Kislev* (November or December) and commemorating the re-dedication of the Sanctuary by the Maccabees (167 b.c.e.) and their victory over the Syrian Greeks who desecrated the Temple. In remembrance of the Maccabean Feast of Lights, candles are lighted in Jewish homes on each of the eight evenings, one candle the first evening, two the second, etc.

329

HAVDALAH ("separation" of the holy and the profane) : benediction pronounced upon the wine, spices, and light at the
conclusion of the Sabbath and holidays.

HAZAN: cantor, the reader of the prayers in the synagogue.

HEAD OF ALL THE SONS OF THE DIASPORA (exilarch, *resh
galuta*) : the secular head of Babylonian Jewry in talmudic
and post-talmudic times.

HILLEL: a great teacher of the first century B.C.E. His life and
teachings were based on the ideal of universal brotherhood.

HOLY BROTHERHOOD (*hevra kaddisha,* holy society) : its members devote themselves to the burial of the dead.

HOLY NAMES: all the elements of the sacred language are understood as living, super-mundane beings.

HOLY GUEST: the patriarchs are said to visit the devout in the
holiday booths (*see* SUKKOT). The devout recite words of
greeting to them.

HOUSE OF STUDY (*Beth ha-Midrash*) : identical, usually, with
the House of Prayer. It is a place of learning and worship.
Travelers without lodgings are put up in the House of Study.

IBN EZRA: *see* ABRAHAM IBN EZRA.

IMMERSION: the ancient bath which, in the Kabbalah and especially among the hasidim, became an important ceremony
with meanings and mysteries of its own. Immersion in a
river or a stream is higher in value than the ordinary ritual
bath.

JERUSALEM OF ABOVE: the heavenly Jerusalem that corresponds to the earthly Jerusalem. In the same way, a heavenly
sanctuary corresponds to the Temple on Zion.

KADDISH ("holy") : a doxology, especially the one recited as
a memorial of the dead.

KAVVANAH, *pl.*, KAVVANOT ("intention, devotion") : the intention directed towards God while performing a (religious)

deed. In the Kabbalah, kavvanot denote the permutations of the divine name that aim at overcoming the separation of forces in the Upper World.

KIDDUSH ("sanctification") : in addition to its other meanings, this term denotes the benediction pronounced upon the wine at the commencement of the Sabbath and holidays. The marriage ceremony, too, is a Kiddush.

KLAUS: the prayer room of a private (usually hasidic) congregation of worshippers.

KOL NIDRE ("All Vows") : the initial words in the solemn formula of absolution from unfulfilled and unfulfillable vows, pronounced on the eve of the Day of Atonement.

LAG BA-OMER: the thirty-third day of a counting of days that begins with the second day of Passover and ends with the Feast of Weeks.

LAMENTATIONS AT MIDNIGHT: the pious are accustomed to rise at midnight from their beds, sit down on the floor, without shoes, put ashes on their forehead, and read lamentations on the fall of Zion and prayers for redemption.

LETTER OF DIVORCE: the only permissible form of divorce.

LILITH: a female demon that seduces men.

LITHUANIA: the more rationalistically minded Lithuanian Jews, strongly opposed to hasidism.

LURIA, ISAAK: *see* ARI.

MAGGID, *pl.*, MAGGIDIM: a preacher. The maggidim were partly itinerant preachers, partly regularly appointed community preachers; some of the latter at times served as wandering preachers. The term also refers to a spirit that appears to the select and reveals to them secrets of the teachings and the future.

MAKOM ("place") : the designation of God, in whom exists all that exists.

MARRIAGE CONTRACT (*tenaim*, "conditions") : written down and signed at the time of the betrothal; just before the marriage, the *ketubah*, a financial agreement, is added.

MASTER OF CEREMONIES: *see* BADHAN.

MATZAH, *pl.*, MATZOT: unleavened bread, eaten during the week of Passover.

MELAMMED: the teacher of the children.

MENORAH: seven-branched candelabrum, especially the one used in the synagogue.

MERCY-RIGOR: the chief attributes of God.

MESSIAH SON OF JOSEPH: a Messiah who will prepare the way, gathering Israel together and re-establishing the Kingdom, and who will then fall in a war against the Romans led by Armilus. Another tradition holds that he reappears "from generation to generation."

MIDRASH, *pl.*, MIDRASHIM ("exposition, interpretation") : books of the talmudic and post-talmudic times devoted to the homiletic exegesis of the Scriptures. They are rich in legends, parables, similes, and sayings.

MINHAH ("offering") : originally, an afternoon sacrifice (Ezra 9:4), later, as its substitute, the Afternoon Prayer.

MISHNAH ("repetition, teaching") : the earliest and basic part of the Talmud.

MITNAGED, *pl.*, MITNAGDIM ("opponent, antagonist") : the avowed opponents of hasidism.

MUSAF ("addition") : originally, an additional sacrifice on the Sabbath and holidays, later, as its substitute, an additional prayer service recited after the general Morning Prayer.

NEILAH ("closing") : the closing prayer of the Day of Atonement.

NEW YEAR: *see* ROSH HA-SHANAH.

332

NINTH DAY OF AV: *see* TISHAH BE-AV.

NOTES OF REQUEST (in Yiddish, *Kvittel*): written on slips of paper containing the name of the supplicant, the name of his mother, and his request.

"ONE": the devout, and especially the martyrs, when they die, avow the Oneness of God.

PASSOVER: *see* PESAH.

PESAH ("passing over," i.e., the sparing of the houses of the children of Israel): eight-day holiday (in Palestine, seven days) beginning on the fifteenth day of *Nisan* (March or April) and commemorating the exodus from Egypt.

PHYLACTERIES: *see* TEFILLIN.

PRAYER SHAWL: *see* TALLIT.

PRESENCE OF GOD: *see* SHEKHINAH.

PRINCE ADAM CHARTORISKY: on his relations to the maggid of Koznitz, as portrayed in the legendary tradition, *see* M. Buber, *For the Sake of Heaven*, Philadelphia, The Jewish Publication Society, 1945, pp. 195 ff.

PRINCE OF THE TORAH: the angel who represents the Torah in heaven. The elements, the forces of nature, and the nations, which, according to Jewish tradition, are seventy in number, are represented by their respective princes, who are either angels or demons.

PURIM: the feast of "lots" (Esther 9:25); the happy holiday commemorating the defeat of the wicked Haman. It is observed by masquerades and games.

RAB (Abba Areka): a third-century Babylonian master of the Talmud.

RAM'S HORN: *see* SHOFAR.

RANSOM MONEY: the hasid visiting the zaddik hands in, together with a Note of Request, a sum of money. This sum is taken to be a "ransom" for the soul of the applicant.

RASHI: abbreviation for Rabbi Solomon (ben) Isaak (of Troyes), the classical commentator on the Bible and the Babylonian Talmud (died 1105).

RAV ("master, teacher"): the leader of the religious community. He teaches the law and, as the "head of the law court," supervises its fulfillment; whereas *rabbi*, in most cases, denotes the leader of the local hasidic group. In some instances the rabbi was also the rav of his town.

READER: *see* HAZAN.

REJOICING IN THE LAW: *see* SIMHAT TORAH.

ROSH HA-SHANAH ("New Year"): observed on the first and second day of *Tishre* (September or October); the days of judgment.

SABBATAI ZEVI: the central figure of the greatest messianic movement in the history of the Diaspora (died 1676). Soon after Sabbatai Zevi proclaimed himself Messiah, the movement broke down and its founder embraced Islam. *See* G. Scholem, *Major Trends in Jewish Mysticism*, Eighth Lecture.

SACRED UNION: a close and helpful attitude to one's fellow men. It promotes a closeness of the separated heavenly spheres.

SAMMAEL: post-biblical name for Satan, the prince of demons.
SANCTIFICATION OF THE NAME (of God): designates every sacrificial act of man; by it man participates in the establishment of the kingdom of God on earth.

SAYINGS OF THE FATHERS (*Pirke Avot*): a tractate of the Mishnah dealing with ethical teachings and sayings in praise of the study of the law. It begins with a genealogy of tradition.

SECTION OF SONGS (*Perek Shirah*): a compilation of scriptural verses said to be spoken by all kinds of living beings as a praise of God, each one speaking a particular verse.

SEDER ("order") : the festival meal and home service on the first and second (in Palestine, only the first) night of Passover. In this celebration, each succeeding generation identifies itself anew with the generation that fled from Egypt.

SEFIROT: the mystical and organically related hierarchy of the ten creative powers emanating from God, constituting, according to the kabbalistic system, the foundation of the existence of the worlds.

SEVEN SHEPHERDS: mentioned in the Bible (Mic. 5:4), and identified by the Talmud (Sukkah 52 b) as Adam, Seth, Methuselah, Abraham, Jacob, Moses, and David.

SHAVUOT ("weeks") : a two-day holiday (in Palestine, one day), seven weeks after Passover. It is the feast of the first fruits and a season dedicated to the memory of the revelation on Mount Sinai.

SHEKHINAH ("indwelling") : divine hypostasis indwelling in the world and sharing the exile of Israel; Divine Presence among men.

SHOFAR: the ram's horn, sounded in the synagogue, principally on the New Year. A blast on the ram's horn will announce the coming of the Messiah.

SHULHAN ARUKH ("set table") : the book of Jewish law, codified in the sixteenth century.

SIMHAT TORAH ("rejoicing in the law") : feast on the day following Sukkot. The Torah scrolls are taken out of the Ark and are carried through the House of Prayer by an enthusiastic procession.

SON OF COMMANDMENT: *see* BAR MITZVAH.

SPARKS: in the primeval creation preceding the creation of our world, the divine light-substance burst and the "sparks" fell into the lower depths, filling the "shells" of the things and creatures of our world.

Sukkah, *pl.*, sukkot ("booths") : tabernacles; an eight-day holiday beginning on the fifth day after the Day of Atonement. It commemorates the wandering in the desert. During this period the houses are abandoned and the people live in booths covered with leaves.

Tabernacles: *see* Sukkot.

Tallit: a rectangular prayer-shawl to whose four corners fringes (*Tzitzit*) are attached.

Tanna, *pl.*, tannaim ("repeater, teacher") : the masters of the Mishnah.

Tashlikh: ceremony of the "casting off" of sins on the New Year. Crumbs of bread symbolizing one's sins are cast into a river.

Tefillin (phylacteries) : leather cubicles containing scriptural texts inscribed on parchment. Following the commandment in Deuteronomy 11:18, Tefillin are attached to the left arm and the head during the weekday morning service. They are a sign of the covenant between God and Israel. An error in the written text disqualifies the phylacteries. There is a talmudic conception (Berakhot 5) of the "phylacteries of God." These phylacteries are said to contain the verse II Samuel 7:23.

Tekiah, *pl.*, tekiot: the sounding of the ram's horn (*see* Shofar) ; in particular, one of the prescribed sounds. The later Kabbalah enjoined a special Kavvanah on the listener for each of the sounds of the shofar.

Third Meal: the principal meal of the Sabbath, eaten after the Afternoon Prayer, and accompanied by community singing and an address by the zaddik.

Tishah be-Av: the "Ninth Day of *Av*" (July or August). A day of fasting and mourning in memory of the destruction of the first Temple by Nebuchadnezzar and the second Temple by Titus. The worshippers sit, like mourners of the dead, without shoes, on the floor of the darkened House of Prayer and recite verses from the Book of Lamentations. According to tradition, the Messiah was born on the Ninth Day of *Av* and will reappear on that day.

TORAH: teaching, law, both the written (biblical) and the oral (traditional) law.

TRAVEL (to the zaddik) : to become a follower of a zaddik, to receive his teaching, and to visit him from time to time.

"TREE OF LIFE" (*Etz Hayyim*) : an exposition of the kabbalistic system of Isaak Luria, written by his most outstanding disciple, Hayyim Vital Calabrese.

TURNING (*Teshuvah*) : man's turning from his aberrations to the "way of God." It is interpreted as the fundamental act by which man contributes to his redemption. (*Teshuvah* is usually translated as "repentance.")

UNLEAVENED BREAD: *see* MATZAH.

WARS OF GOG: the prophecy of Ezekiel (Ezek., chap. 39) is interpreted as a vision of great wars of nations in the time preceding the coming of the Messiah.

WINE OF LIFE: "preserved" from the days of Creation for the pious men in paradise.

YOHANAN THE SANDAL-MAKER: a disciple of Rabbi Akiba.

YOHANAN BEN ZAKKAI: according to a talmudic legend, this leading teacher of the first century C.E. had himself placed in a coffin and carried out of Jerusalem into the presence of Vespasian in order to secure permission to establish a Jewish academy of learning after the fall of Jerusalem.

YOM KIPPUR: the Day of Atonement, the last of the Days of Awe, which commence with the New Year. It is a day of fasting and uninterrupted prayer for atonement.

ZADDIK: the leader of the hasidic community (*see* RAV).

ZECHARIAH: identified by the Targum as "the priest and prophet" who, according to the Bible (Lam. 2:20), "was killed in the sanctuary."

GENEALOGY OF THE EARLY MASTERS OF HASIDISM

THE FOUNDER

Israel ben Eliezer, the Baal Shem Tov (abbrev. the Baal Shem), 1700-1760

GRANDSONS OF THE BAAL SHEM

Moshe Hayyim Efraim of Sadylkov
Barukh of Mezbizh, d.1811

GREAT-GRANDSON OF THE BAAL SHEM

Nahman of Bratzlav, d.1810

DISCIPLES OF THE BAAL SHEM

Dov Baer of Mezritch, "the Great Maggid," d.1772
HIS SON:
    Abraham "the Angel," d.1776

Yaakov Joseph of Polnoye, d.1782
HIS DISCIPLE:
    Arye Leib of Spola, "the Spola grandfather," d.1811

Pinhas of Koretz, d.1791
HIS DISCIPLE:
    Rafael of Bershad, d.1816

Yehiel Mikhal of Zlotchov, "the Maggid of Zlotchov," d. about 1786
HIS SONS
    Zev Wolf of Zbarazh, d.1800
    Mordecai of Kremnitz
HIS DISCIPLES
    Mordecai of Neskhizh, d.1800
    Aaron Leib of Primishlan

338

Nahum of Tchernobil, d.1798
  HIS SON:
    Mordecai (Motel) of Tchernobil, d.1837

David Leikes
Wolf Kitzes
Meir Margaliot
Zevi the Scribe
Leib, son of Sarah

DISCIPLES OF DOV BAER OF MEZRITCH

Menahem Mendel of Vitebsk, d.1788
Shmelke of Nikolsburg, d.1778

Aaron of Karlin, d.1772
Levi Yitzhak of Berditchev, d.1809
Meshullam Zusya of Hanipol, d.1800
Elimelekh of Lizhensk, Zusya's brother, d.1786
Shneur Zalman of Ladi, "the Rav," d.1813
Shelomo of Karlin, d.1792
Israel of Koznitz, the Maggid of Koznitz, d.1814
Yaakov Yitzhak of Lublin, "the Seer," d.1815

SELECTED BIBLIOGRAPHY

(Only works in English and Hebrew are listed)

Agus, Jacob B., "Hasidism," in *The Evolution of Jewish Thought*. London-New York, 1959, ch. XI.

Baron, Salo W., *A Social and Religious History of the Jews*, vol. II. New York, 1937, ch. X.

Bromberg, Abraham Isaac, *Migedole ha-Hasidut* (a series of monographs). Jerusalem.

Buber, Martin, *Be-Fardes ha-Hasidut*. Jerusalem, 1945.

Buber, Martin, *Or ha-Ganuz*. Jerusalem-Tel Aviv, 1946. (A Hebrew edition of the "Tales of the Hasidim.")

Buber, Martin, *Ten Rungs. Hasidic Sayings*. New York, 1947.

Buber, Martin, *Hasidism*. New York, 1948.

Buber, Martin, *The Way of Man According to the Teachings of the Hasidim*. Chicago, 1951.

Buber, Martin, *For the Sake of Heaven. A Chronicle*. New York, 1953.

Buber, Martin, *The Legend of the Baal-Shem*. New York, 1956.

Buber, Martin, *Darko shel Adam al-pi Torat ha-Hasidut*. Jerusalem, 1957.

Buber, Martin, *Hasidism and Modern Man*, ed. Maurice Friedman. New York, 1958.

Buber, Martin, *The Origin and Meaning of Hasidism*, ed. Maurice Friedman. New York, 1960.

Bunin, H., "Ha-Hasidut ha-Habadit." *Hashiloah* XXVIII, XXIX, XXXI, 1913-15.

Dinaburg, Benzion, "Reshitah shel ha-Hasidut," *Zion* VIII, IX, X, 1934-1945.

Dresner, Samuel H., *The Zaddik*. London-New York, 1960.

Dubnov, Simon, *History of the Jews in Russia and Poland*, vol. I. Philadelphia, 1916, ch. VI and XI.

Dubnov, Simon, *Toledot ha-Hasidut*. Tel Aviv, 1930-32.

Haberman, A. M., "Shaarei Habad." In *Ale Ayin*. Jerusalem, 1953, 293-370.

Halpern, I., *Ha-Aliyot ha-Rishonot shel ha-Hasidim le-Eretz Yisrael*. Jerusalem-Tel Aviv, 1946.

Halpern, I., "Associations for the Study of the Torah and for Good Deeds and the Spread of the Hasidic Movement." *Zion* XXII, 1957, 194-213.

Heschel, A. J., "R. Gershon Kotover." *The Hebrew Union College Annual* XXIII, 1950-51, Part Two, 17-71.

Horodezky, S. A., *Leaders of Hasidism*. London, 1928. *Ha-Hasidut veha-Hasidim*, 3rd ed. Tel Aviv, 1951.

Judaism: A Quarterly Journal, Hasidism Issue, IX, 3 (Summer 1960).

Kahana, Abraham, *Sefer ha-Hasidut*, 2nd ed. Warsaw, 1922.

Kazis, Israel J., "Hasidism Re-examined." *The Reconstructionist*, XXVIII, 8 (May 1957), 7-13.

Kranzler, Gershon, *R. Shneur Zalman of Ladi, Founder of Chabad*. New York.

Marcus, Aaron, *Ha-Hasidut*. Tel Aviv, 1953.

Minkin, Jacob S., *The Romance of Hasidism*. New York, 1935.

Mordecai ben Jeheskel, "Le-Mahut ha-Hasidut." *Hashiloah*, XVII, XX, XXII, XXV, 1909-1912.

Newman, Louis I., and Spitz, Samuel, *A Hasidic Anthology*. New York, 1934.

Newman, Louis I., "The Baal Shem Tov." *Great Jewish Personalities*, ed. Simon Noveck, Washington, D.C., 1959.

Schechter, Solomon, "The Chassidim." *Studies in Judaism* I (1896), 1-45.

Schneersohn, Joseph I., *On the Teachings of Hasidus*. New York.

Schneersohn, Joseph I., *Some Aspects of Hasidus*. New York.

Scholem, G. G., "R. Adam Baal Shem." *Zion* VI, 1941, 89-93.

Scholem, G. G., "The Two First Testimonies on the Relations Between Chassidic Groups and the Baal-Shem-Tov," *Tarbiz* XX (1949), 228-240.

Scholem, G. G., "Dvekuth, the Communion with God in Early Hassidic Doctrine," *Review of Religion* XV, 1950.

Scholem, G. G., *Major Trends in Jewish Mysticism*, 3rd ed., New York, 1954 (Ninth Lecture).

Scholem, G. G., "The Polemic Against Hasidism and its Leaders in the Book Nezed ha-Dema." *Zion* XX, 1955, 73-81.

Scholem, G. G., "New Material on Israel Loebel and his Anti-Hasidic Polemics." *Zion* XX, 1955, 153-162.

Schochat, A., "On Joy in Hasidism." *Zion* XVI, 1951, 30-43.

Spiegel, Shalom, *Hebrew Reborn*. New York, 1930.

Tishby, I., "Beyn Shabtaut le-Hasidut." *Keneset* IX, 1945, 238-268.

Weiss, Joseph, "Beginnings of Hasidism." *Zion XVI*, 1951, 46-105.

Weiss, Joseph, "A Circle of Pneumatics in Pre-Hasidism." *Journal of Jewish Studies* VIII, 1957, 199-213.

Werfel, Yitzhak, *Ha-Hasidut ve-Eretz Yisrael*. Jerusalem, 1940.

Werfel, Yitzhak, *Sefer ha-Hasidut*. Tel Aviv, 1947.

Wilensky, Mordecai L., "The Polemic of R. David of Makow against Hasidism," *Proceedings of the American Academy for Jewish Research*, XXV, 1956.

Zeitlin, Hillel, *Ha-Hasidut*. 1922.

Zweifel, E. Z., *Shalom al Yisrael*, 4 vols. Shitomir, 1868-73.

INDEX TO THE TALES

INDEX TO THE TALES

BARUKH OF MEZBIZH

YEHIEL MIKHAL OF ZLOTCHOV

FROM THE CIRCLE OF THE BAAL SHEM TOV

MENAHEM MENDEL OF VITEBSK

SHMELKE OF NIKOLSBURG

ZUSYA OF HANIPOL